Praise for Richard Rhodes's

ARSENALS OF FOLLY

"Detailed and dramatic.... Devastating commentary on the perilous nature of the nuclear arms race." —*Houston Chronicle*

"An up-close look at people we elected to lead us and the advisers they trusted, the theories we believed in, how they worked and the consequences we bear today." —*The Denver Post*

"His artful narrative contains some real gems." —*The New York Times*

"Using an impressive range of sources, clean writing and a clear sense of the dramatic, Rhodes triumphs." —*Rocky Mountain News*

"An absorbing account of the arms race [and] a suspenseful narrative." —*The Baltimore Sun*

"Rhodes has done his usual excellent job." —*The Boston Globe*

"Rhodes performs the remarkable feat of reconstructing all the niggling, the misunderstanding, the moments of obtuseness in a way that proves dramatic precisely in its repetitiveness and frustration." —*Newsday*

"A terrifying overview of the global potential for killing." —*The Economist*

"Highly detailed and gripping.... A chilling conclusion." —*Scientific American*

"Rhodes is not only an outstanding researcher and historian, he is a superb writer who enraptures the reader with a gripping narrative."
—*The Star-Ledger*

"Stylistically, *Arsenals of Folly* is often quite distinguished. . . . It is alarmingly relevant."
—*The Tennessean*

"[There is] no finer manual for learning from the mistakes of our past than [this] valuable book."
—*Seed* magazine

"Intriguing insight. . . . Rhodes masterfully dissects decades of what he considers reckless and misguided policy decisions that led the United States and the Soviet Union to expand their nuclear arsenals beyond all logic. . . . An engrossing narrative."
—*American Heritage*

"Absorbing."
—*The Seattle Times*

RICHARD RHODES
ARSENALS OF FOLLY

Richard Rhodes is the author or editor of twenty-two books, including novels, history, journalism, and letters. *The Making of the Atomic Bomb* won a Pulitzer Prize, a National Book Award, and a National Book Critics Circle Award. *Dark Sun*, about the development of the hydrogen bomb, was one of three finalists for a Pulitzer Prize in History. An affiliate of Stanford University's Center for International Security and Cooperation, he lectures to college and professional audiences. He lives with his wife near Half Moon Bay, California.

www.richardrhodes.com

ARSENALS OF FOLLY

ARSENALS
OF FOLLY

THE MAKING OF THE
NUCLEAR ARMS RACE

VINTAGE BOOKS
A DIVISON OF
RANDOM HOUSE, INC.
NEW YORK

RICHARD RHODES

FIRST VINTAGE BOOKS EDITION, NOVEMBER 2008

The Library of Congress has cataloged the Knopf edition as follows:
Rhodes, Richard.
Arsenals of folly : the making of the nuclear arms race / by Richard Rhodes.
p. cm.
Includes bibliographical references and index.
1. Nuclear Weapons.   2. Arms race.   I. Title.
US64.R48 2007   355.02'1709045—dc22   2007017613

Vintage ISBN 978-0-375-71394-1

Author photograph © Nancy Warner
Book design by M. Kristen Bearse

www.vintagebooks.com

Printed in the United States of America
10   9   8   7   6   5   4   3   2   1

For Chuck Hansen, 1947–2003

A grant from the Alfred P. Sloan Foundation supported the research and writing of this book.

Reality is that which, when you don't believe in it, doesn't go away.

PETER VIERECK

CONTENTS

<table>
<tr><td>PART
ONE</td><td># A RIGID SYSTEM</td></tr>
</table>

What happened in this country was that a rigid system was created, and then life was herded into it.

MIKHAIL GORBACHEV

ON THE SATURDAY MORNING IN APRIL 1986 when the alarms went off at the Institute for Nuclear Power Engineering of the Byelorussian Academy of Sciences, in a forest outside Minsk, the nuclear physicist Stanislav Shushkevich thought the institute's reactor was bleeding radiation. Its fuel assemblies, sealed inside aluminum cassettes at the bottom of a deep, stainless-steel tank full of distilled water, might have sprung a leak. Or something might have spilled in the institute's radiochemistry lab. Dosimeter operators began working their way methodically through the labs and offices and found radiation everywhere. It was in people's hair and clinging to their clothes. It registered two hundred times normal on the air filters. It was near danger levels at the front door.

The dosimetrists moved outside and discovered it there as well: on the sidewalk, on the grass, on the periwinkle crocuses pushing up through the dark litter of the forest floor. So the institute wasn't the source. An order over the public-address system warned everyone to stay indoors. Someone called the Lithuanian nuclear-power complex at Ignalina, one hundred miles northwest, and radiation was everywhere there too. Chernobyl, in the Ukraine, was farther away, two hundred miles southeast, where four big RBMK* thousand-megawatt reactors were lined up end to end in a building almost a mile long. Hundreds of people worked there, but the phones rang unanswered. Something was wrong at Chernobyl.

By afternoon, institute chemists had found radioactive iodine in the fallout, which confirmed that a reactor had exploded. For radioactive gas and

---

* In Russian, an acronym for "reactor, high-power, boiling, channel type." The RBMK reactor is essentially a large block of graphite drilled with hundreds of channels into which uranium fuel elements are inserted. Water also circulates through the channels to cool the fuel elements and transfer heat out of the block. Reactors use light elements to slow and reflect neutrons to sustain a slow-neutron fission chain reaction, the source of their energy; in the RBMK design, both the graphite (carbon) and the circulating water (hydrogen) moderate the reaction.

smoke from Chernobyl to have reached Minsk, the explosion must have occurred sometime during the night. How much radioactivity had been released? How much more would follow? Why had no one warned them?

Shushkevich, fifty-two, a solid, ample man with a ruddy face and a high, domed forehead fringed with graying brown hair, was friendly and avuncular but shrewdly intelligent. He was vice-provost of the Byelorussian University in Minsk, a liberal humanist in the tradition of Andrei Sakharov. The Soviet Union's change of direction since the death of Konstantin Chernenko in March 1985, just thirteen months before, had filled him with hope. Chernenko, an emphysemic general secretary with the soul of a retired file clerk, had served as a placeholder between the reform-minded but ailing former KGB chief Yuri Andropov and his vigorous young heir apparent, Mikhail Gorbachev. At Chernenko's death his private safe had turned up no personal diary or other intimate record, only a large cache of money no one could account for. Good riddance, Shushkevich had thought: "I was the first at the university to put a portrait of Gorbachev on the wall."

The night of Chernenko's death, Raisa Maksimovna, Mikhail Gorbachev's wife and partner, pacing beside him in the garden of their country house near Moscow, heard him say resolutely, "We just can't go on like this." The next day, 11 March 1985, Gorbachev had been elected general secretary at a meeting of the Communist Party Central Committee. In his acceptance speech immediately after his election he had called for open government and accountability: "I emphasized the need for transparency (*glasnost*) in the work of Party, Soviet, state and public organizations," he wrote later. He had laid out in detail his other fundamental goal, perestroika—economic restructuring, salvaging the nearly moribund Soviet economy—at a Central Committee plenum the following month, stressing "the elimination of everything that interferes with development."

The huge Soviet military-industrial complex, which insinuated itself into every corner of the Soviet economy and consumed at least 40 percent of the state budget, headed his list for cutbacks, and in a letter delivered to President Ronald Reagan on 15 January 1986 he had broached a proposal without precedent across the four dangerous decades of the U.S.-Soviet nuclear-arms race: "A concrete program," as he described it during a press conference in Moscow later that day, ". . . for the complete liquidation of nuclear weapons throughout the world . . . before the end of the present century." Opening to such unprecedented initiative, 1986 had seemed a year of immense possibility. Now a disaster loomed, of consequences yet unknown, and radiation blew north from Chernobyl.

At 2:30 on Saturday afternoon someone finally called the institute to report an accident at Chernobyl. In the early hours after midnight, Chernobyl Reactor Number Four had run away in four seconds from 7 percent of maximum rated power to about one hundred times maximum rated power, an event called a prompt critical excursion that had flashed the reactor's thousands of gallons of circulating water to high-pressure steam. The graphite core of the massive, concrete-encased reactor was an enclosed cylinder forty feet in diameter and twenty-three feet tall, set on end, with blocks of concrete and a water pool beneath it to absorb the fierce radiation its zirconium-clad uranium fuel elements produced, and a two-million-pound, disk-shaped upper biological shield of concrete blocks set over it like a lid to protect workers from radiation exposure. In the same spirit of bravado that had prompted the scientists at Los Alamos during the Second World War to nickname the atomic bomb they were building the "gadget," the men who operated the RBMKs called the upper biological shield the *pyatachok,* Russian for one of the smallest Soviet coins, the five-kopek piece.* When the water flashed to superheated steam and the reactor's steam pipes started exploding, an eyewitness reported later, the *pyatachok* "began to bubble and dance."

Then two explosions in the space of less than four seconds tore open the reactor and blew out the building. The reactor core was sealed within a metal tank filled with a mixture of helium and nitrogen to prevent the graphite moderator—four million pounds of pure carbon—from burning. The prompt critical excursion had heated the graphite red hot. The first steam explosion lifted the two-million-pound *pyatachok.* At the same time the steam burst down through the metal tank and penetrated the red-hot graphite. Steam combines ferociously with hot carbon to make carbon monoxide, liberating hydrogen; the second and more powerful explosion combined steam and exploding hydrogen gas, tilted up the *pyatachok* nearly vertical, shattered the upper half of the reactor core, and blew tons of its red-hot radioactive debris—a rubble of highly irradiated uranium-oxide fuel as well as radioactive graphite and zirconium—past the *pyatachok,* through the roof, and half a mile into the air.

It fell out by size. Big blocks of hot graphite landed on the roofs of Number Four's turbine hall and Reactor Number Three. To lower construction costs, the roofs had been covered with flammable asphalt; the hot graphite set them on fire. Blocks and smaller pieces of graphite landed on the grounds

* One hundred kopeks equal one ruble.

around the building and splashed hissing into the four-mile-long cooling pond that lay between the plant and the Pripyat River. The cooling pond was fed by and drained into the river, which drained in turn into the big reservoir downstream that stored the water supply of the city of Kiev, the Soviet Union's third-largest city, with a population of some 2.5 million people.

Graphite pieces and soot-like particles scattered across a stand of pines southeast of the complex; several weeks later, when the radiation had killed the trees and their chlorophyll had faded, people started calling the dead stand "the Red Forest." About half the total radioactive fission products jettisoned from the reactor fell within a two-mile radius of the building. The gases released in the explosion diluted and dispersed into the upper atmosphere, but the wind carried the finest aerosols and hot, intensely radioactive particles (which lofted on their own heat like microscopic hot-air balloons) northwest toward Minsk, on to Ingalina and then across the Baltic Sea to Finland and Sweden. The explosions also blew out the shield elements below the reactor; with the water channels through the graphite blocks drained, the hot graphite chimneyed air up the channels through the remaining lower half of the reactor core and the graphite began to burn. It burned efficiently, the soot and ash carrying more and more radiation high into the air.

A containment structure such as the concrete-and-steel dome that protects all Western and Japanese power reactors would probably have confined the Chernobyl explosions and their radioactivity, but Soviet reactors of the RBMK type lacked such containment.

In the 1950s, when the RBMK design was developed and approved, Soviet industry had not yet mastered the technology necessary to manufacture steel pressure vessels capacious enough to surround such large reactor cores. For

Source: Nuclear Energy Institute

that reason, among others, scientists, engineers, and managers in the Soviet nuclear-power industry had pretended for years that a loss-of-coolant accident was unlikely to the point of impossibility in an RBMK. They knew better. The industry had been plagued with disasters and near-disasters since its earliest days. All of them had been covered up, treated as state secrets; information about them was denied not only to the Soviet public but even to the industry's managers and operators. Engineering is based on experience, including operating experience; treating design flaws and accidents as state secrets meant that every other similar nuclear-power station remained vulnerable and unprepared.

Unknown to the Soviet public and the world, at least thirteen serious power-reactor accidents had occurred in the Soviet Union before the one at Chernobyl. Between 1964 and 1979, for example, repeated fuel-assembly fires plagued Reactor Number One at the Beloyarsk nuclear-power plant east of the Urals near Novosibirsk. In 1975, the core of an RBMK reactor at the Leningrad plant partly melted down; cooling the core by flooding it with liquid nitrogen led to a discharge of radiation into the environment equivalent to about one-twentieth the amount that was released at Chernobyl in 1986. In 1982, a rupture of the central fuel assembly of Chernobyl Reactor Number One released radioactivity over the nearby bedroom community of Pripyat, now in 1986 once again exposed and at risk. In 1985, a steam relief valve burst during a shaky startup of Reactor Number One at the Balakovo nuclear-power plant, on the Volga River about 150 miles southwest of Samara, jetting 500-degree steam that scalded to death fourteen members of the start-up staff; despite the accident, the responsible official, Balakovo's plant director, Viktor Bryukhanov, was promoted to supervise construction at Chernobyl and direct its operation.

Now in the night someone called Bryukhanov from the power plant to tell him that "something awful has happened—some sort of explosion." He rushed to the scene thinking he would have to deal with another steam-valve rupture, but when he saw Number Four ruined and smoking, fires burning on the roof, fire trucks everywhere, he said later, "my heart stood still." He claimed he called Moscow for permission to order an immediate evacuation, without finding anyone in authority willing to believe that such an accident could happen to an RBMK. Whether he contacted Moscow or not, he waited until four in the morning—three and a half hours after the explosions—to alert the authority nearest the plant, Kiev Regional Civil Defense, and then reported only the roof fires, which he told Kiev would soon be extinguished.

They were, by firemen from Pripyat and from Chernobyl town, eleven miles from the power station. Firemen arrived within seven minutes of the explosions; by four a.m. eighty-one engines and 186 firemen had joined the first responders, most of the men working on the roof in ordinary fireman's gear, directing water onto the fires and moving intensely radioactive blocks and chunks of graphite over the side with wheelbarrows, shovels, and their bare hands. Despite the danger, no one ordered Reactor Number Three shut down. Doing so might have been unsafe. It continued operating through the night, the control-room operators wearing respirators for the little protection they gave. Saving Number Three's roof from collapse became the firefighters' first priority. By seven a.m. they had extinguished all the roof fires, but Number Four was still a red-hot crater, billowing smoke.

The first information known to have reached Moscow was a coded signal, "1-2-3-4," sent to Soviet civil-defense headquarters about two hours after the explosions. The numbers invoked the highest state of emergency, an accident involving nuclear, radiation, fire, and explosion effects. The Soviet nuclear-power industry was managed by the Ministry of Medium Machine Building, the branch of the Soviet military-industrial complex that was also responsible for producing nuclear weapons. That ministry contacted Nikolai Ivanovich Ryzhkov, the Politburo member responsible for Soviet industry, and he in turn alerted Gorbachev. Gorbachev hastily assembled the Politburo in an emergency meeting. By noon on Saturday, just as Shushkevich, in Minsk, was learning that a reactor had exploded, the Politburo had appointed a government fact-finding commission whose members—scientists, physicians, engineers, and high Party officials—were instructed to meet at Moscow's Vnukovo Airport at four p.m. From there they flew to Kiev, where a long line of black government ZIL limousines waited to deliver them to Pripyat. It was eight o'clock Saturday evening before they arrived. A member of the commission, a fifty-year-old physicist named Valery Legasov, the first deputy director of the Kurchatov Institute of Atomic Energy in Moscow and a former member of the RBMK reactor design team, described the conditions they found: "The reactor premises were destroyed, several hundred people had received radiation injuries, two people had been killed and the remainder of the shift of workers on duty at the time of the accident were hospitalized."

Legasov was detailed by the commission leader to organize putting out the reactor fire. He saw immediately that the station managers and local officials were unprepared for a disaster on such a major scale and had no idea what to do; "they had no guidelines written earlier and were incapable of making any decisions on the spot." The government commissioners improvised, discussing options among themselves and consulting by phone with the Kurchatov Institute and the Ministry of Energy in Moscow. With the roof fires out, they could confirm that the reactor itself was burning, "a *white pillar* several hundred meters high," Legasov emphasized, "consisting of burning products constantly flying from the crater of the reactor," and down in the reactor itself "individual spots of deep crimson luminescence." A large mass of graphite burns at the rate of about 2,200 pounds per hour; since there were about 5.5 million pounds of graphite in the reactor, if it was allowed simply to burn itself out it would continue to spew its radioactivity into the environment for more than ten days.

In some desperation, lacking any other means of limiting the fire—water would dissociate in the intense heat into oxygen and hydrogen, feeding combustion—Legasov and his colleagues decided to try to smother it from the air. The only immediately available material with which to do so was sand from a riverside quarry. The Pripyat town committee was delegated to round up 150 spades and an equivalent number of local young people. At around eleven on Saturday evening a truckload of sacks arrived at the quarry, but the load included no twine for tying the sacks once they were filled. Someone remembered a stock of red calico the town kept for festival decorations, and strips of red calico soon brightened the mounting pile of sandbags.

Early on Sunday morning, 27 April, the Kiev district chief of air staff, Major General N. T. Antoshkin, arrived by car to supervise the assault. Antoshkin called in a squadron of big Soviet Mi-8 workhorse helicopters. The drops began on Sunday afternoon. "The first flights were the most difficult," Antoshkin told the Tass news service later. "Picture a crater of very limited proportions, to which one must first select the shortest possible route, after which one must try to drop a bag of sand in a precise spot, all in a matter of seconds. The pilots proved to be topnotch in these peaceful bombing runs." A flight engineer, speaking of his pilot, described a grimmer scenario:

[At 110 meters (360 feet) above the blown-out reactor] the radiometer registered 500 roentgen* per hour. . . . The helicopter hung over the crater . . . he opened the door. He could feel the heat from below. A mighty torrent of radioactive gas . . . rose up. All this without respirators. The helicopter was not protected underneath with lead. They only began to think about that later,

---

* Roentgen, rad, and rem are roughly comparable measures of radiation. A whole-body exposure of 20–100 rem will result in a temporary reduction in white blood cells; of 100–200 rem, vomiting, diarrhea, fatigue, and reduction in resistance to infection; of 200–300 rem, serious radiation sickness with symptoms as with 100–200 rem and 10 to 35 percent mortality in thirty days; of 300–400 rem, serious radiation sickness, destruction of bone marrow and gastrointestinal tissue, and 50 to 70 percent mortality in thirty days; of 400–1,000 rem, acute illness and 60 to 95 percent mortality in thirty days. Above 1,000 rem, 100 percent of the victims will die within days. (Source: The Atomic Archive.)

when hundreds of tonnes [i.e., metric tons] had already been off-loaded. At first, however, they stuck their heads out through the open door to aim at the nuclear crater and threw the sacks. . . .

Pilots protected themselves by stuffing lead plates under their seats. They coined a slogan to suit the circumstances: "If you want to be a dad, cover your balls with lead."

Despite the late start, the helicopter crews flew ninety-three drops on that Sunday, dumping about one hundred thousand pounds of sand into the crater. Each crew member received 20 to 80 rads of radiation on each flight. "The first twenty-seven crews," the flight engineer concludes, "soon had to be sent to Kiev for treatment" of radiation sickness. Chernobyl death and disability figures have never included military personnel, even though as many as 340,000 would participate in the resulting area-wide cleanup by the end of 1986; despite the promises of glasnost, the number of those who died or were disabled has not been revealed. "They flung us there," one soldier said, "like sand onto the reactor." Helicopter dumping operations continued throughout June, with several other materials added to the formula: clay to quench the fire and absorb hot particles; boron carbide to capture neutrons to slow what was presumed to be a continuing chain reaction; crushed dolomite, a soft marble that releases carbon dioxide when heated, to blanket the fire with inert gas; lead shot to melt and boil (at 3,172°F.) to absorb heat. Up to 10 May, more than eleven million pounds of material were dumped into the reactor; another twenty-six million pounds were dumped through the end of June.

NOT ONLY PREPARATIONS FOR HELICOPTER DROPS began on Saturday night. Pripyat, with a population of forty-five thousand, was only two miles northwest of the burning reactor. No one had warned the people to stay indoors that day; many had gone about their business, shopping, walking dogs, encouraging their children to play outside in the warm spring sunlight. Radiation levels were low in the morning in Pripyat, about 0.1 rem per hour. But as the burning reactor got hotter, the melting fuel elements vaporized an increasing inventory of radionuclides. By nine p.m., the level in the Pripyat street nearest the power station had reached 1.4 rem per hour. Physicists on the government commission warned of higher levels to come, and at about eleven p.m. the commissioners decided to order the town evacuated. Not long after midnight a column of 1,216 large city buses—most of them yellow Icarus double buses—and about three hundred trucks left Kiev for Pripyat, a column of transport almost ten miles long. The drivers had been sworn to secrecy.

On Sunday morning, the evacuation was announced four times on local radio. It was set for two p.m. "Have your papers, indispensable things and, if possible, rations for three days, with you," the townspeople were told. The evacuation turned out to be permanent, as the authorities who ordered it probably knew in advance it would be; whatever was left behind—savings passbooks, family photographs, clothing, furniture, family pets—was lost. By the time the townspeople boarded the buses, many of the women wearing only light dresses or even bathrobes, the radiation level in the streets had reached a dangerous 10 rem per hour. The convoy carried them west into the villages of the Polissia and Ivankiv districts of the Ukraine, where they were housed uncomfortably among the population. Someone realized the buses would have to be decontaminated before they could be returned to Kiev; in a day and a half the Ukraine Republic Motor Repair and Construction Association assembled a fully equipped open-air decontamination center in a field outside the city to receive them. Chernobyl town (with a population of 12,000), the rural countryside and, eventually, an exclusion zone thirty kilometers (nineteen miles) out in every direction from the power station were permanently cleared of people and livestock. Family pets that were left behind in the zone either suffered the depredations of a burgeoning population of wolves or were shot.

During the morning of the Pripyat evacuation, the town council sent high school girls door-to-door dispensing potassium-iodide tablets to the townspeople. The tablets came from civil-defense supplies. They were meant to protect the population from a radioactive form of iodine that made up fully half the volume of the radionuclides boiling out of Reactor Number Four in the first days after the explosions—iodine-131 (^{131}I), a fission product that emits beta and gamma radiation when it decays. The half-life of ^{131}I is only eight days (meaning that half of the atoms in a given quantity decay away every eight days, transmuting into xenon), but the shorter half-life indicates that its radiation is correspondingly more intense. The thyroid gland, wrapped around the neck below the larynx, takes up iodine from the bloodstream and uses it to make thyroid hormone. The gland does not discriminate between stable and radioactive forms of iodine. In theory, then, flooding the thyroid with stable iodine from potassium-iodide tablets should protect the gland from taking up radioactive iodine, being irradiated and irradiating the surrounding tissue. Thus the Pripyat Sunday morning distribution.

It was well intended, but it was probably too late. Potassium iodide administered up to two days before exposure to ^{131}I protects the thyroid gland almost completely. But potassium iodide taken more than eight hours after exposure is only marginally effective, especially if normal dietary iodine intake is inadequate—as it was in the Chernobyl region, where goiter (thyroid enlargement) is still common because low levels of iodine in the soil leave locally grown food and milk deficient.

Potassium-iodide prophylaxis had been one of Stanislav Shushkevich's urgent first thoughts when he and his colleagues at the institute had confirmed on Saturday afternoon that a reactor had exploded at Chernobyl. "In every civil-defense shelter in the Soviet Union there was information on what to do to deal with radioactive fallout," he told me, "and a supply of potassium iodide tablets. They were supposed to be distributed as quickly as possible in appropriate doses, especially to children." The director of the institute, Valery Nesterenko, happened to be visiting Moscow when he learned of Chernobyl. "I called Nikolai Slyunkov, the general secretary of the Central Committee of the Byelorussian Communist Party in Minsk," Nesterenko said later. He kept calling for two hours before Slyunkov's assistant put him through. He told Slyunkov the accident was serious and a radioactive cloud was moving toward Byelorussia. "We need to immediately perform an iodine prophylaxis of the population," he warned, "and evacuate everyone near the station."

Slyunkov was unimpressed. "I've already received reports," he informed Nesterenko. "There was a fire, but they've put it out."

Nesterenko exploded. "That's a lie! It's a blatant lie!" Slyunkov wouldn't budge. Greatly worried, Nesterenko took the first train home. In Minsk he measured his son's thyroid—"that was the ideal dosimeter then," he told the journalist Svetlana Alexievich bitterly—and found it slightly radioactive. He, Shushkevich, and the other scientists at the institute began warning people.

When Nesterenko finally got to see Slyunkov in person, the following week, the Party boss challenged him: "Why are your men running around town with their dosimeters, scaring everyone? I've already consulted with Moscow, with Professor Ilyin, chairman of the Soviet Radiological Protection Board. He says everything's normal. And there's a government commission at the station, and the prosecutor's office is there. We've thrown the army, all our military equipment, into the breach."

"Every political entity had a civil defense unit," Shushkevich explained, "that was supposed to know what to do with a radiation incident. They had rules developed by scientists and supported by government agencies. But everybody waited for an order, and none came, only a statement that it had been 'an insignificant accident.'"

Nesterenko discovered that the Byelorussian leadership was secretly taking iodine. "When my colleagues at the institute gave them checkups, their thyroids were clean. Without iodine that's impossible. And they quietly got their kids out of there too, just in case." At the same time, he said, "they took away all the institute's radiation-measuring equipment. They just confiscated it, without any explanations. I began receiving threatening phone calls at home. 'Quit scaring people, professor. You'll end up in a bad place.' "

Shushkevich and Nesterenko both blamed Gorbachev. "I'd bet there'd been a call from the Kremlin," Nesterenko speculated, "right from Gorbachev, saying, you know, 'I hope you Byelorussians can keep from starting a panic.' . . . And of course if you didn't please your higher-ups, you didn't get that promotion, that trip abroad, that dacha." Shushkevich underwent what he calls "a sad evolution." If he had been the first at the university to hang Gorbachev's portrait on the wall, the attempted cover-up of Chernobyl in those first days and weeks after the accident made him furious: "I understood that was treason." When Gorbachev finally spoke publicly about Chernobyl in mid-May, claiming that "the worst is over" and "the most serious consequences have been averted," Shushkevich was appalled. "That was the end of my respect for Gorbachev. His advisers had to have told him of the seriousness of the accident. From that day on I hated him." In time, Shushkevich's "sad evolution" would lead him into politics, and his loss of faith in Gorbachev would have the largest consequences.

THROUGH SATURDAY AND SUNDAY, despite the frantic efforts at Chernobyl, the evacuation of Pripyat's entire population, the extensive casualties, and the plume of radiation advancing into Finland and Sweden, no public announcement issued from the Kremlin. In his memoirs, Gorbachev implicitly blames the government commission for the delay, writing that its reports "consisted mainly of preliminary fact-finding, with all kinds of cautious remarks but without any conclusions at all." Whether or not Gorbachev was misled, a better measure of the Soviet government's initial response is that sometime on Sunday, the editors of *Izvestia*, the government-controlled newspaper, were ordered to suppress a story about the accident. Kiev went unwarned. So did Minsk. So did Europe. "In those first days," a village teacher in Byelorussia wrote later, "there were mixed feelings. I remember two: fear and insult. Everything had happened and there was no information: the government was silent, the doctors were silent. The regions waited for directions from the *oblast* [i.e., province], the *oblast* from Minsk, and Minsk from

Moscow. It was a long, long chain, and at the end of it a few people made the decisions. We turned out to be defenseless. That was the main feeling in those days. Just a few people were deciding our fate, the fate of millions."

Curiously, a U.S. spy satellite had passed over the Chernobyl complex on Saturday morning only twenty-eight seconds after the explosions and had imaged it. American intelligence thought at first that a missile had been fired, reports health physicist and Chernobyl expert Richard Mould. When the image remained stationary, "opinion changed to a missile had blown up in its silo." Consulting a map corrected the mistake. By Sunday the British government had been informed, but neither the United States nor Britain warned the public.

The plume of radionuclides from Chernobyl had continued moving northward and westward throughout the weekend of 26 to 27 April, its fall-out dusting Poland, the Baltics, and Finland. Finland detected plume radiation early Sunday afternoon, when Helsinki recorded levels of six times normal background,* but the Finns decided to investigate more thoroughly before announcing their finding. At about the same time, the plume crossed into Sweden. It went undetected until early Monday morning, 28 April, when staff arriving at a Studsvik corporation energy research laboratory on the Baltic coast about fifty miles southwest of Stockholm measured radiation levels higher than normal. Morning arrivals at the Forsmark nuclear-power plant sixty miles north of Stockholm made a similar discovery, measuring radiation levels 150 times background. Forsmark contacted the Studsvik lab midmorning, and samples retrieved from air filters, Studsvik scientists later reported, "combined with a knowledge of the wind direction, allowed us to confirm . . . that the contamination was caused by a release from a nuclear reactor east of Sweden and not from nuclear weapons." Though the Soviet government might prefer to keep its nuclear accidents secret, the plume of radiation pouring out of Reactor Number Four was broadcasting the truth.

The samples ruled out an exploding nuclear weapon because nuclear weapons and nuclear power plants each produce a characteristic and distinct spectrum of fission products. Studying filter samples, Studsvik determined that the reactor fuel had been in active use for about four hundred days.

---

* Radiation occurs everywhere on Earth. It issues from long-lived elements such as uranium and thorium that permeate the earth's crust and are dissolved in seawater. Cosmic rays continually rain down from space, their intensity varying with altitude. The human body carries a load of radioactive potassium acquired from food and drink. Radon gas, a natural decay product of radium (itself a decay product of uranium), spills from house foundations and granite walls. These and other sources produce "background" radiation—naturally occurring rather than man-made (the two kinds are indistinguishable)—that varies at different locations across the earth from extremely low levels below 1 millisievert (0.1 rem) to above 280 mSv (28 rem). (One sievert equals 100 rem.) (Source: Jaworowski, 1999, p. 25.)

(Chernobyl Reactor Number Four had reached the end of a fuel cycle and had been scheduled for a maintenance shutdown the week after the accident.) The lab found highly radioactive microscopic particles of fallout—"hot spots"—contaminating the grounds, some of which consisted of spheres of pure ruthenium, a silvery metal fission product. Ruthenium melts at 4,082°F.; uranium at 2,070°F.; and zirconium, the metal of the fuel's cladding, at 3,360°F.; all three had melted and vaporized. That morning, Sweden announced to the world that a Soviet reactor had melted down and was spreading its radiation across Europe. The world media responded; for the next weeks Chernobyl was the lead story of print and broadcast news.

The government commission had reported to Moscow on Sunday. Ryzhkov carried the report into the regular Monday morning Politburo meeting. What to do about the report occasioned intense debate. In the past, every nuclear accident had been treated as a state secret; acknowledging the accident publicly would be an unprecedented change of policy. Eduard Shevardnadze, Gorbachev's foreign minister and old friend, had quoted the general secretary at a public event just the previous week speaking out in favor of glasnost: "We categorically oppose those who call for releasing public information in doses," Gorbachev had said; "there can never be too much truth." Denying Chernobyl was absurd, Shevardnadze argued, an affront to common sense: "How can you conceal something that can't be hidden? How could people complain about 'washing our dirty linen in public' when it was radioactive and had slipped out in spite of us?" From the standpoint of politics, Shevardnadze thought that trying to maintain secrecy would be "outright sabotage of the principles of the new thinking."

The Soviet system's seemingly pathological obsession with secrecy had emerged from its messianic conception of authority. "Possessed by a unique sense of its own destiny," the former Soviet military economist Vitaliy Shlykov wrote, "and hoping to establish a new world order 'free of capitalistic exploitation,' the communist leadership of the country saw a military confrontation with the rest of the world as inevitable. To be prepared for that confrontation, the Soviet State had to be turned into a permanent military camp." This ideological interpretation of reality, which emerged in the 1920s, had far-reaching consequences:

> It was decided that the equipment of the Red Army had to be based on dual-use technologies, i.e., those applicable to both military and civilian needs. The civilian aviation and automobile and tractor industries were expected to provide the basis for mass production of military aircraft and tanks, and they were explicitly organized and equipped to do so. For instance . . . new types of auto-

mobiles were allowed to go into production only if [the factories] could meet the standards of tank production. This was supposed to make the mobilization of civilian industry in wartime relatively easy.

The RBMK reactor was a dual-use design. It was developed in the 1950s as a production reactor to produce plutonium for nuclear weapons, then adapted for civilian power operation in the 1970s; Like its graphite core, its *pyatachok* was punctured with multiple channels from which irradiated fuel rods could be removed via an overhead crane while the reactor was operating. If the military needed plutonium, on-line refueling would allow fuel rods to be removed early to maximize their bloom of military-grade plutonium.* A safety containment structure around such a reactor, which would probably have prevented an accident like the one at Chernobyl, would have also greatly reduced its military value. Military needs thus competed with civilian needs in the choice of the RBMK design when the Soviet Union decided to greatly expand electricity production with nuclear power in the early 1970s; a competing light-water reactor design, the Soviet VVER, was safer but less suitable for the production of military-grade plutonium. The RBMK design was adapted for civilian use primarily for economic and logistic reasons—the concrete and graphite reactors drew on different industrial resources than the steel VVERs did—but their dual-use potential weighted the decision as well. From the perspective of the Politburo's old guard, then, publicly discussing an accident at a Soviet nuclear power plant, especially one that revealed such serious design flaws, would be no less subversive than revealing the location and fitness of an army in the middle of a war.

Unfortunately, Gorbachev knew very little about nuclear physics or the Soviet nuclear-power industry. His adviser Anatoly Chernyaev, who attended every Politburo meeting on Chernobyl that year, insists that the champion of glasnost made no effort to cover up the accident but made the mistake, common to the Soviet leadership, of trusting the experts. Faced with what Shevardnadze would call the "unsheathed . . . claws" of the Politburo opposition, Gorbachev relied on the advice of senior scientists and managers such as Anatoly Alexandrov, the eighty-three-year-old president of the U.S.S.R.

---

* Uranium-238, the bulk of the uranium in a nuclear reactor, does not undergo fission under slow-neutron bombardment and does not chain-react; the active portion of natural uranium is a rare isotope, uranium-235. When ^{238}U absorbs a neutron, however, it can transmute to a man-made element of atomic number 93, neptunium, which transmutes further within days to a man-made element of atomic number 94, plutonium, which does chain-react and is an even more efficient explosive for atomic bombs than the rare fissile form of uranium, ^{235}U. A ton of natural uranium fuel in the American World War II–era graphite-moderated production reactors produced, after several months' operation, about a dime's volume of plutonium.

Academy of Sciences and the physicist who had directed RBMK design. Gorbachev complains bitterly in his memoirs that immediately after the accident Alexandrov and the powerful minister of Medium Machine Building, Yefim Slavsky, misled the Politburo, claiming (in Gorbachev's sarcastic parody): "Nothing terrible has occurred. These things happen at nuclear reactors. Just drink a little vodka, have a bite to eat, have a good night's sleep—forget it."

Confronted with stiff resistance within the Politburo, ill-informed himself, and badly advised by his experts, with the Swedish ambassador clamoring for more information, Gorbachev compromised and agreed to the broadcast of a simple, misleading statement on national television at nine p.m. that Monday night:

> From the USSR Council of Ministers: An accident has occurred at the Chernobyl nuclear power plant—one of the atomic reactors has been damaged. Measures are being undertaken to liquidate the consequences of the accident. Those affected are being given aid, and a government commission has been created.

It was a grudging beginning, but it opened a crack in the monolith that the full flood of world attention soon forced wide.

Hans Blix, the Swedish diplomat, who had trained at Columbia University in international law, was the director-general of the United Nations' International Atomic Energy Agency (IAEA) at that time. Blix, in Vienna, remembers hearing about the Chernobyl accident on the same Monday that the Politburo met. "I was phoned by the Swedish minister of energy," he told me. "I then phoned around to Poland and other places, and on about Monday evening I heard from the Russians. Then they went public about it." One outcome of the Monday Politburo meeting was the appointment of a strategic group to follow and direct Chernobyl recovery operations from day to day. The group met for the first time on Tuesday. Its chairman was Nikolai Ryzhkov, a Gorbachev ally. Another prominent member was Central Committee secretary Alexander Yakovlev, one of the principal theoreticians behind Gorbachev's ambitious program of reforms. They more than counterbalanced Yegor Ligachev, a conservative who favored Gorbachev's reforms only so long as they sustained the Communist Party's leadership over the U.S.S.R. Blix told the Soviets that the IAEA was prepared to help in any way possible. Before the week was out, he was invited to travel to Moscow with a team of experts. Whether he and his team would be allowed to view the accident scene he did not yet know, but he prepared to pack his bags.

Pravda began publishing regular reports on the Chernobyl accident on 30 April—a major breakthrough for glasnost. On 1 May, Thursday, it reported that "the emission of radioactive substances has decreased, and radiation levels in the area of the atomic power station and in the station settlement [i.e., Pripyat] have gone down," which was true—temporarily. *Pravda* also claimed that as a result of the accident "two people died and a total of 197 were hospitalized; 49 of them have been discharged from the hospital after examination. Enterprises, collective farms, state farms and other institutions are operating normally." But evacuations of the rural areas around the Chernobyl plant were ongoing that week, so that by the next day, Friday, a ten-kilometer (6.2-mile) exclusion zone had been emptied of people and domestic animals, and there would soon be evidence that more casualties had been sustained than the numbers cited in official reports.

Ryzhkov and Ligachev traveled to Chernobyl that Friday to review the situation firsthand. They were just in time to hear of a new and imminent threat. By then the helicopters had dumped more than eleven million pounds of materials onto the reactor. The tons of sand, clay, lead, dolomite, and boron piled into the crater failed to seal it completely, however; the reactor was still sufficiently exposed to allow the chimney of air pulled up through the core's empty water channels to continue fanning the graphite fire. And since the pile of material was now so massive that it held in the heat, the temperature of the core had begun to rise, eventually reaching about 4,500°F. Superheated gas and particulates filtered up through the ruins, renewing the radioactive plume, and the level of radioactivity, which had been declining steadily, began again to increase. (On Monday it reached a level nearly as high as it had been on the first day of the accident.) Ryzhkov and Ligachev acted immediately: they ordered the exclusion zone enlarged from a ten-kilometer to a thirty-kilometer (nineteen-mile) radius, increasing the area to be evacuated by more than 1,000 square miles, including the town of Chernobyl, which dated back to the twelfth century and was a center of Hasidism. The journalist Svetlana Alexievich later interviewed a soldier who participated in the evacuations and remembered them vividly:

At first there was disbelief, this sense that it was a game. But it was a real war, an atomic war. We had no idea—what's dangerous and what's not, what should we watch out for, and what ignore? No one knew.

It was a real evacuation, right to the train stations. . . . We helped push kids through the windows of the train cars. We made the lines orderly—for tickets at the ticket window, for iodine at the pharmacy. In the lines people were swearing at one another and fighting. They broke the doors down on stores and stands. They broke the metal grates in the windows. . . .

Our system, it's a military system, essentially, and it works great in emergencies. You're finally free there, and necessary. Freedom! And in those times the Russian shows how great he is. How unique. We'll never be Dutch or German. And we'll never have proper asphalt and manicured lawns. But there'll always be plenty of heroes.

In a matter of days, about 116,000 people and eighty-six thousand head of cattle were evacuated from the larger exclusion zone, haphazardly, because housing and pasturage in which to resettle them were scarce. "We didn't just lose a town," one of the evacuees said. "We lost our whole lives."

AT THE SAME TIME THAT THE HEAT from the burning reactor intensified the radioactive plume by then circumnavigating the globe, it also threatened to melt down the fuel elements remaining in the reactor core. The massive seal weighed down on the core and crushed it against the weakened concrete lower shield, which was suspended above the water-filled shielding pool. Under these conditions, the Chernobyl historian Zhores Medvedev writes, the core could give way:

> It could burn down and drop into the large bubbler pool of water which was below the reactor vault. This would cause a new, more powerful explosion and complete dispersal of the full inventory of uranium, plutonium and large quantities of other radioactive products. By 3 May only about 3 or 4 percent of the total inventory of radionuclides had been released into the environment. . . . Probably not less than 10 percent of the core was blown out and scattered close to the reactor. . . . The main part of the destroyed reactor core was still trapped inside. . . . To prevent a second, even greater catastrophe there were now two urgent tasks: to drain the bubbler pool and to freeze the earth beneath the reactor building to make it solid.

By Sunday, 4 May, Soviet Army engineer units had brought in oil-drilling equipment and had begun drilling into the soil below the reactor. Through these channels they pumped liquid nitrogen at the rate of about one thousand cubic feet—fifty-five thousand pounds—per day to freeze the soil against a possible core meltdown. Liquid nitrogen injected into the spaces around the core vaporized to a cold cloud that soon smothered the fire. But putting out the fire had no effect on the increasing heat generated by the decaying fission products in the reactor's remaining fuel. Over the night of 6 to 7 May, sharply shadowed in floodlights, sweat-soaked in dark green ZZK protective suits and echoing gas masks that allowed only twenty-four minutes each of exposure to the intense radioactivity of the blown-out reactor, the engineers pumped five million gallons of water out of the bubbler pool. In the coming days they used shaped-charge explosives to blow holes through the concrete foundation, laid pipe into the empty pool, and pumped in enough concrete to fill it to a solid block. To prevent flooding in the late May rains, which might wash radioactivity down the Pripyat River into the Kiev Reservoir, engineer units built five miles of earthen dams and barriers along the river and lined them with polyethylene sheeting. That spring, half a million cubic yards of mud and sand were dredged from the Pripyat riverbed and replaced with gravel to trap radioactive runoff.

Eight days after the accident, on Sunday, 4 May, Gorbachev had still not discussed Chernobyl publicly. "We sat in front of the television for days," a young woman who lived just outside the thirty-kilometer exclusion zone told Alexievich, "waiting for Gorbachev to speak. The authorities didn't say anything." *Pravda,* citing the U.S.S.R. Council of Ministers, continued to underplay the numbers of casualties. On 2 May it had admitted to eighteen people "in serious condition" and said there were "no foreign citizens among the victims." But secret protocols of the Politburo strategic group's meetings reveal much higher numbers. One of the few protocols made public, dated 4 May, reported that "1,882 people were treated in hospital [on that day]. The total number of people treated reached 38,000. Two hundred four people were discovered to have been affected to greater or lesser degrees by irradiation syndrome, of whom 64 were children. Eighteen are in serious condition."

Blix arrived in Moscow on Tuesday, 6 May, with two IAEA nuclear experts, an American and a Russian. The delegation, thoroughly briefed by Soviet officials and scientists, watched a film shot from one of the helicopters that surveyed the damaged reactor and heard from eyewitnesses who had reached the Chernobyl complex within a few hours of the explosions. But the vital question for Blix was whether or not he would be allowed to visit the accident site itself. "I know in retrospect," he says, "that the question went to the Politburo and that Mr. Gorbachev himself had argued that, yes, they should be invited, while others felt that the traditional policy of secrecy should be continued." Gorbachev won the argument, extending glasnost that much further; Blix and his team would fly to Kiev on Thursday.

Tuesday also saw the first official news conference devoted to the disaster, organized by the Soviet Ministry of Foreign Affairs. Shevardnadze sponsored such an unprecedented revelation, he writes, "so that the truth about Chernobyl would be known to the country and to the whole world." He adds that he "was not able to do much." At least Kiev was apprised that day—for the first time, ten days late—about the fallout risk. Tuesday's secret Politburo strategic group protocol reported that "the number of people treated in hospital [on 6 May] rose to 3,454; among these, 2,609 were admitted, of whom 471 were children. According to more precise figures, the number of people affected by irradiation syndrome is 367 people, of whom 19 are children. Of these, 34 are in a serious condition. One hundred and seventy-nine people have been admitted to six Moscow hospitals, of whom two are children." Gorbachev himself attended the Wednesday meeting of the strategic group and heard that "in one day, the list of people treated in hospital rose by 1,821. By . . . 7 May the number of people admitted to hospital had reached 4,301, of whom 1,351 were children. In 520 of these, irradiation syndrome was diagnosed, including people working for the Ministry of the Interior of the USSR [i.e., the KGB]. The number of people whose condition is serious is 34." He could not claim not to have been informed.

The IAEA team toured Kiev and then helicoptered north to the Chernobyl complex. "We circled the whole site," Blix told me, "and saw the black smoke coming up from the graphite, and then we had extensive briefings by the Russians about what had happened." Andranik Petrosyants, the head of the Soviet atomic energy program, who was traveling with Blix, remembered that "the helicopter made two rounds of the destroyed reactor building. We did not fly directly over the reactor itself, but circumvented it to avoid the high radioactivity. The reactor was smothered with debris, including lead, dropped from helicopters, and though smoke was still seeping from the burning wooden and other structures, it was clear the fire was over." Blix's dosimeter registered a hazardous 3.5 rem per hour, however, fire or no. "And then we went back to Moscow and we had a huge press conference there," Blix recalls. "We thought our main job was to inform the outside world by objective statements and understanding and we did. However, somewhat to my surprise I found that maybe our impressions were even more important in Russia, because the Russian population had not believed a word of what their own authorities said. But they believed outside people coming from an international organization. So it calmed the atmosphere, because they thought it was even worse than it was. It was bad enough."

In our conversation about Chernobyl, Blix emphasized twice that he had not gone to Moscow to "scream" at the Soviet leaders but to help them. Certainly the rest of the world was screaming by then, with minimal but measurable quantities of Chernobyl radionuclides falling out around the world and particularly on Western Europe; the Chernobyl fallout was roughly equivalent to the fallout from a twelve-megaton nuclear explosion (the explosions themselves had been equivalent to about thirty to forty tons of TNT). Blix's statements did help, and in exchange for them he extracted historic agreements from Gorbachev to make available timely information about the accident and its aftermath. "The Soviet authorities agreed," he said later, "to provide daily information on radiation levels from seven measurement stations, one close to Chernobyl and the other six along the Western border of the USSR." They agreed as well to participate in a post-accident review meeting and to increase cooperation in the field of nuclear safety. "It is sad, but a common experience," Blix concludes, "that only big accidents or other setbacks will provide the necessary impetus to move governments and authorities to act."

In this context, as in so many others, Chernobyl was exceptional. "It was the first time in Soviet history," Zhores Medvedev comments, "that an offer was made to put records of Soviet technology and details of an accident before the international scientific community for analysis and judgment."* Gorbachev judged the political effects of the accident to be mixed. On the one hand, it "shed light on many of the sicknesses of our system as a whole. Everything that had built up over the years converged in this drama: the concealing or hushing up of accidents and other bad news, irresponsibility and carelessness, slipshod work, wholesale drunkenness. This was one more convincing argument in favor of radical reforms." On the other hand, Chernobyl "severely affected our reforms by literally knocking the country off its tracks."

After their press conference on Friday, 9 May, Blix and his colleagues left Moscow to return to Vienna. And finally, on the following Wednesday, 14 May, eighteen days after the accident and one day after preparations had been announced to end school early for the 370,000 children of Kiev Province and send them south for the summer to work-and-recreation camps, a haggard Gorbachev appeared on Moscow evening television to deliver an unprecedented speech. "A misfortune has befallen us," he began,

---

* A conference for this purpose was held in Vienna under IAEA sponsorship in August 1986, where the physicist Valery Legasov spoke without notes and in unprecedented detail for almost five hours. Ultimately, however, the accident was blamed on the Reactor Number Four operators. Since it occurred in the course of an equipment test that should have been carried out before the reactor was certified for operation, and resulted from disconnecting the reactor's safety backup systems, the operators and plant management were certainly at fault, and were punished accordingly, with prison terms. But the reactor's flawed design, which made it unstable at low power and prone to running away to prompt criticality, should have indicted its designers and sponsors in the military-industrial complex as well. (See Yaroshinskaya, 1995, pp. 94–99.)

but with the old guard looking over his shoulder he went on to assert, falsely, that "this is the first time we have had to deal with a force as powerful as nuclear energy that has gone out of control." The secret Politburo protocol for 12 May had listed 10,198 people "admitted to hospital for observation or treatment, of whom 345 [including thirty-five children] show symptoms of radiation syndrome," but in his speech Gorbachev claimed that only 299 people had been hospitalized, "diagnosed as having radiation sickness at varying degrees of gravity." He praised the workers who were struggling "to eliminate the consequences of the accident" and the neighbors in the provinces outside the exclusion zone who received the evacuees into their homes. Implicitly he revealed the reason he had delayed so long before speaking publicly about the accident: to be able "to say today that the worst is over. The most serious consequences have been averted." He thanked Blix and the IAEA and "our friends in socialist countries" for their support.

Then, reverting again to old-style Cold War rhetoric, he warned the Soviet people that "certain NATO [North Atlantic Treaty Organization] countries, especially the USA," had launched "a wanton anti-Soviet campaign" that had piled up "a veritable mountain of lies—most brazen and malicious lies" about Chernobyl, such as "thousands of casualties," "mass graves of the dead" and "Kiev deserted." They were looking for a pretext, he said, that could be used "to try to defame the Soviet Union and its foreign policy, to lessen the impact of Soviet proposals on the termination of nuclear tests and on the elimination of nuclear weapons"—referring to the voluntary Soviet moratorium on weapons tests, begun in 1985, that the United States had pointedly not matched, and his bold January proposal to Ronald Reagan to eliminate all nuclear weapons before the end of the century.

Swinging back to his program of reform, Gorbachev then spoke with feeling of the impact of the Chernobyl nuclear accident on his understanding of the perils of nuclear war:

> For all this, it should not be forgotten that in our world, where everything is interrelated, problems with the military atom exist alongside those of the peaceful atom. . . . The accident at Chernobyl showed again what an abyss will open if nuclear war befalls mankind. The stockpiled nuclear arsenals are fraught with thousands upon thousands of disasters far more horrible than the one at Chernobyl.

Whereupon he announced that his government would extend its unilateral moratorium on nuclear tests until 6 August 1986, the forty-first anniversary of the U.S. atomic bombing of Hiroshima—a pointed reminder of the destructive force of even a small nuclear weapon, as the thirteen-kiloton bomb exploded over Hiroshima had come to seem.

THE STRUGGLE TO DEAL WITH THE fallout of radionuclides that had contaminated large areas of Soviet territory continued through the summer and fall and across the next winter. When the leaves fell from the chestnut trees that are the glory of Kiev, proud on its high bluff above the Dnieper River, they had to be raked up, all three hundred thousand tons of them, baled and buried outside the city as low-level nuclear waste. "Liquidators" by the hundreds of thousands, perhaps half a million in all—340,000 soldiers, many of them recently returned from service in Afghanistan, new draftees, minor government employees such as teachers and inspectors—were pressed into service and took their brief turn scraping away topsoil, paving over roads, spraying plastic coatings onto schoolyards and fallow fields, burying gardens, houses, equipment, wells. "We buried the forest," one of them told Alexievich. "We sawed the trees into meter-and-a-half pieces and packed them in cellophane and threw them into graves. . . . It was just your average Russian chaos. That's how we live." In November 1986, after a heroic effort, workers finished entombing Reactor Number Four within a sarcophagus made of half a million cubic yards of reinforced concrete, and only then did it cease releasing radiation into the environment.

"More than 500 residential communities, nearly 60,000 buildings and structures, and several tens of millions of square meters of exposed surfaces of technological equipment and internal surfaces at the [nuclear-power plant] itself have been decontaminated," Colonel-General Vladimir Pikalov of the U.S.S.R. Chemical Forces summarized a year later. "Tens of thousands of cubic meters of contaminated soil has been removed and the same amount brought in and several thousand insulating screens have been laid down. Dust has been suppressed on vast territories and several thousand samples have been taken for radioactive isotope analysis."

Shevardnadze came to call 26 April 1986 "Chernobyl Day." It "tore the blindfold from our eyes," he wrote later. It tore the blindfold as well from the eyes of hundreds of thousands of Soviet citizens living in the western Soviet Union. "Chernobyl happened," a Byelorussian biologist told Alexievich, "and suddenly you got this new feeling, we weren't used to it, that everyone has his separate life. Until then no one needed this life. But now you had to think: what are you eating, what are you feeding your kids? What's dangerous, what isn't? Should you move to another place, or should you stay? Everyone had to make her own decisions. And we were used to living—how? As an entire village, as a collective—a factory, a kolkhoz [i.e., a collective farm]. We were Soviet people, we were collectivized. . . . Then we changed. Everything changed."

Eastern Europe changed. The European Community banned imports of Soviet, Polish, Czechoslovakian, Hungarian, Romanian, and Bulgarian agricultural products worth $500 million annually as of 7 May 1986, inflicting great economic hardship on populations already restive in response to Gorbachev's relaxation of authoritarian control. Ironically, the purpose of recent Soviet nuclear-power development had been to increase electrical capacity available to Eastern Europe. "The decision to accelerate the nuclear-energy program had been taken in 1974," Zhores Medvedev explains, "when the international price of oil rose sharply and export demand increased. Oil became the main source of foreign exchange after 1974. Poor [Soviet] harvests meant that large imports of grain and food were necessary. As a result, the replacement of oil by nuclear energy became a priority." More than any other natural resource, oil propped up the stagnant Soviet economy, but the oil the Soviet Union supplied to Eastern Europe went at subsidized rates. Replacing most of that oil with nuclear electricity would free it up for foreign trade. The new Five-Year Plan that Gorbachev's government had introduced at the 27th Party Congress in February 1986 had called for doubling nuclear-generated electricity, primarily by building reactors in the Ukraine. Those plans were now in doubt.

Shevardnadze concluded that "Chernobyl was the first test of *glasnost,* and it failed." Certainly the disaster was never discussed publicly with the candor that Gorbachev and his advisers claimed. But as the affected population was changed by it, as Eastern Europe was changed, so also was Gorbachev changed. He had been "profoundly realistic" in his attitude toward nuclear proliferation even before Chernobyl, writes the Soviet historian Dmitri Volkogonov: "In April 1985 he had ordered that the North Korean leadership be told that a nuclear reactor being built with Soviet help must be under the control" of the IAEA. "In July of the same year he had informed Colonel Qaddafi that he would not agree to the Soviet-built nuclear research center in Libya being used for the production of heavy water, which could lead to Libya's acquiring nuclear weapons." In the months after Chernobyl, the American analyst William Potter reports, "senior Polish and Hungarian Communist Party officials who had contact with the Soviet political leadership" told him that the accident had a "profound impact . . . on Gorbachev's thinking about the consequences of nuclear war." Gorbachev had said as much in his speech to the Soviet people on 14 May, but the West had dismissed the statement as propaganda. It went much deeper than propaganda, deep as a wound. George Shultz, the secretary of state under the Reagan administration, saw its lasting effect on Gorbachev at a dinner in 1988 and noted it in a memo:

> I was struck by how deeply affected Gorbachev appeared to be by the Chernobyl accident. He commented that it was a great tragedy which cost the Soviet Union billions of rubles and had only been barely overcome through the tireless efforts of an enormous number of people. Gorbachev noted with seemingly genuine horror the devastation that would occur if nuclear power plants became targets in a conventional war much less a full nuclear exchange.

"His mind was undergoing a sweeping 'de-ideologization,'" Gorbachev's adviser Anatoly Chernyaev thought. The Soviet deputy foreign minister Alexander Bessmertnykh commented later that "Chernobyl . . . was something like one-third of the smallest nuclear explosive. And if it caused such great damage to almost half of Europe, what would happen if we should use all those arsenals we now have in our hands?" Gorbachev told a Politburo meeting in July 1986, "Global nuclear war can no longer be the continuation of rational politics, as it would bring the end of all life, and therefore of all politics." And thinking perhaps of Chernobyl, he added, "What happened in this country is that a rigid system was created and then life was herded into it."

TWO MOSCOW DOES NOT BELIEVE IN TEARS

MIKHAIL SERGEYEVICH GORBACHEV, a son of southern Russian farmers, was born in a time and place of neomedieval horror—corpses strewn along the roads and across the fields and starving families reduced to eating horse manure or the flesh of the dead. In medieval times such disastrous conditions would have measured an outbreak of the Black Death; in March 1931, in a western corner of the Stavropol steppe lands of the North Caucasus, over the mountains from Georgia, it measured Joseph Stalin's deliberate starvation of the independent farmers ("peasants," "middle peasants," "kulaks") who dared to resist giving up their hard-won land, animals, and machinery for the unrewarding serfdom of the collective farm. The name of the village where Gorbachev was born, on 2 March 1931, in a two-room wattle-and-daub house with a dirt floor, was Privolnoye, meaning "free and easy," but free and easy it had not been since the late 1920s, when forced collectivization began.

The Communist Party had first given what it was now taking away. "My [maternal] grandfather [Panteli Yefimovich Gopkalo] had been a poor peasant," Gorbachev says, "and beginning from a very early age, after the death of his father, had to be concerned about a family in which there were five children. During World War I my grandfather was on the Turkish front, and he returned from the war with a definitely radical outlook, which was typical of the soldiers at that time. Then after the revolution, when the family was given the land it worked on, my grandfather was won over completely to the side of the Soviet government. In the oral history of our family it was constantly repeated: *the revolution gave our family land.*" (Raisa Maksimovna Titorenko, whom Gorbachev would marry, heard a similar appreciation at home in western Siberia: "*Lenin gave my parents land—that is what my mother always says. . . .*"

Land or not, grandfather Gopkalo cast his lot with the Party from the beginning. The first version of collective farming that the Party endorsed, in the early 1920s, was the Association for the Joint Cultivation of Land, known by its Russian initials as a TOZ; the TOZ were "not really collective farms at all," the historian Robert Conquest notes, "but merely associations for joint tillage, ploughing, harvesting and sharing the proceeds." Gopkalo had signed on immediately, and Gorbachev's mother, Maria Panteleyevna, had worked on a TOZ as a young woman. In 1928, Gopkalo joined the Party. "He participated in organizing our *kolkhoz,* 'Khleborob,' " Gorbachev says of the collective farm his grandfather then helped to establish in Privolnoye, "and was its first chairman." He must have been an exceptional leader: Many if not most kolkhoz chairmen were Party members sent out from the city who couldn't tell a harrow from a plow. "Loyalty to the Party and to its policy in dealing with the farmers," writes a Ukrainian émigré who lived through this era, "were valid enough recommendations for this office." Kolkhoz chairmen were subservient in any case to resident Party leaders, whose veto authority paralleled that of political commissars in the Red Army. But Gopkalo knew farming, which gave him an advantage in trying to fulfill Moscow's increasingly draconian requisitions of grain; in the 1930s, when Gorbachev lived with his maternal grandparents, Gopkalo was promoted to the chairmanship of the larger Red October kolkhoz in a village twelve miles from Privolnoye.

Ironically, the campaign to decapitate the leadership of the rural communities of the Soviet Union, which Stalin called "the liquidation of the kulaks as a class," interfered with collectivization. (Kulaks were supposed to be "the capitalists of the village," but the net was cast wide. Conquest estimates the value of the average kulak's property at $150. "A typical kulak," he says, "would have something like 12 acres, a cow, a horse, 10 sheep, a hog and about 20 chickens, on a farm supporting four people." So-called middle peasants like Gorbachev's grandparents owned even less.) Early in 1930, some ten million small farms were forcibly collectivized in a matter of months, while millions of "kulaks" whose property had been expropriated—40 percent of them children—were packed into railroad freight cars with little food or water, transported north of the Arctic Circle or into Siberia, and crowded together, starving, in churches, monasteries, and temporary barracks while the able-bodied among them struggled in the northern forests in deep snow and cold to build one of the first bitter islands of the Gulag archipelago. Dmitri Volkogonov, the Soviet historian, estimates that 8.5 to 9 million "men, women, old people and children . . . were affected by dekulakization, most of them torn root and branch from their native habitat. Many were shot for resisting, many died en route. In some places . . . the process also swept up many middle peasants. . . . One way or another something like 6 to 8 percent of peasant households were sucked into the vortex."

The farmers responded to forced collectivization—state appropriation of their property without compensation—and the threat of being designated kulaks and exiled by selling or slaughtering their animals; by March 1930, Conquest writes, "even by official figures, over 40 percent of the country's cattle and 65 percent of the sheep had gone" and "Stalin's policy lay in ruins." When the breaker of nations lifted away his hammer, more than half the farmers who had submitted to collectivization returned to independent farming. Stalin attacked again with orders to deport resisters beginning in February 1931, a month before Gorbachev was born. Conquest specifically mentions "the Stavropol area in the North Caucasus" as a place where farmers trying to escape "drove herds of oxen, dairy cows, horses and sheep from district to district," to no avail. "It is to an activist of this period," Conquest notes, "that the well-known saying is attributed: 'Moscow does not believe in tears.'"

Forcing families to give up their property, forcing them onto collective farms or into exile, was brutal business. If Gorbachev's grandfather Gopkalo participated in organizing and leading a collective farm, he could not have escaped complicity. Nor did collectivized farmers necessarily work willingly. One of Gorbachev's Moscow University roommates, the Czech political leader Zdenek Mlynar, remembers Gorbachev explaining to him "how insignificant farm legislation was in everyday life and how important, on the other hand, was brute force which alone secured working discipline on the collective farms."

"Up to the end of 1931," writes the Ukrainian émigré Miron Dolot, "the Communists fought their war against the farmers under the guise of fighting against 'the [kulaks] as a social class.' But by 1932, the situation had already changed: the so-called [kulaks] had already been physically liquidated, and collectivization had been completed except for a small number of farmers who were still clinging to their freedom. Thus, the battle now was fought between the Communist forces and the collective farmers; the Collectivization Campaign now changed into the Grain Collection Campaign."

In the 1930s, the new Soviet state pursued a program of rapid industrialization, primarily to prepare itself for the war against Fascism and capitalism that Marxist theory declared to be inevitable. "With collectivization" of agriculture, writes Martin Malia, ". . . economically the regime was guaranteed a food supply independent of the caprices of the market, a supply for which the regime therefore did not have to pay. With this assured, they could then

advance on the second, and more important, front—the Promethean development of heavy industry. . . ." Stalin particularly feared the Japanese, who
had invaded Manchuria in 1931 and were poised to invade China. Industrialization drew 8.5 million farm workers into the city among 12.5 million new
industrial recruits in the Soviet Union between 1929 and 1932. "This increase
in the urban population meant, among other things, that more food was
needed to supply them," Conquest writes, adding that "26 million urban
persons were provisioned by the State in 1930. In 1931, this had risen to
33.2 million, nearly 26 percent." Grain requisitions from the kolkhozy increased accordingly, more than doubling between 1929 and 1932, while production had in fact greatly declined—mostly because of the disruptive
reorganization of agriculture, partly from the passive resistance of the
kolkhozniks. As Nikita Khrushchev remembered, "All too frequently the
peasants would have to turn everything over they produced—literally everything! Naturally, since they received no compensation whatsoever for their
work, they lost interest in the collective farm and concentrated instead on
their private plots to feed their families."

In retaliation, as of October 1931, a new law required the kolkhozy to meet
their requisitions from the state before they met their own needs, and in July
1932, when Gorbachev was a sixteen-month-old toddler, Stalin set an impos-
sibly high goal for the year's grain requisitions: nearly half the harvest. Since
as much as 30 percent of the total harvest was routinely lost to inadequate
collection, transportation, and storage, the 1932 requisitions programmed
deliberate mass starvation. Famine had already broken out among the most
vulnerable part of the population, Dolot writes:

> I remember the endless procession of beggars on roads and paths, going from
> house to house. They were in different stages of starvation, dirty and ragged.
> With outstretched hands, they begged for food, any food: a potato, a beet, or at
> least a kernel of corn. Those were the first victims of starvation: destitute men
> and women; poor widows and orphaned children who had no chance of sur-
> viving the terrible ordeal.

The final twist of the knife was an August 1932 decree that Stalin himself
drafted. Dolot assesses its effect:

> One of the cruelest laws of all was enacted on August 7, 1932. This law decreed
> that all [kolkhoz] and cooperative property such as the crops in the fields, com-
> munity surpluses and storehouses, livestock, warehouses, stores and so forth
> were hereupon to be considered as state owned. The protection of such prop-

erty from theft was to be enforced in every possible way. The penalties for theft were execution by firing squad and confiscation of all property of the guilty one. The alternative sentence was no less than ten years of penal servitude in a labor camp as well as confiscation of property. . . .

This law . . . was aimed at the starving farmers. No other interpretation is possible. Only those poor, hungry wretches in quest of food were driven and forced by hunger to steal from the communal, and now state-owned, property. . . . Not only petty thievery of a potato or a couple of heads of grain from the communal fields was considered a grave offense against the state: it was considered a great crime to even glean the already harvested fields, to fish in the rivers, or to pick up some dry branches in the forest for firewood. After the passage of this law, everything was considered socialist, state-owned property, and thus everything was protected by law.

Guard towers went up in the fields, manned by watchmen armed with shotguns. A further attack followed in December when a new decree imposed an internal passport system that the rural population was denied, preventing the starving from evacuating their villages for the city, where work and food might be found, a restriction more extreme than any that had prevailed for serfdom under the czars. A German agricultural attaché, Otto Schiller, traveled through the North Caucasus that spring and reported to Berlin in May 1933 on the appalling conditions he found there; the report, which included the Stavropol district, is worth quoting at length:

> The famine is not so much the result of last year's failure of crops as of the brutal campaign of State Grain Collection. Therefore even such localities as the Northern districts of North Caucasia in which the crops were quite satisfactory, did not escape. . . .
>
> In the villages I visited the number of deaths varied between 20–30 a day. Those still alive are enfeebled in the extreme through semi-starvation, and also by the eating of such unnatural food as grass, roots, charred bones, dead horses, etc. And the majority will doubtless die from malaria with the arrival of the warm weather, this disorder having prevailed to an unprecedented extent since last Autumn. The typhus which now appears sporadically will probably become an epidemic. . . .
>
> The villages stricken by famine give an impression of utter hopelessness. The abandoned homes are rapidly falling to ruin. . . . In the forsaken courtyards the present inventory is seen lying, perishing in disorder. . . . The kitchen gardens are for the most part unworked. . . . A dog or cat is extremely rarely met with—most of them had been eaten. . . .
>
> The present situation in Northern Caucasus may be summed up as follows:

In some of the villages the population is almost extinct. In other about half the population have died out. And there are still villages in which death from famine is not so frequent.

But famine reigns everywhere, at least in those regions which I have visited. . . .

People have become callous and indifferent to the fate of those near to them. One meets people with legs swollen from starvation who move with difficulty. Others have already become so weak that they lie about in the road waiting for death. Several days usually elapse before a chance passerby endeavors to help them.

One can therefore see bodies of those dead from famine not only on the highroads, but even in the streets of the towns. . . .

In Krasnodar a German living there told me that bodies from which pieces had been cut off to serve as human food had been found. Personally, however, I cannot vouch for this.

What strikes one in all the villages is the small percentage of men. They have evidently less power of resistance, and more easily fall victims to the famine. The women who have children die sooner than others, therefore single women predominate in the villages which have suffered most severely.

Gorbachev would acknowledge these events at various times, if briefly and impatiently. His paternal grandfather Andrei Moiseyevich Gorbachev, he said, had resisted collectivization, unlike Panteli Gopkalo, and had been denounced "for not fulfilling the sowing plan in 1933, a year when half the family died of hunger. They took him away to Irkutsk to a timber-producing camp, and the rest of the family was broken, half-destroyed in that year." Three of Andrei Moiseyevich's children starved to death, Gorbachev reveals in his memoirs. "The famine was terrible. A third, if not half, of the population of Privolnoye died of hunger. Entire families were dying, and the half-ruined ownerless huts would remain deserted for years." His father, Sergei, carried the burden of supporting his grandmother Stepanida and two aunts until grandfather Gorbachev returned from Irkutsk after serving only two years of a nine-year sentence, in 1935—"bearing two letters of appreciation for his work," Gorbachev notes, adding without irony that he "joined the *kolkhoz* immediately." Evidently Gorbachev lived with his maternal grandparents in his preschool years because the Gopkalos, unlike the Gorbachevs, had found a way not to starve.

Then in 1937, in the further brutal repression of the Great Terror, when executioners with axes were splitting skulls in prison basements all over the Soviet Union, when at least a million people were "purged" and murdered among more than five million arrested as Stalin consolidated his power, it was Gorbachev's grandfather Panteli Gopkalo's turn. Gorbachev calls his grandfather's arrest in the middle of the night when Gorbachev was only six years old his "first real trauma."

"After Grandfather's arrest," Gorbachev remembers, "our neighbors began shunning our house as if it were plague-stricken. Only at night would some close relative venture to drop by. Even the boys from the neighborhood avoided me. . . . All of this was a great shock to me and has remained engraved in my memory ever since."

Raisa's grandfather Petr Stepanovich Parada was arrested at about the same time as Gorbachev's grandfather, interrogated at about the same time, found guilty and executed. Gopkalo was luckier; the NKVD* itself was purged while his case was in process, "the head of our regional department committed suicide, and in December 1938 Grandfather was released from prison." Within a year the popular and resourceful Gopkalo was back running the kolkhoz.

He had suffered for his sins:

> I remember well the winter evening when Grandfather returned home. His closest relatives sat around the hand-planed rustic table and Panteli Yefimovich recounted all that had been done to him.
>
> Trying to get him to confess, the investigator blinded him with a glaring lamp, beat him unmercifully, broke his arms by squeezing them in the door. When these "standard" tortures proved futile, they invented a new one: they put a wet sheepskin coat on him and sat him on a hot stove. Panteli Yefimovich endured this too, as well as much else.

Gorbachev's grandfather never again spoke of his ordeal. And like many others of that era who were imprisoned and tortured, "he was convinced that Stalin did not know about the misdeeds of the NKVD and he never blamed the Soviet regime for his misfortunes." Shaken by the cognitive dissonance of having been tortured and imprisoned for crimes he did not commit by representatives of the ideology to which he had wholly dedicated himself, Gopkalo reduced the dissonance by dividing the Party and its leader off from its army of enforcers, blaming the enforcers for his mistreatment and idealizing the leadership. This early experience, Gorbachev's "first real trauma," is a point of origin for his similar mental separation of the Leninist ideal he believed in from the failing and corrupt bureaucracy he confronted when he

* The secret police, predecessor to the KGB.

came to power himself in 1985. As the writer David Remnick characterizes it, "The tragedy of the Stalin era and the farce of the Brezhnev period represented for Gorbachev not the failure of ideology, but rather its perversion."

Similar compartmentalization helped prepare Gorbachev to bury his doubts during the years of his rise to power and to conceal his radicalism from his Politburo colleagues even after they elected him general secretary. Dolot describes how the process worked on a Ukrainian kolkhoz:

> In the collective farm, our personal existence became completely dependent upon the dictates of the Communist Party, and on the whims of the local officials. Every detail of our life was supervised. Our daily routine was subject to the strictest regimentation. We had to obey orders without any protest, and without giving any thought as to their sense or purpose. A vast system of secret police, spies and *agents provocateurs* watched our every move.
>
> We were always suspected of treason. Even sadness or happiness were cause for suspicion. Sadness was thought of as an indication of dissatisfaction with our life, while happiness, regardless of how sporadic, spontaneous or fleeting, was considered to be a dangerous phenomenon that could destroy the devotion to the Communist cause. You had to be cautious about the display of feelings at all times, and in every place. We were all made to understand that we would be allowed to live only as long as we followed the Party line, both in our private and social lives.

But in Gorbachev's case, the local official whose "whims" he and his family depended upon was his grandfather, so that what was oppression for people like this Ukrainian émigré was opportunity for Gorbachev—and in any case, the only reality he knew. "Not only I," he reminisced once, "but the generation before me, took as an existing reality, as a given, everything that had taken place under Communist rule; we took it as a given that the system we lived under was socialism. . . . Thus we developed the outlook, in reference to the reality in which we were living, that no alternative was possible."

Conditions on the kolkhozy improved in the later 1930s, partly because the millions of executions in the years of the Great Terror had reduced the number of mouths to feed. "The shops had calico and [kerosene] to sell," Gorbachev remembers. "Grandfather Panteli replaced the thatched roof with tiles. Gramophones appeared in the shops. On rare occasions, 'silent' movies would be shown on portable film projectors. And the height of bliss for us children would be the ice cream brought into the village now and then." In those years, Gorbachev's quiet, hardworking father, Sergei, found a niche as a machine operator attached to a Machine Tractor Station, harvesting grain with a tractor-drawn combine, a new implement introduced into cereal farming in the 1930s that combined into one field operation the two previously separate functions of binding and threshing. Conquest calls the Machine Tractor Station—a centralized depot for farm machinery established by government decree in 1929—"the third great element of socialization in the countryside." (The other two elements were the collective and state farms.) Some 2,500 MTS's were operating by 1932, and since they controlled not only the schedule of farmwork on the kolkhozy but also the deliveries of grain and other crops from the kolkhozy to the Soviet government, they were quickly infested with Party officials and secret police. As such, they offered security and opportunity to farmers like Sergei Gorbachev who made themselves useful.

Nazi Germany invaded the Soviet Union on 22 June 1941. Having achieved complete surprise, the Wehrmacht troops rapidly swept eastward. "The village was drained of its inhabitants within weeks," Gorbachev remembers— "all the men had gone." For the rest of the war, the women and children worked the fields. "Gorbachev passed through the formative years of puberty working shoulder to shoulder with women," the writer Gail Sheehy points out, which was one source of his immense self-confidence. "He was a male child, a robust and energetic male child, and as such, prized beyond any possession. . . . One out of every three Soviet males between the ages of eighteen and twenty-one watered the ground of Russia with their dying blood" during the Second World War. "So it is easy to understand why mothers of that generation treated their living sons like gold." On the rare occasions when a batch of newspapers reached Privolnoye, Gorbachev read the news to the illiterate adults of his village, who even asked his advice about their problems. But he was young enough (twelve years old in 1943) that an evening among the women at someone's home, when fear for their lives and a reading of their husbands' letters started them weeping, left him feeling "unbearable terror."

The fighting front passed around Privolnoye in August 1942, close enough that Gorbachev saw a volley of the Red Army's Katyusha rockets for the first time, "fiery arrows crossing the skies with a frightening whistling sound." After the rockets, silence, and then on the third day the sound of German motorcycles approaching. The Wehrmacht troops crowded the village, uprooted its orchards for camouflage materials and soon passed on, pushing southeast along the Caucasus toward the Baku oil fields, leaving behind a sixty-man garrison. "Rumors of mass executions in the neighboring towns circulated," Gorbachev recalls, "and of machines that poisoned people with gas." Himmler's killing squads, the SS Einsatzgruppen, which followed behind the German Army murdering Jews, were just then changing their methods from shooting their victims into killing pits to poisoning them in mobile gas vans, but another Privolnoye resident, Grigory Gorlov, told Sheehy that some 370 Jewish families, both local and refugee, were shot to death into pits dug beside the river that edged the village. There were rumors that Communist families would be murdered as well; to protect their golden child, Gorbachev's mother and grandmother hid him on a farm outside Privolnoye until the village was liberated in late January 1943, after a five-month occupation.

The problem for the rest of the war was simple survival. The women grew hemp, processed it into thread, and wove cloth for clothing. (A shirt made from such rough thread, writes Gorbachev, "felt as if it was made of wood.") They spun wool for coats and made hides into shoes. Matches made of TNT from tank mines lit their fires; salt evaporated from a salt lake thirty miles away seasoned their food. Famine struck in the winter and spring of 1944; Gorbachev's mother organized an ox-cart mission to a distant district rumored to have a store of grain and sold a suit her husband had never worn and two new pairs of his boots for a hundred-pound sack of corn that saved their lives.

That summer, notice arrived from the front that Gorbachev's father had been killed in the Carpathians after surviving battles in Rostov, Kursk, Kiev, and Lvov. "The family cried for three days," Gorbachev writes. "Then a letter arrived from Father saying he was alive and well." The boy's response was typical: "I wrote to him to express my indignation at the death notice sent to us." Don't be so hard on us, his father responded: Anything can happen in a war. A shrapnel wound to the leg in Czechoslovakia sent Sergei Gorbachev to the hospital and then home not long before the German surrender in May 1945. During the war he had joined the Party.

Gorbachev's worst memory of the war, he says—he still had flashbacks in his sixties—was encountering the rotting remains of Soviet soldiers killed in battle in a forest near Privolnoye in 1943, when he was not quite twelve, his first unprotected look at the "unspeakable horror" of war: "decaying corpses, partly devoured by animals, skulls in rusted helmets, bleached bones, rifles protruding from the sleeves of the rotting jackets. . . . There they lay, in the thick mud of the trenches and craters, unburied, staring at us out of black, gaping eye-sockets." His generation, he adds, was "the generation of wartime children." The war had scorched them, "leaving its mark both on our characters and on our view of the world."

Like many of his peers, Gorbachev missed two years of school during the war. He studied all the harder afterward to make up for the loss, in a school knocked together from various village outbuildings, where students had to make their own ink and the horses kept for hauling firewood so nearly starved each winter that for weeks at a time they could not even stand. He joined the Communist Union of Youth, the Komsomol, as soon as he turned fourteen, in 1945, initiating his political career. The Komsomol was charged with "spreading the ideas of communism and involving worker and peasant youth in the active construction of Soviet Russia." Though it had become a mass movement by 1945, it still served as a Communist Party farm team. Gorbachev took it seriously, unlike many of his peers, already understanding that the Party was his only route to a future beyond Privolnoye. Could he have thought otherwise after what his father and grandfathers had survived?

At fifteen, in 1946, Gorbachev became an assistant at the Machine Tractor Station where his father worked. For the next four years and during university summer vacations, father and son labored together combining grain throughout the district from late June to late August, usually away from home. They slept with their machinery in the fields even when it rained, and when the weather was good they worked twenty hours a day—comfortable work in the cool of morning, hot, hard work in the blazing afternoon sun and then winding down to the buzz of cicadas in the cooling evening. Father and son could trade off at the controls without stopping the combine, and as all good farmers do, Gorbachev learned to judge the complicated machine's condition by listening to the sounds it made. But he was a teenage boy, not a grown man, and he suffered nosebleeds from the dusty dryness of the fields, sometimes fell asleep at the wheel, and lost at least ten pounds every summer.

In their downtime father and son talked about "a great variety of topics, work and life alike. Our simple father-son relationship . . . developed into a bond between two persons who shared a common cause and a common job. Father treated me with respect and we became true friends." From someone—perhaps his father, perhaps the women who had surrounded him in his formative early adolescence during the war—Gorbachev learned to substitute argument for violence. His high school girlfriend remembered him "correcting teachers in history class, and once he was so angry at one teacher he asked, 'Do you want to keep your teaching certificate?' He was the sort of man who felt he was right and could prove it to anyone, be it in the principal's office or at a Komsomol meeting." An American journalist couple who followed him closely after he became general secretary confirm his old girlfriend's observation; they remark on Gorbachev's "dislike of violence and his reliance on words as his main political weapon." They explain:

> In difficult situations he was given to hectoring and lecturing; he believed that, if his conclusion was logical and based on good evidence, others should accept it automatically. For those who ignored or discounted his views, he was ready to explain them one more time, but his tone would suddenly acquire an authoritarian edge. . . . Among his most beguiling qualities were a self-deprecating humor and a sense of proportion, both of which he used to win people over. But he also showed himself unrelenting and profane when necessary, which, in the setting of his native province, was often. Classmates remembered him during his student days as being an extrovert southerner who relished the *ruski mat* (Russian mother), as the rich compendium of Russian obscenities is known generically.

Unlike so many of the men around him, particularly among the veterans and the secret police, Gorbachev was never violently socialized. He could swear like a southern farmer when need be, but he carried the *ruski mat* in his bag of tricks partly to avoid the "brute force" that he told Zdenek Mlynar was necessary to motivate work discipline on a kolkhoz. Obvious physical strength, quick intelligence, confident authority supported by good political connections, psychological astuteness, and a knack for the bold, colorful swearing that can be at the same time a form of bullying and an aesthetic performance that defuses potentially violent confrontations: these traits, a gift to the world from the women who raised him and the calm father who finished shaping his character in adolescence, substituted in Gorbachev's case for brutality.

Famine approached again in 1946 when drought limited the grain harvest to only 37 million tonnes, of which the state took 17 million—"very, very hungry and hard times here for eight more years," a villager told Sheehy. (For comparison, the grain harvest in the United States in 1946 totaled 120 million tonnes.) The country had a better harvest in 1947—70 million tonnes—but around Stavropol the yield was low. "We somehow managed to make it through the winter," Gorbachev recalls stoically. The next year looked to be as bad—dust storms in April, "the terrible companions of drought"—but warm rains followed and raised a bountiful harvest. In 1947, the Supreme Soviet had decreed that medals would be awarded to combine operators who set records for threshing: a Hero of Socialist Labor for a thousand tonnes threshed in a season, an Order of Lenin for eight hundred. In 1948, Sergei Gorbachev and his energetic son threshed 889 tonnes. Sergei received the Order of Lenin, Gorbachev himself the Order of the Red Banner of Labor, a handsome bronze medal hung on a red-and-white-striped ribbon with a red banner enameled over its bronze-on-white hammer and sickle. "I was seventeen then," Gorbachev writes, "and this has been the most cherished of all my awards." As well it should be: Along with the endorsement of his Komsomol and an outstanding school record, it qualified him for a free university education. He chose the best school in the country, Moscow University, and traveled to Moscow for the first time at nineteen, in the autumn of 1950, to claim his future.

MOSCOW WAS NOT YET A MODERN CITY, although by 1950 postwar reconstruction had finally begun. The Soviet Union had suffered terribly from the war; the civilian population continued to suffer for years afterward as billions of rubles were diverted to the military and to the crash program to build the atomic bomb and stockpile a nuclear arsenal. Mlynar, arriving from Czechoslovakia and about to become one of Gorbachev's roommates, claims not to have been shocked by his first sight of Moscow, but his description is brutal:

> The problem was not chiefly the fact that Moscow was a huge village of wooden cottages, that people scarcely had enough to eat, that the most typical dress, even then, five years after the war, was old military war-issue uniforms, that most families lived in one room, that instead of flush toilets there was only an opening leading to the drain pipe, that both in the student residences and on the street people blew their noses into their hands, that what you didn't hang onto tightly would be stolen from you in a crowd, that drunks lay unconscious in the streets and could be dead for all the passers-by knew or cared, and that there were dozens and dozens of similar phenomena. All these facts seemed somehow explicable by the past. We did not go to the Soviet Union expecting to find a consumers' paradise, and, in any case, such was not to be found anywhere in Europe five years after the war. On the contrary, we considered the poverty and wretchedness we saw in Russia as a direct consequence of the war and of the terrible backwardness of czarist Russia.

(The problem, Mlynar concludes, was the cynicism and hypocrisy of the Party officials, the "absence of values that the faith itself considered as primarily necessary to the future of communism.")

Gorbachev had hoped to study physics. The astrophysicist Roald Sagdeev, a contemporary of Gorbachev's at the university (and later one of his advisers), believes that the physics course was closed to him because admission required proof that a student could qualify for a security clearance: Physicists were likely to be recruited for nuclear-weapons work, as Andrei Sakharov had been while still a postdoc working with his mentor Igor Tamm. Gorbachev's residence in Privolnoye during its four and a half months of wartime German occupation was probably what disqualified him, Sagdeev speculates. If so, the implication that Gorbachev might have been turned by the Germans was absurd: He was only eleven at the time.

Barred from studying physics, Gorbachev chose law, a distinctly minority choice in a country run by an absolute dictator but a choice that Lenin had also made. "I had only a rather vague idea what jurisprudence and law were all about," Gorbachev writes. "But the position of a judge or prosecutor impressed me." Even before he left Privolnoye he had understood that whatever he would do with his life would have to be done through the Communist Party; he had applied for full membership as soon as Party rules allowed, when he turned nineteen.

A classmate characterizes the hayseed law student from Privolnoye as romantic and innocent; in his university years Gorbachev's entire wardrobe consisted of one suit jacket, a few shirts, and a pair or two of pants. Housed in an old czarist barracks, first-years like Gorbachev lived twenty-two to a room (down to eleven in their second year and six in their third). "The Soviet state had added two extra floors" to the old building, Mlynar recalls, "to make room for 10,000 students . . . and for the several hundred on each floor there was only one collective latrine with a washing area and a single common kitchen. For everyone in the building there was a single Russian *banya* (bathhouse) in the courtyard." But a cup of tea cost only a few kopeks in the student cafeteria, and there was always bread on the table. At the end of the month, when they waited, broke, for the next month's stipend, a one-ruble can of beans offered subsistence. For a provincial born in the midst of famine who had survived the Great Patriotic War, these were conditions of luxury, set among wonders. "Everything was new to me," Gorbachev reminisces—"Red Square, the Kremlin, the Bolshoi Theatre (my first opera, my first ballet), the Tretyakov Gallery, the Pushkin Museum of Fine Arts, my first boat trip on the Moskva River, excursions to the countryside around Moscow, my first October demonstration. . . . And every time, I was overwhelmed by an incomparable sensation of novelty." Most of all he was hungry to learn. "University studies captivated me from the start and they took up all my time. I studied eagerly and passionately."

He did not neglect the Party. If he studied much longer and later than his more sophisticated Muscovite classmates, he also made time to participate actively in the student Komsomol; alumni from his era remember that he could be shrill and dogmatic about even minor deviations from the

Party line. First he was chosen *komsorg* of his class—its Party monitor and organizer—and then, in 1952, the year he was admitted to full Party membership, *komsorg* of the entire law school student body. In his memoirs he calls the Party education he endured a "massive ideological brainwashing," which "was designed to prevent us from developing a critical mind." Yet he notes ironically that "the first authors who sowed the seeds of doubt about the unquestionable 'ultimate truth' presented to us were Karl Marx, Friedrich Engels and Vladimir Lenin." Their works contained "a detailed criticism of their opponents' theses, a system of counter-arguments and theoretically sustained conclusions" that contrasted sharply with Stalin's argument from authority or simply from ad hominem abuse. Farmers can be skeptical of abstract thought: They know how much the world depends on rain and weather. With Mlynar and his war-veteran roommates, Gorbachev debated what could be debated, what they dared debate even in the relative privacy of their room. "Before the university I was trapped in my belief system in the sense that I accepted a great deal as given, as assumptions not to be questioned. At the university I began to think and reflect and to look at things differently. But of course that was only the beginning of a prolonged process."

Stalin had been off-limits—even, perhaps, to thought. At the beginning of March 1953, in the hard cold of Russian winter, the breaker of nations suffered a cerebral hemorrhage that left him unconscious and partly paralyzed. With his drunken son Vasili storming around the room and the members of the Politburo helplessly wringing their hands, he died at 9:50 a.m. on Thursday, 5 March 1953. Word spread quickly. Gorbachev and Mlynar heard the news together in a university lecture hall. "The instructor came in," Gorbachev writes, "and informed us with a tragic voice, tears veiling his eyes, of Stalin's untimely death, in the seventy-fourth year of his life. Later, talking to Gorbachev, Mlynar recalled that, while they stood for the two minutes of silence the instructor had requested, he had whispered to his roommate, " 'Misha, what's going to happen to us now?' And you in a voice full of alarm and uneasiness, answered, 'I don't know.' " Like hundreds of thousands of others, they decided they must view the leader in his open coffin in the white-and-gold Hall of Columns, the grand ballroom of the House of Trade Unions on Okhotny Ryad, where Lenin had lain in state in 1924 with Stalin among his ceremonial guards. A huge crowd converged on central Moscow. "We advanced slowly," Gorbachev remembers, "all day, stopping for hours in one place." Mlynar takes up the tale:

> The density of the crowd became that of a streetcar full to bursting at rush hour. At the same time there was a continual influx of tens of thousands from

behind, in front were the horses and soldiers, and on each side the barrier of trucks and the buildings. It was cold and the slush was slippery underfoot; anyone who fell down had little hope of ever getting up again, and help was impossible. Naturally, no statistics have ever been released about the number of people trampled to death or wounded, and it is difficult to estimate the total toll. But that night I myself saw dozens of wounded and unconscious people, and some I saw were dead. The casualties were loaded into trucks and gradually taken away.

Gorbachev had never seen Stalin before. Now he saw him dead, "a stony, waxen face, devoid of any signs of life. I searched for traces of his greatness, but there was something disturbing in his appearance that created mixed feelings."

Of equal or greater importance to Mikhail Gorbachev's future evolution into the charismatic reformer he became was his discovery, among the ten thousand other students in his dormitory, of a beautiful young woman from western Siberia named Raisa Maksimovna Titorenko. Raisa—Raya to her friends—was a year younger than Gorbachev, but she had entered the university a year ahead of him, in 1949, among what she called "the generation of the seventeen-year-olds." She won her university education by graduating at the top of her class. Her childhood had been nearly as impoverished as Gorbachev's and as marked by political repression.

Her Ukrainian father, Maxim, was a railroad construction worker who moved with his work. Raisa remembered with some bitterness "the neverending moves the family had to make in the wake of my father the railwayman, the trouble that this caused, the various flats we found to live in—goodness knows how many such 'nests' we occupied, and huts and wooden-frame houses. . . . So can you imagine what our life was like?" In a conversational memoir published in 1991 she described in some detail the expulsion of her father's family from their land as kulaks "at the beginning of the 1930s." Somewhat later, she said, her maternal grandfather was arrested and executed, as a result of which her grandmother "died of grief and hunger as the wife of an 'enemy of the people.' " So traumatic was this experience to Raisa that she associated it in the memoir with the vicious gossip and scheming she and Gorbachev had encountered in the years of his leadership of the Soviet Union:

> I do not deny it: there are sometimes, it is true, bitter lessons to be learned. For example, if fate had not handed us the burden of *perestroika* I would probably never have known the many different shapes and forms human beings can

take. This is serious, you understand. For me this is one of the most difficult moral tests of *perestroika:* the specific way people behave, what they say and what they do. What they were yesterday and what they are today. What they are when they are with you, and what they are with other people. What they are when it is their advantage, and what they are when it is not. Sometimes I even see, or rather feel, that they are not faces but masks, but masks of the real world, not the fantastic world of fairy tales. And, do you know, the masks I see will suddenly disappear and I can see quite clearly the faces of the people who informed on my grandfather in the 1930s. And of those who destroyed him. And of those who, with their tails between their legs, would not approach a dying woman, just because she was from the family of an "enemy of the people."

But Raisa's father was transferred to Chernigov in the Ukraine, 1,800 miles from the two-year-old's maternal grandparents, in 1934, and his family moved with him, which means Raisa could not have seen "the faces of the people who informed on my grandfather," nor have experienced the mistreatment of her grandmother firsthand. Her grandfather was certainly purged and murdered. There is good reason to believe, however (though Raisa seems never publicly to have acknowledged the fact), that her father himself was purged in 1935, arrested and imprisoned for four years, leaving Raisa, her mother, and her two younger siblings to struggle for survival without support. That would explain the intensity of Raisa's feelings more than fifty years later about hypocrites who inform on innocent men and avoid the family of an "enemy of the people." It would also explain her mother's curious overresponse to what was supposedly her father's departure for "the front"—into Army service—in the following recollection:

I remember the scene when we accompanied my father off to the front. The overcrowded railway station—I really do recall from childhood so clearly and so sharply the railway stations with that unrepeatable sad atmosphere— women, children and tears. Many women even fainted. And I remember my mother, frozen in her grief. Her words were: "Who's going to support us? We must hold out."

A sad atmosphere is appropriate to a railroad station where young fathers are going off to war, but why would Raisa's mother be "frozen in her grief"? And since soldiers are required to assign pay allotments to their families, why would she be concerned about support? These inconsistencies immediately make sense if Maxim's departure was not to the front but to the Gulag, as a Trotskyite enemy of the people, and not in 1939 or 1941 but in 1935. He returned four years later, in 1939, in a railwayman's uniform because men who could construct railroads were suddenly in great demand as the Soviet Union made preparations to defend itself against Nazi Germany, itself gearing up toward war.

The Titorenkos suffered through the war, as everyone did. Raisa's school lunch was "a daily bowl of watery soup." Because they moved around so much she experienced "a sort of internal constraint, a feeling of diffidence, sometimes of isolation. . . . But the situation of being 'always the new girl' led me at the same time to develop contact with people. I simply had to become more social."

She arrived at the university a provincial, in a peasant blouse with her head wrapped in braids, but she adapted even more rapidly than Gorbachev, so that in a photograph from 1951 she already looks slim and sophisticated, with styled hair and a wristwatch. Classmates remember her coat, which seemed to announce her prosperity, but the effort of the coat was collective. "I received my first real overcoat as a present from my mother and father," she recalled, "when I was already a university student. It had a small fur collar—a 'Boston,' according to my mother. I wore it for a long time. The whole family remembers that coat. . . . It really was a milestone in the family history."

She studied philosophy as a way of studying sociology, then still marginalized as an aberration. "In our country," she would explain, "sociology practically ceased to exist as a science somewhere in the 1930s. It turned out . . . to be 'unwanted' and perhaps even 'dangerous' in conditions where a bureaucratic command system was being formed. Sociology is the embodiment of what we call 'feedback,' and for that reason alone a system of command is organically alien to it. Just as it is alien to the system." Like Gorbachev, then, and independently, she probed the system cautiously for an explanation of the suffering it had inflicted on her family and her country, splitting off the ideal from the real. Two handsome people, both intelligent, both provincial strivers, both with high ambitions, both with grievances: How could they not have found each other even in the crowd?

Gorbachev wanted her the first time he saw her. It took him three months to get her attention, at a student dance, but once they connected they were inseparable. They went to the theater, they read and discussed books, they took long walks together around the city, Raisa remembered:

> Our relationship and our feeling were from the very outset perceived by us as a natural, inseparable part of our fate. We realized that our life would be

unthinkable without each other. Our feelings were our very life itself. . . . We didn't know if our relationship would be lasting. . . . Whether our marriage would be harmonious. We didn't even think about it. It didn't worry us. Financial considerations didn't concern us: legacies, family connections, somebody's position, protectionism. No. There were no legacies and no family connections. All we had was ourselves. All we had was with us. *Omnia mea mecum porto*— "Everything I have I carry with me."

We were friends for a long time before we got married.

People who come from nowhere feel that way, that the world begins with them.

The first thing they bought together was her wedding dress—"a beautiful Italian crepe dress," Gorbachev writes, ". . . made for Raya at a dressmaker's shop on Kirovskaya Street. She simply looked gorgeous in it." He worked overtime in the summer of 1953 to raise the money. "You've got a new work incentive," his father kidded him. In her memoir Raisa quotes one of his letters:

> "I know, Rayechka, I haven't written to you. Our work team consists almost entirely of Gorbachevs. Papa is the combine operator, I do the steering and Semen Grigorievich Gorbachev is the tractor driver. There is a girl on the straw collector—Anna Mikhailovna Gorbachev, and the grain is transported from the combine in a truck by Vasili Alekseyevich Gorbachev. Our team is known as 'The Gorbachevs.' Papa, Semen and Vasili are cousins. . . . I must finish now. . . . Warmest greetings from the sphere of production to the sphere of the intellect."

Gorbachev and his father sold a thousand pounds of grain at the end of the summer; with his salary, Gorbachev took home nearly a thousand rubles. "I had never had so much money in my hands before." It bought the wedding dress, but Raisa had to borrow the white shoes. On 25 September 1953, twelve days after Nikita Khrushchev became first secretary of the Communist Party of the Soviet Union, Gorbachev and Raisa were married in a Moscow registry office.

THREE A HIERARCHY OF VASSALS AND CHIEFS

AFTER HIS GRADUATION FROM LAW SCHOOL in June 1955, Mikhail Gorbachev had hoped to work in Moscow, but he was not allowed that privilege. He was assigned instead to the Prokuratura—the public prosecutor's office—in Stavropol. Traveling out to the old city ahead of his wife, he found a room in a house occupied by two retired teachers and their children. The room was barely eleven by eleven feet, with an iron bed and a huge stove for heating, but its three windows looked out onto a luxuriant garden. The crate in which the Gorbachevs had shipped their belongings became a combination table and bookshelf; to round out the furnishings Gorbachev built a clothes rack and bought two chairs. The small room would be their home for the next two years. Their daughter and only child, Irina, would be born there on 6 January 1957, one day after her mother's twenty-fifth birthday. "Stavropol struck me by its greenery," Raisa recalled. The city had originated as an imperial fortress in 1777, and the old stone houses were overgrown with hops and grapevines, "a flood of green. It seemed as though the city had been decked out in luxurious green clothes. Lombardy poplars and such a lot of chestnuts. And willows and oaks and elms. And lilac. And flowers everywhere."

Gorbachev disliked the cold formality of the Prokuratura. A career there looked like a dead end. But Moscow had initiated an ambitious program of agricultural reforms in the fall of 1953 that had opened up promising positions within the district Party apparatus. Gorbachev talked his way out of the Prokuratura and into Komsomol work, winning appointment as deputy head of the Stavropol Department of Propaganda and Agitation. In practice that meant touring the countryside assessing conditions, solving problems, and promoting the Party; his first month's salary, 840 rubles, went for a pair of sturdy boots. He found no flood of green in the Stavropol outback but "sheer misery and complete devastation everywhere." Wading through the mud to a hilltop above one remote village he looked down on "low, smoke-belching huts [with] blackened dilapidated fences" stretched out twenty kilometers along both sides of a river:

> Down there, in those miserable dwellings, people led some kind of life. But the streets (if you could call them streets) were deserted. As if the plague had ravaged the entire village, no contacts or ties existed between these shanty-town microcosms, just the everlasting barking of the dogs. And I told myself that this was the reason why the young fled. . . . They fled from desolation and horror, from the terror of being buried alive. . . . People deserve a better life—that was always on my mind.

His birth village was only a little better off, he wrote Raisa during one of his tours:

> I don't know how many times I've been to Privolnoye hearing them talk of just twenty rubles—where were they going to find such a sum? Despite the fact that my father works day and night the whole year round. I am simply overwhelmed with shame. Honestly I can't keep back my tears. . . . There's a great deal yet to be done. Our parents and thousands like them really deserve a better life.

Khrushchev's reforms offered Gorbachev a first version of how the Soviet people might achieve the better life he believed they deserved. An early and important reform had been the abolition, in 1953, of the Special Board of the Ministry of Internal Affairs, which the American legal scholar Harold Berman calls "the chief instrument of [Soviet] terror." Since 1934, the secret three-man committee had dispatched hundreds of thousands of people to labor camps without legal representation, a hearing, or the right of appeal. Along with abolishing the Special Board, Khrushchev ordered all political convictions reviewed and many prisoners released; although the Gulag continued to function, large-scale amnesties followed in 1953 and again in 1957. A major liberalization of the Soviet legal system began in 1955 and continued throughout the rest of the decade, Berman notes, involving "hundreds, indeed thousands, of needed reforms," most of all the restoration of due process in political cases.

Renouncing wholesale domestic terror as a means of governing, Khrushchev and his followers worked to replace terror with law and with a degree of popular participation in political debate. Though Khrushchev's cultural gestures are better known—his approval of the publication of Aleksandr Solzhenitsyn's *One Day in the Life of Ivan Denisovich* in *Novy Mir* in November 1962, for example—his proto-glasnost effort to outmaneuver the Stalinist old guard by encouraging the Soviet people to support his reforms was more influential in the long run. Certainly it influenced Gorbachev. Berman reports "a substantial increase in the powers of the local municipal councils and a vast amount of activity of local government organizations, involving the participation of literally hundreds of thousands of Soviet citizens." Working through the Komsomol, Gorbachev facilitated that participation:

> The main thing for me at that time was the sense of hope being born. . . . I tried to function in such a way as to arouse people's interest and activism. I organized a discussion club for young people. There was a great deal of interest, and we had to rent larger and larger meeting rooms in order to fit everyone that wanted to attend. This success and the feeling that people were waking up, as though they were being released from shackles that had bound them and were beginning to lose the sense of fear and lack of self-confidence—I was completely inspired by such things at the time. . . . It was quite an extraordinary development.

Gorbachev felt something more wrenching than inspiration in the spring of 1956 when he read a transcript of Khrushchev's indictment of Stalin at the 20th Party Congress that February. Stalin "practiced brutal violence," Khrushchev charged; he authorized "barbaric tortures"; he originated the concept of an "enemy of the people," which "made possible the use of the most cruel repression . . . against anyone who disagreed with [him]." (But "Lenin had used the term," says Dmitri Volkogonov, "having borrowed it from the lexicon of the French Revolution.") "How were confessions extracted?" Khrushchev asked rhetorically. "Only one way, by beating, torture, deprivation of consciousness, deprivation of reason, deprivation of human dignity by means of physical violence and intimidation."

Khrushchev's speech "morally discredited totalitarianism," Gorbachev writes, "arousing hopes for a reform of the system." It staggered him. "I was shocked, bewildered and lost. It wasn't an analysis, just facts, deadly facts. Many of us simply could not believe that such things could be true. For me it was easier. My family had itself been one of the victims of the repression of the 1930s." The Komsomol sent him around to explain the speech to its local leadership. "I had no real idea of the true state of affairs up until the Khrushchev revelations," he said later. Such naïveté may seem unlikely, but his more sophisticated Czech friend Zdenek Mlynar was equally uninformed, acknowledging that "the concrete details of crimes committed by the Soviet security organs" that Khrushchev revealed, "of torture and forced confessions in political trials . . . had never crossed my mind."

The speech allowed Gorbachev for the first time "to understand the inner connection between what had happened to our country and what had happened to my family. My memories and associations from childhood became interwoven with the beginnings of an awareness of what Stalinism was." His grandfather Panteli Gopkalo had convinced himself that Stalin could not have known about the Terror famine and the purges (Stalin's apologists blamed the NKVD); such denial was no longer possible for Gorbachev. But young and ambitious as he was, he followed Khrushchev's lead in assigning responsibility narrowly to Stalin and the Stalinist system while exonerating Communism itself.

Yet he was no barren dogmatist. The Communist ideal connected him emotionally to his family and his family's struggles. "Am I supposed to turn my back on my grandfather, who was committed to the [socialist] idea?" he asked rhetorically in 1990. ". . . And I cannot go against my father, who defended Kursk, forded the Dnieper River knee-deep in blood, and was wounded in Czechoslovakia. When cleansing myself of Stalinism and all other filth, should I renounce my grandfather and my father and all they did?" Part of what they did was to embrace the Communist Party as a way past their mistreatment at its hands; and so now did Gorbachev: "I did not perceive [Khrushchev's speech] as a catastrophe or as the collapse of everything that had existed up until then. On the contrary, I perceived it as the beginning of something new, as providing tremendous new opportunities for the future."

GORBACHEV MOVED UP TO FIRST SECRETARY of the Stavropol city Komsomol committee in September 1956. At a session of the Komsomol Central Committee in Moscow he met a kindred spirit, his Georgian counterpart, Eduard Shevardnadze. "We had the same peasant roots," Shevardnadze says, explaining their instant friendship, "had worked on the land at a tender age, and had the same knowledge of folk life." Like Gorbachev, Shevardnadze had been "shaken . . . by the direct connection between the politics of terror and Stalin's activity. . . . It shattered my life and my faith." But Shevardnadze had experienced a more immediate trauma as well: the brutal suppression in March 1956 of protest demonstrations in the Georgian capital of Tbilisi, the beginning of what Shevardnadze calls "the East European upheavals of the 1950s and 1960s."

That summer, Soviet tanks massed on the Polish border in response to large-scale demonstrations by Polish workers demanding "bread and freedom." Khrushchev had barely finished negotiating an accommodation with the new Polish Communist Party chief, Wladyslaw Gomulka, when student demonstrations in Hungary enlarged into a full-scale anti-Soviet revolution. Shevardnadze had been there before. "It is not true that the first time heavy military vehicles were used against civilians was in Budapest in October 1956," he writes. "The tank was first deployed as an argument against dissent in Tbilisi in March of that year." As a result, Shevardnadze adds significantly, "My generation and I acquired a '1956 complex' for the rest of our lives— rejecting force as both a method and a principle of politics." When, much later, Gorbachev would refuse to use force to keep Eastern Europe within the Soviet fold, it was partly the example of these early experiences that he and his foreign minister, Shevardnadze, heeded.

Pressure on Khrushchev to order Soviet troops, tanks, and strafing and bombing aircraft into Budapest to put down the Hungarian Revolution came especially from the Soviet ambassador to Hungary at that time, Yuri Andropov, a tough, smart Second World War partisan leader and Party functionary who happened to have been born near Stavropol (in 1914). Distracted by Poland and the Suez Crisis, concerned to follow his new policy of rallying popular support, Khrushchev was reluctant to use force to crush the Hungarian uprising. Khrushchev's advisers, including Andropov, emphasized the importance of a show of force at a time when Britain, France, and Israel were preparing to invade Egypt to wrest the Suez Canal back from Gamal Abdel Nasser, the Egyptian leader, who had abruptly nationalized it. Khrushchev seized on their argument to justify his abrupt reversal: "If we depart from Hungary," he said, addressing a meeting of the Central Committee Presidium on 31 October, when Egypt was under active attack, "it will give a great boost to the Americans, English and French—the imperialists. They will perceive it as weakness on our part and will go onto the offensive. . . . To Egypt they will then add Hungary." Andropov had been exiled to the Hungarian ambassadorship during the struggle for Politburo leadership that followed Stalin's death in 1953; after his work suppressing the Hungarian Revolution, he was recalled to Moscow and renewed his rise to power.

By 1962, Gorbachev had found a mentor, Fedor Kulakov, the new first secretary of the Stavropol region (*krai*)—a position similar to governor of a U.S. state, but appointed rather than elective. Kulakov encouraged Gorbachev to switch from Komsomol work to a newly created post as a Communist Party organizer responsible for managing production in three *krai* agricultural districts. Young, highly intelligent, motivated, personable, seemingly committed to the Party system, Gorbachev appealed to the paternal feelings of one powerful Soviet leader after another in the course of his advancement to leadership. Kulakov was the first; Andropov, whom Gorbachev would meet in 1969, was the most influential. The younger man gave good value:

> I was totally committed to my job. I spent days, and often nights, traveling around the districts, visiting farms and trying to develop new management structures. I was deeply convinced that we had embarked upon the right path and once the technocrats were free to do their job it would soon bear fruit. Being a candidate member of the [district] Party committee bureau, I had frequent dealings with Kulakov. . . . He would entrust me with all kinds of tasks and invite me on trips through the krai.

But if Gorbachev made use of the Mafia-like system that manipulated the formalisms of Communist Party rule, he did not necessarily approve of it. "Both the general secretary at the center and the various first secretaries in the regions repaid support with protection," he writes. "This hierarchy of vassals and chiefs of principalities was in fact the way the country was run. The democratic façade did not change the essence of the matter. It was a caste system based on mutual protection. To me this was a distortion of socialism and by no means a defect inherent in that system."

He and Raisa both felt the need for more education. Raisa was teaching philosophy, including sociology, at the Stavropol Agricultural Institute; her husband began studying agricultural economics in night school there, eventually writing a thesis on the economics of milk production. She pursued the equivalent of a Ph.D. in sociology. Her dissertation work gave both of them a deeper understanding of the conditions of rural life in the Soviet Union twenty years after the end of the immensely destructive war with Nazi Germany. It also, by its methodology, added to Gorbachev's understanding of democratic process.

Raisa chose to study "the peasant family, its material condition, daily life, cultural demands and the nature of relationships in the family." She used statistics, documents, and archives, but also—and significantly—questionnaires and interviews. "I personally collected about 3,000 questionnaires in those years. . . . On the collective farms I visited the farm workers' homes, the working brigades, the farms, schools, libraries, shops, medical centers, preschool nurseries and old people's homes." She interviewed "hundreds of people . . . on a whole variety of subjects. . . . I know what their daily life is like and what their problems are. I have traveled hundreds of kilometers along country roads, in a passing car, on a motorcycle or a cart, and sometimes on foot in rubber boots." It was from such meetings with real people, she believed, "and not from books or newspapers, not from plays or films, that I came to understand many of our [Soviet] misfortunes and the questionable nature of many undisputed assertions and established concepts." So did her husband. Contempt for ordinary people—for the difficulties of their lives and for their hopes—was the characteristic attitude of Party leadership at every level in the Soviet Union (Gorbachev writes critically of "the traditional concept of the peasant as a second-class citizen"). The Gorbachevs' personal histories and their extended encounter with rural life enabled them to avoid the narrowing corruption of such contempt.

NIKITA KHRUSHCHEV WAS OUSTED FROM POWER in October 1964 partly for the debacle of the Cuban Missile Crisis, when the United States and the Soviet Union came within hours of all-out nuclear war, but more immediately for his disastrous agricultural policies. Moscow no longer dared to impose food rationing when crops failed in the early 1960s; Khrushchev's attempt to ration meat and butter by raising their retail prices in 1962 provoked a riot in one Soviet city that the Red Army put down violently, leaving more than sixty dead. Instead of rationing, the Soviet government increased its imports of food grains from the West. "The leadership of the USSR in effect was challenged by its own 'revolution of rising expectations,' " writes an agricultural economist, "in which it could [no longer] 'run an industrial society on a diet of pickled cucumbers and black bread.' " To pay for grain imports in the previous decade, the government had drawn down its gold reserves, which declined, says Volkogonov, "from 13.1 million tonnes in 1954 to 6.3 million in 1963." It paid for the increased imports of the next two decades with oil revenues from new fields opened up in Siberia.

Kulakov moved to Moscow as the head of the Central Committee's agricultural department in October 1964, his reward for having connived with Leonid Brezhnev, Khrushchev's successor, to force Khrushchev's "retirement." In his place as Stavropol *krai* first secretary arrived a more sophisticated apparatchik, Leonid Yefremov, who was being banished to the provinces for the sin of having been an enthusiastic Khrushchev supporter. Yefremov spent two years brooding on his misfortune before he finally got down to work. Gorbachev, whose capacity for absorbing information was limitless, describes Yefremov ironically as "a refined product of the system" and judges "the years I spent working together with him [to have been] a most instructive experience for me."

In Volkogonov's view, Brezhnev was "a mild, indecisive man" whose favorite activity was big-game hunting. He allowed Khrushchev's programs of reform to be halted and eventually reversed. "We . . . did not [esteem] highly enough what Khrushchev had done," Gorbachev judges, "and what later on disappeared with him. With the advent of Brezhnev there gradually occurred a transfer of power to those who had an interest in restoring essentially the old order, although of course without the harshest methods of Stalinism."

Before the walls closed in, in 1966, the Gorbachevs made their first trip abroad together, part of a group of Soviet managers sponsored by a wealthy French businessman interested in promoting East-West relations. Three couples in three Renaults covered five thousand kilometers around Europe, and it is easy to believe that they were wide-eyed. The following year the Gorbachevs vacationed in Italy, living in Sicily for a time and then visiting Rome, Florence, and Turin. In the 1970s Gorbachev would travel officially or by invitation to Italy, France, Belgium, and East Germany. Travel also opened his eyes:

> My previous belief in the superiority of socialist democracy over the bourgeois system was shaken as I observed the functioning of civil society and the different political systems. Finally, the most significant conclusion drawn from the journeys abroad: people there lived in better conditions and were better off than in our country. The question haunted me: why was the standard of living in our country lower than in other developed countries?

With reform fading and Yefremov uncooperative, Gorbachev took a reduction in pay and became first secretary of the Party's Stavropol city committee, where he plunged into urban industrial development. He finished his agricultural economics study in 1967, the same year that Raisa earned her doctorate in philosophical sciences. The couple furnished a two-room flat and bought their first television set. Yefremov was further frustrated and angered when Moscow appointed Gorbachev second secretary of the Stavropol *krai* in August 1968—his immediate second in command—without consulting him, but the two men eventually contrived to work together.

The Prague Spring—Czechoslovakia's attempted liberalization in the spring and summer of 1968—came to its brutal conclusion on 21 August, only days after Gorbachev's appointment as second secretary. Zdenek Mlynar, his old roommate, had visited him in Stavropol the previous year and alerted him that Czechoslovakia was simmering. Mlynar himself was active in the movement toward liberalization and was eventually forced into exile in Austria. Gorbachev says the suppression of Czechoslovakia set him thinking critically about his government. He visited the country in 1969 and was shocked when workers in a defense plant he toured turned their backs on him. "I suddenly understood that despite all the global, strategic and ideological justifications, we had suppressed something that had grown up within our own society. From that time on I began to think more and more about our own situation and I came to rather unconsoling conclusions—that something wasn't right among us."

(According to the former Washington KGB station chief Oleg Kalugin, "the KGB stirred up fears . . . that Czechoslovakia could fall victim to NATO aggression or a coup" unless the Czech dissent was violently suppressed, one reason that the Brezhnev Politburo reacted so excessively. More ominously, Brezhnev may have put Soviet nuclear forces on full alert during the August invasion to warn off the West. The evidence that he did so—a declassified U.S. intelligence document—is provocative but not conclusive; a former Soviet general who was deputy commander of the invasion agrees that an alert was considered but denies that it was actually ordered. The Soviet government was extremely cautious about nuclear alerts during the Cold War, and stood down even during the Cuban Missile Crisis; an alert during its invasion of Czechoslovakia would have been a rare exception and a strong indication of Kremlin panic.)

The suppression of the Prague Spring, Gorbachev writes, "engendered a very harsh reaction in the Soviet Union, leading to a frontal assault against all forms of free thinking. . . . Soviet society . . . entered a stage of profound stagnation." Yuri Andropov, who became the chairman of the KGB in 1967, directed that frontal assault. Besides stifling dissent, Gorbachev adds, the Brezhnev reversal "practically put an end to all subsequent quests for ways and means to transform the existing system of economic management." Although Gorbachev was promoted to replace Yefremov as the Stavropol *krai*'s first secretary in 1970, he discovered "gradually, and more and more tangibly . . . that although I held positions of high authority, in fact there was little I could do, because I was bound hand and foot by orders from the center."

Gorbachev's concerns for the next ten years were largely agricultural: drought, crop failures, dust storms, irrigation projects, road building. His work brought him into regular contact with Moscow and frequent conflict with Kulakov, who by then was the Politburo member responsible for agriculture. Gorbachev saw the economy stagnate, saw regional initiatives rejected, saw "manipulators" become "the heroes of the day," and found himself increasingly disenchanted: "Should you come up with your own ideas—be prepared for trouble. You could even land in jail. It was actually impossible to do something sensible while complying with all the regulations and instructions. A popular adage hit the mark: 'All initiative is punishable.' "

GORBACHEV FIRST MET YURI ANDROPOV in the immediate aftermath of the Prague Spring invasion of 21 August 1968; supervising its brutalities had prevented the KGB chairman from taking his annual vacation. The North Caucasus region was famous for its mineral springs, and in April 1969 Andropov turned up at one of its spas, where Gorbachev was delegated to welcome him. Thereafter Gorbachev cultivated Andropov, not cynically but certainly realistically, understanding that the only way to power in his country was through alliances with its leaders, however black their souls. Gorbachev "was a great charmer," his biographers Dusko Doder and Louise Branson say of him at this period; "his extrovert personality and humor, bold ideas expressed in moderate language, and perpetual references to specific material achievements disarmed the old men of the Kremlin.... By then he was a totally political creature." As time passed and the friendship, or mentorship, deepened, the Andropovs and the Gorbachevs sometimes vacationed together. Gorbachev wrote:

> We made family excursions to the surroundings of Kislovodsk and went to the mountains. Sometimes we stayed late, cooked shashlik and sat around a bonfire. Like me, Andropov did not favor noisy parties. The southern night was magnificent, it was quiet and we talked openly.... Yet he never opened up completely, and his trust and frankness did not exceed the established framework. More than anyone else, Andropov knew what was going on [in the Soviet Union]. But I would think that he reasoned like many others: deal with the cadres, introduce tighter discipline, and the rest will be all right.

Mikhail Suslov, the Party's leading ideologist and effectively Brezhnev's second in command, was another important mentor. Suslov had been first secretary of the Stavropol *krai* during the Second World War and, like Andropov, often vacationed in the region. Andropov described Gorbachev to a colleague as one of "the entirely new people coming up . . . who can bear our hopes into the future," and on another occasion as "a brilliant man working in Stavropol."

Even Brezhnev seemed to like the young go-getter from Stavropol. David

Remnick cites the assessment of Anatoly Sobchak, a law professor and former mayor of Leningrad, on what might seem Gorbachev's sycophancy:

> Gorbachev could tell us much we do not know about how a man feels, doomed to daily renunciation of his own will in favor of that of his superiors, compelled to daily self-abasement for the sake of his career. . . . To me, the greatest mystery is how Gorbachev managed to retain his individuality, the ability to shape his own opinion and set it against the opinion of others. Evidently, it was to preserve his own self that he developed his almost impenetrable mask. He learned to conceal his disdain for those whom he must have despised, to speak with them in their own language.

Remnick adds: "Gorbachev appears to have few illusions about his double face. Years after coming to power, he told [the journalist] Vitaly Korotich . . . 'In those days, we all licked Brezhnev's ass—all of us!' " Ass-lickers are a staple of middle bureaucracies, of course, and are certainly not unique to the former Soviet Union. The activist and strategic analyst Daniel Ellsberg identifies the same pattern of behavior in American bureaucrats. The U.S. government, he points out, "does not require true believers to run it. . . . The system consciously runs by men who—in order to stay in the game, to be close to the center of power, to have the hope that someday the moment may come when their own true values will be served—will go on for years serving values that are the opposite of what they privately believe." Hence the frequent phenomenon of recantation from retirement.

Election to the Central Committee in 1971 opened other sources of information to Gorbachev. Foreign publications forbidden to officials of lower rank were now made available to him in translation, including essays on the Prague Spring and articles by the West German chancellor Willy Brandt and the French Socialist Party leader and future president François Mitterrand. His travels continued as well. "My trips abroad were of no small importance to me," he recalls, "accompanied by numerous contacts, conversations and discussions on the most varied themes." The scope of his interest and concern enlarged beyond Stavropol as he talked through his ideas with Andropov, with Shevardnadze, and, most of all, with Raisa. "I am very lucky with Mikhail," she would say later. "We are really friends, or if you prefer, we have great complicity." She noticed the change in her husband's focus in their last years in Stavropol:

> I heard Mikhail Sergeyevich speak ever more frequently not only about the difficulties involved in the social development of the villages and towns in the region, the provision of materials and technology, the lack of balance in the

terms of exchange of agricultural and industrial output, and the shortcomings in the system of payment for work done. He also talked about the need for profound changes in the country as a whole.

Finally, in July 1978, Fedor Kulakov, sixty years old, overdosed on vodka after major surgery and a position opened up for Gorbachev in Moscow. Not long after Kulakov's death, Georgi Arbatov, the director of the Institute for the United States and Canada, overheard Andropov complain in a telephone conversation, "those bastards don't want Gorbachev transferred to Moscow." Who "those bastards" were, Andropov did not say, but he found a way around them. On 19 September 1978, Gorbachev and Andropov, vacationing with their families at Mineral'nyye Vody, a historic spa in the foothills of the Caucasus, met a train carrying Leonid Brezhnev and his aide Konstantin Chernenko to Baku. "The train's departure was delayed for two hours," write Doder and Branson, "as the four men who would rule the country in succession—Brezhnev, Andropov, Chernenko and Gorbachev—met and talked on the narrow platform of the old tsarist railway station. . . . This was, in effect, Gorbachev's job interview, and it went well."

Gorbachev's appointment on 27 November 1978 as Central Committee secretary for agriculture was announced on the front page of *Pravda* the next day. Early in December, he and Raisa left Stavropol permanently for Moscow. (Their daughter, Irina, now twenty-one, and her new husband, Anatoly—the young couple had married the previous April—followed them at the end of the year.) On their last day in Stavropol, the Gorbachevs drove into the dense Russky Forest northwest of the city, where they had walked together in times past. "My character and my entire perception of the world were to a large extent shaped by nature," Gorbachev writes in his memoirs, recalling his childhood play in a mature orchard his grandfather Panteli had left to his parents. In that Eden of apple, apricot, cherry, plum, and pear trees, "there was always enough in the summer and the autumn," and he had improvised adventures in the jungle of elms and undergrowth that darkened beyond the fruit trees. Later, farther afield, he and his father had brought in the grain harvests together. The people in their poverty, the land, the cycle of the seasons, drought and flood and the precarious security of a full grain bin were not abstractions to him; they were real.

GORBACHEV'S FIRST GOAL AS secretary of agriculture was to try to understand why a country so rich in resources could not feed itself. The cost of food imports into the Soviet Union had increased from $700 million in

1970 to $7.2 billion in 1980, while gross domestic agricultural output had declined annually from about $26 billion in 1978 to about $24 billion in 1980. After a destabilizing wheat deal between the United States and the Soviet Union in 1972, when the Soviet purchase of $700 million worth of American wheat had helped push U.S. consumer food prices up by as much as 30 percent, the two countries had signed a Long-Term Grain Agreement in October 1975 that set a minimum for Soviet purchases of wheat and corn of 6 million metric tons per year. The Politburo met this drain on hard currency by selling oil, gas, and armaments ($20 billion in hard currency for armaments from Libya alone); in 1980, the Soviet Union led the world in the production of petroleum and natural gas, extracting 12 million barrels per day equivalent. (The United States followed at 10.8 million barrels per day equivalent, with Saudi Arabia next at 10.3.) And since the world price of oil tripled between 1973 and 1974 and again in 1979 through 1980, petrodollars staved off serious shortages—and serious reforms.

Gorbachev found ignorance, indifference, and neglect in Moscow's management of rural life and production. In Central Asia, he writes, "the careless expansion of cotton fields and the non-observance of crop rotation led to diseases of both the soil and the people." Farmers were treated as second-class citizens, with the rural population of 100 million people—38 percent of the total 1980 Soviet population of 266 million—receiving only 10 percent of national electrical production. Gorbachev cites many other examples as well:

> Despite the enormous growth in coal mining, the rural population was forced to use all sorts of devious ways to get fuel, because only one-third of their needs was met through official channels. I was shown a map of gas pipelines crisscrossing the country in every possible direction. A gas network was introduced in urban areas but the farmers were deprived of it, and there were no plans in prospect to make gas available to them. Rural areas were badly off for roads, schools, medical services, public utilities, newspaper and magazine supplies, cinemas and cultural entertainment.

Doder and Branson cite an official Soviet survey indicating that negligence and the lack of storage facilities led to the loss annually of "one-fifth of the grain harvest and one-third of the potato crop." More than half of the rural villages in the Soviet Union lacked paved roads. "Trucks broke down so frequently that four times as many men were engaged in repairing them as in making them." The half-million tractors produced annually were so poorly made that the total number of machines actually operating remained constant from year to year. Gorbachev summarizes: "Much more was siphoned off from agriculture than invested in it. And . . . the nation's economic development had been achieved largely at the expense of the countryside."

The chickens came home to roost in 1979, when the Soviet invasion of Afghanistan led the American president, Jimmy Carter, to embargo grain sales to the U.S.S.R. Limited sales of wheat and corn continued under the Long-Term Grain Agreement, but the immediate consequence of the embargo was a shortfall in 1980 of seventeen million tonnes. The Soviet government had to scramble to meet its needs with purchases from other grain-producing countries such as Canada and Argentina, and more petrodollars flew out the door. "The growing holes in the economy," writes Georgi Arbatov bitterly, "were being plugged by the barbaric plunder of our enormous, but not limitless, natural resources."

In January 1980, Gorbachev had his first taste of huddling with the men of the small inner circle who actually ran the country—in this case, Brezhnev, foreign minister Andrey Gromyko, and defense minister Dmitry Ustinov. "Gromyko and Ustinov began first," Gorbachev recalls, "by giving their optimistic view of the situation in Afghanistan. It was left to me to speak about the alarming grain shortage." He did, and was ordered to prepare various studies and documents, but then he raised a larger strategic question, "the problem of preparing a plan to free us from the necessity of importing grain." In Gorbachev's hands, that question led to the development of what came to be called the Food Program, which authorized changes in Soviet agricultural policy and practice that anticipated the changes of early perestroika: profit-like mechanisms that encouraged initiative, bonuses for increased output, increased production of consumer goods so that farmers might have something on which to spend their bonuses, prefabricated metal storage buildings to protect the expected bounty from rotting in the fields, and increased importation of advanced agricultural technology.

Exploring these possibilities, Gorbachev came up against the hard truth that the state had not a kopek to spare. Since increasing food prices led to riots (the Polish union Solidarity was born in Gdansk in September 1980 in demonstrations against meat-price increases), the only way the Soviet government could increase payments to farmers for their products was by subsidy. Agricultural subsidies already cost the state 40 billion rubles a year. "This problem dominated our debates," Gorbachev writes. "All agreed that the collective and state farms could no longer subsist on a starvation diet." The finance ministry was not moved. " 'The State has no money,' V. F. Garbuzov, the minister, repeated, countering all of my arguments. He knew the real state of the budget. Its mainstay was such sources of income as covert price increases, increases in the rate of vodka production, and, finally, petro-dollars. But even these could no longer make ends meet. The yawning deficit was covered by State Bank loans at the expense of citizens' savings."

It was in the course of this 1980 debate within the Soviet government that Gorbachev encountered for the first time the idea of cutting defense spending to free up resources for domestic programs. "N. K. Baibakov," he writes, "Chairman of the State Planning Committee of the Council of Ministers, was the first to hint to me at the possibility of cutting the defense budget. The growth in military expenditure was far ahead of the growth in national income. Yet no attempt had ever been made to analyze that budget rationally, with a view to an optimal redistribution of means and resources."

Neither Baibakov nor Gorbachev was yet prepared to question the defense budget, however. "We both knew perfectly well that even a mention of this subject would mean immediate dismissal. It was the General Secretary's turf." The day would come when Mikhail Gorbachev would occupy that turf. In the meantime, the idea of reviewing defense needs and priorities had been planted, well before Ronald Reagan became president. What originally spurred Mikhail Gorbachev to think hard about arms reduction was not Reagan administration pressure in the form of increased U.S. defense spending, but the pressure of Soviet domestic need. Gorbachev summarized this development succinctly in a 1996 symposium:

> With technological progress and the improvement of the educational and cultural level, the old system began to be rejected by people who saw that their initiative was suppressed, who saw they were not able to realize their potential.
>
> Therefore, the first impulses for reform were in the Soviet Union itself, in our society which could no longer tolerate the lack of freedom, where no one could speak out or choose their own party or select their own creed. In the eyes of the people, especially the educated, the totalitarian system had run its course morally and politically. People were waiting for reform. Russia was pregnant.

NOT ONLY SECOND-RANK OFFICIALS SUCH AS Baibakov and Gorbachev feared usurping Brezhnev's prerogatives where the military was concerned; so also did Gromyko and Andropov. One consequence of military influence over the Soviet leadership, ultimately devastating, was the 1979 decision to invade Afghanistan. Arbatov believes that "the military-industrial complex had grown to such proportions [by then] that it escaped political control." Brezhnev, Arbatov points out, had been the Central Committee's secretary of defense industries before he became the general secretary, and "treated the military as a very important power base." Ustinov, the minister of defense, "matched Brezhnev in his sycophancy toward the military." Brezhnev's failing health, exacerbated by an addiction to sleeping pills, added to the confusion.

Anatoly Chernyaev, an international analyst for the Central Committee who would become one of Gorbachev's most trusted advisers, points to Ustinov as the instigator of the December 1979 invasion:

> I learned that the intervention in Afghanistan was initiated by Ustinov. The project to present this "idea" to Brezhnev was organized by a group of four: Ustinov and Gromyko, plus Andropov and [the Central Committee secretary for international affairs Boris] Ponomarev. Andropov was reserved but didn't object, only noting certain "possible complications." Ponomarev also expressed some doubts, but then quickly joined in.

Both Arbatov and Chernyaev note that the senior military staff objected to the war, "arguing," says Chernyaev, "that it would be impossible and senseless," but according to Arbatov, the Ministry of Defense nevertheless promoted and even insisted upon the intervention, which he calls "a pretty typical escalation of military aid." With the United States covertly supporting the anti-Soviet Afghan mujahideen, Afghanistan in the 1980s became the Soviet Union's Vietnam.

An unintended consequence of military-industrial dominance of government policy was the piling up of Soviet arms during the 1970s, when both the Soviet Union and the United States were pursuing policies of détente. "As a result," Arbatov points out, "we reached absurdly high ceilings in many areas [including] such important components of conventional forces as the number of people under arms; tanks; artillery; tactical missiles; many types of aircraft; submarines; and many other weapons systems." In nuclear weapons "we surpassed the Americans in the number of delivery systems, megatonnage, and throw weight in strategic arms, and also in medium-range weapons"— as if more nuclear weapons meant more security.

The excesses of the Soviet military-industrial complex in the 1970s were as much the consequence of internal policy as they were of external threat. The complex was "something like a bull in a china shop" according to a former Soviet defense official named Vitaliy Katayev—"a sort of Soviet Texas." It "always demanded as much weaponry as possible." The decision to produce a new weapons system was usually made "not on the basis of military needs or technical merit . . . but rather on the basis of [the] authority of its sponsors" and their personal relationships with the political leadership. And since the complex was expected to increase its output by at least 3 percent annually, "production of many types of weapons was not stopped even after the army was saturated with them." The purpose of this overproduction, a former Soviet military economist explains, was "to keep the production base 'warm' "—to be ready to mobilize production in case war broke out. If mobilizing production—that is, preparing to fight a long war—looks like antiquated 1930s policy in a nuclear world, he adds, it was.

Massively overproducing arms, Arbatov concludes, "undermined Western trust toward us. Right-wingers and militarists in the United States and other NATO countries waged a successful campaign to create public mistrust of us.... More than that, our actions encouraged Americans to intensify the arms race."

By the early 1980s, the Soviet dissident Vladimir Bukovsky told a British journalist, "the regime was obviously in crisis. You can imagine that it was obvious to the Politburo sitting there and receiving all the reports about politics and economics. They knew the contempt for them of the entire country, they knew they were in trouble." The price of crude oil had begun declining as well, and by U.S. estimates every dollar per barrel the price declined cost the Soviets about $1 billion annually. "The creaky Politburo of Leonid Brezhnev began to panic," writes Thomas Reed, a former Reagan special assistant. "It demanded the immediate production of oil regardless of the long-term cost. It was this full-throttle, devil-take-the-hindmost approach to oil production that was a key indicator [of Soviet economic troubles] to us at the White House."

Mikhail Suslov died in January 1982. Yuri Andropov, then sixty-seven, moved from his position as the chairman of the KGB to replace Suslov as Central Committee secretary. The move was a necessary step if Andropov was to succeed Brezhnev, says Arbatov, since the election of a leader "straight from the ... KGB would have been unprecedented and almost certainly would have been stopped by the apparat." When Brezhnev died, on 10 November 1982, Andropov immediately assumed the general secretaryship. As Andropov's protégé, Gorbachev saw his prospects improve accordingly. Even before Andropov's advanced kidney disease forced him into the hospital, limiting his ability to administer the country, he pushed Gorbachev to prepare himself for leadership:

> Andropov and I were drawn even closer together in our work during his early months as General Secretary. I sensed his trust in me and his support. At the very end of 1982 he suggested meaningfully: "You know what, Mikhail, don't limit your work to the agrarian sector. Try to look at other aspects."

He fell silent and then added: "In general terms, act as if you had to shoulder all the responsibility one day. I mean it."

Under Andropov's protection, Gorbachev reached out to what Chernyaev calls "leading reformist thinkers" for information and support. The agricultural economist Vladimir Tikhonov, the sociologist Tatyana Zaslavskaya, the physicist Yevgeny Velikhov, Arbatov, and others extended his knowledge of his country and its problems. It was a painful education. "The relations between town and country, the fate of the peasantry, the land and the people on the land, the preservation of nature—these ancient questions did not give me any rest," Gorbachev wrote. "The further I delved into them, the more I was overcome by alarm about the situation in the country, the more I began to doubt the wisdom of the economic policy being implemented in the country." He commissioned studies of necessary reforms and invited contributions; some 110 memoranda resulted, sent in by individuals as well as institutes and ministries. "Their analysis then became the basis for the documents of *perestroika*," Gorbachev notes.

In May 1983, invited to visit Canada by the Canadian secretary of agriculture, Gorbachev formed a crucial alliance with Alexander Yakovlev, a philosophic but outspoken Soviet apparatchik whose criticism in the early 1970s of a burgeoning Brezhnev personality cult had earned him a decade's exile as the Soviet ambassador to Canada. A small, balding man with a pronounced limp from severe war injuries, Yakovlev had begun losing faith in the Soviet system when he saw Soviet prisoners of war returning from Germany in 1945 hauled off to prison camps at Stalin's behest. He was "terribly ashamed," he said later; and further ashamed when he heard Khrushchev's speech on Stalin's crimes. A year studying at Columbia University in the Communist witch hunt days of the 1950s had left him unimpressed with American democracy, but ten years in Canada had given him time to study and reflect on Western values and Western prosperity. Like Gorbachev, he was a son of farmers—his father had been a kolkhoz chairman—which prepared him to admire the bounties of Canadian agriculture.

He and Gorbachev spent eight days touring the country, talking nonstop along the way. "We spoke very frankly about everything," Yakovlev said later. ". . . The main point was that society had to change, that it had to be constructed on different principles." They visited a state animal-husbandry research center, a dump-truck factory, a canning factory, family farms, a cattle ranch. "My Canadian travels served as a powerful impetus for thought," Gorbachev remembers. One of his thoughts was to return Yakovlev from exile. Within two months, Gorbachev's new ally was back in Moscow and installed as the director of the prestigious Institute of World Economy and International Relations.

Yuri Andropov died of complications of kidney failure in February 1984. Gorbachev in his memoirs expresses doubt that his mentor would have pursued serious reform had he not been ill, as some believe: "He realized the need for changes, yet Andropov always remained a man of his time. . . . Apparently the years spent in KGB work had left an imprint on his attitudes and perceptions, making him a suspicious man condemned to serve the system." Arbatov puts it more bluntly, listing among Andropov's negative traits "indecisiveness, faintheartedness and cowardice," which he speculates resulted from being "deeply traumatized, frightened for life," by his years working under Stalin, "like the majority of his generation."

Gorbachev's name was bruited for general secretary, but the elderly seniors of the Politburo considered him too young (he was fifty-three) and untested—and too independent—to promote to leadership; they chose Brezhnev's dull, ailing, seventy-two-year-old former aide Konstantin Chernenko instead, despite his advanced emphysema. Andropov's personal aide Arkady Volsky testified later to having overheard the defense minister, Dmitry Ustinov, tell another Politburo member, "Kostya [Chernenko] will be more amenable than Misha." "That," Volsky added bitterly, "is how the leader of our great country was chosen." Anatoly Chernyaev wrote in his journal at the time that he "looked at the members of the [Politburo] and thought I saw embarrassment in their faces, as if they were ashamed of dashing our hopes. Really, no matter who you talked to in those days, Gorbachev's name always came up. We didn't want to believe that it could be someone else."

Gorbachev himself had not felt ready to lead the country in 1984; he told a colleague, reports one of his biographers, Archie Brown, that he was "not psychologically prepared for the role of first person" after Andropov's death. He finished preparing himself in the inert thirteen months of Chernenko's lethargic reign, vigorously ("brilliantly," Gromyko would say) chairing meetings of the Politburo, deflecting efforts by the old guard to have him demoted, delivering what amounted to a campaign speech at a national conference on science and technology, visiting Britain and winning an endorsement from the British prime minister, Margaret Thatcher—"I like Mr. Gorbachev. We can do business together"—that brought him international attention. Behind the scenes, he talked through his ideas with Raisa and with Yakovlev. His old friend Eduard Shevardnadze assessed the situation bluntly when they met on vacation at a Black Sea resort in Georgia: " 'Everything's rotten. It has to be changed.' I really did say that to Gorbachev on a winter evening in 1984 at Pitsunda."

In his speech to the national conference on science and technology on 10 December 1984, "The People's Vital Creativity," Gorbachev called for carrying out "profound transformations in the economy and in the entire system of social relations." Sandwiched between the de rigueur boilerplate of tributes to Lenin and Chernenko and claims of a "crisis of capitalism" was a bold assertion of the necessity of reform:

> Life is setting before us a task of enormous political significance—to raise the economy to a qualitatively new scientific-technical and organizational-economic level and to achieve a decided improvement in the intensification of social production and an increase in its efficiency.
>
> The course aimed at intensification is dictated by objective conditions and by the entire course of the country's development. There is no alternative to it. Only an intensive economy developing on the basis of the latest scientific and technical achievements can serve as a dependable material base for improving the working people's well-being, ensure the strengthening of the country's positions in the international arena and allow it to worthily enter the new millennium as a great and prospering power.

Gorbachev introduced in this speech the words that would name his reforms and become known throughout the world. He spoke of "the *perestroika* of the forms and methods of economic management," using the Russian word for reconstruction or restructuring; he said that "*glasnost* is an integral aspect of socialist democracy and a norm of all public life," using the untranslatable Russian word that means both openness and publicity. "Extensive, timely and candid information," he continued, "is an indication of trust in people and of respect for their intelligence, feelings and ability to comprehend various events on their own." He spoke of a radical economics that would utilize "prices, profit [and] credit." He warned of "unfavorable trends in the economy" and threatened "implacability toward shortcomings."

The speech " 'was unambiguously perceived as a claim to political leadership,' " Archie Brown writes, quoting one of Chernenko's aides, and "both Gorbachev's 'champions and his opponents understood it that way.' " It was also, according to a Gorbachev ally, "regarded by quite a number of people as dangerous, as having gone too far." If Gorbachev put himself at risk in speaking out so publicly, he also practiced what he preached: glasnost, trust in people and respect for their intelligence.

Konstantin Chernenko died on Sunday evening, 10 March 1985, and this time Gorbachev was ready. Yevgeny Chazov, Chernenko's personal physician, called Gorbachev first to deliver the news. He in turn called Andrey Gromyko and two other members of the Politburo. He arranged to meet them at the Kremlin at eleven p.m., but contrived to see Gromyko privately before the meeting. Though they spoke in euphemisms, the message was clear: Gromyko, the old hard-liner, the Soviet foreign minister for twenty-eight years, would propose the young reformer at the Central Committee plenum to be called for five p.m. the next day. The meeting at the Kremlin ran on through the night; Gorbachev finally got home at four a.m. Raisa was waiting:

> Mikhail Sergeyevich returned home very late—we were then living in the country house near Moscow. We went out into the garden. There was something oppressive in the late-night air, still untouched by the spring. Three deaths in three years. The death of three General Secretaries, the country's top leaders, one after another. Mikhail Sergeyevich was very tired. At first he remained silent. Then he said: "Tomorrow there will be a full meeting of the Central Committee. The question may arise of my taking over the leadership of the party." . . .
>
> We strolled around the garden where the snow was still lying. My husband again remained silent. Then he appeared quietly to be thinking aloud. "I worked so many years in Stavropol. This is my seventh year in Moscow. But it is impossible to achieve anything substantial, anything on a large scale, the things the country is waiting for. It's like coming up against a wall. Yet life demands it and has done for a long time. No!" I heard him say. "We just can't go on like this."

That afternoon, says Chernyaev, when Gromyko pronounced Gorbachev's name, "the hall exploded with applause."

PART TWO

APES ON A TREADMILL

It may be that we are jogging in tandem on a treadmill to nowhere.

PAUL WARNKE

FOUR

"THE BOMBER WILL ALWAYS GET THROUGH" (I)

MIKHAIL GORBACHEV INHERITED A FORMIDABLE nuclear arsenal when he claimed the general secretaryship of the Communist Party of the Soviet Union (CPSU) on 11 March 1985. In that first year of the second term of Ronald Reagan's presidency, the Soviet Union faced an even more formidable nuclear arsenal arrayed against it by the United States, as well as the smaller but deadly arsenals of Britain, France, and Israel. Although no nuclear weapons had been exploded in anger since the Second World War, the total world stockpile had increased by the mid-1980s to about fifty thousand bombs and warheads with a combined explosive force of about 22,500 million tons of TNT equivalent (1.5 million Hiroshimas). "A few hundred of the fifty thousand," former secretary of defense Robert McNamara wrote in 1986, "could destroy not only the United States, the Soviet Union and their allies but, through atmospheric effects, a major part of the rest of the world as well." All mechanical systems risk failure, accident, criminal appropriation, or misuse; what fears and ambitions had justified such an apocalyptic accumulation?

NUCLEAR FISSION WAS DISCOVERED in Nazi Germany in December 1938, nine months before the beginning of the Second World War. News of the unexpected discovery of a physical reaction that liberated the enormous energy known to be latent in the nuclei of atoms quickly spread around the world. Physicists everywhere immediately understood that nuclear energy might now be harnessed to generate power or released explosively in bombs several million times more destructive, pound for pound, than ordinary high explosives. Such a weapon could assure victory in war or reverse an impending defeat.

It might also, paradoxically, protect against attack. "It must be realized," two physicists working in Britain advised the British government secretly in

1940, "that no shelters are available that would be effective [against a nuclear explosion] and could be used on a large scale. The most effective reply [to a threat of attack] would be a counter-threat with a similar weapon." Given these conditions, could any government that could afford nuclear weapons afford not to have them? Within three years of the discovery of nuclear fission, programs of research into the military potential of the reaction had begun in Germany, Britain, France, the United States, the Soviet Union, Canada, and Japan.

Only the Anglo-American program was successful before the end of the war, but the atomic bombings of Hiroshima and Nagasaki catalyzed the Soviet program and stimulated the initiation or renewal of bomb research in postwar Britain, France, Sweden, Norway, Switzerland, Yugoslavia, and Australia. The Soviet Union tested its first atomic bomb in August 1949. Britain followed in October 1952, France in February 1960, China in October 1964, India in May 1974, and Pakistan in May 1998. Every test was successful, and Israel and South Africa confidently built nuclear arsenals during the same period without testing at full yield. Yugoslavia, Sweden, Australia, Norway, Taiwan, South Korea, Indonesia, Turkey, Greece, Romania, Libya, Canada, Brazil, Argentina, and Switzerland interrupted weapons-development programs under diplomatic pressure from one or more of the nuclear powers or from the international community. South Africa dismantled its small nuclear arsenal of six uranium bombs at the end of the Cold War when the sizable and threatening army of Cuban forces stationed in nearby Angola went home.

Even before the end of the Second World War, the scientists in the Anglo-American program had begun investigating the development of thermonuclear weapons as well as fission bombs. Bombs that fused hydrogen to helium, releasing nuclear energy, would be orders of magnitude more destructive even than fission weapons, their fireballs measured in miles rather than feet, their yields measured in megatons (millions of tons of TNT equivalent) rather than kilotons (thousands of tons of TNT equivalent). The United States tested its first thermonuclear device—a bulky two-story experimental unit named Mike—in November 1952. It yielded 10.5 megatons (seven hundred Hiroshimas). A first Soviet thermonuclear test of a yield-limited but deliverable weapon (four hundred kilotons) followed in August 1953, and of a so-called true thermonuclear—a 1.5-megaton two-stage design like Mike of potentially unlimited yield—in November 1955. Britain tested a thermonuclear weapon in November 1957, China in June 1967, and France in August 1968. None of the smaller nuclear powers is known to have fielded hydrogen bombs, but tritium, a radioactive isotope of hydrogen, is also commonly used in fission weapons to produce fusion reactions to boost fission yields, and Israel at least is believed to have developed such boosted-fission weapons.

In February 1963, McNamara prepared an estimate for President John F. Kennedy of potential nuclear powers. McNamara's list included West and East Germany, Belgium, the Netherlands, Canada, Sweden, Switzerland, Japan, India, Israel, the United Arab Republic (Egypt), Brazil, Australia, Norway, China, Czechoslovakia, and Poland. McNamara also included Romania, Bulgaria, and Hungary on a supplemental list as countries with "a scientific community and industry to support nuclear programs." When Kennedy was asked at a press conference on 21 March 1963, five months after the Cuban Missile Crisis, if he was still hopeful of achieving a nuclear test ban, he referred to the information in McNamara's estimate to justify continuing to negotiate with a Soviet Union reluctant to allow U.S. inspections on its territory: "Personally, I am haunted by the feeling that by 1970, unless we are successful, there may be ten nuclear powers instead of four, and by 1975, fifteen or twenty. . . . I see the possibility in the 1970s of the President of the United States having to face a world in which fifteen or twenty or twenty-five nations may have these weapons. I regard that as the greatest possible danger and hazard."

Kennedy immediately stepped up efforts to limit nuclear-weapons testing as one approach to limiting proliferation; without tests it would be difficult if not impossible for nonnuclear powers or threshold nuclear powers to develop the miniaturized, high-yield weapons required for delivery by ballistic missile. The Soviet Union had offered a first proposal to limit weapons tests at the United Nations in 1955. President Dwight D. Eisenhower had tried hard during his second term (1957–1961) to achieve a comprehensive nuclear-test ban. In February 1960, after extensive negotiations among the United States, Britain, and the Soviet Union had stalled because of Soviet resistance to intrusive inspections, Eisenhower had brought forward a proposal banning tests in the atmosphere, the oceans, and outer space—which could be policed from outside the Soviet Union—as well as "all nuclear weapons tests beneath the surface of the earth which can be monitored." Nikita Khrushchev had accepted Eisenhower's proposal, and the signing of a test-ban treaty was expected to highlight a May 1960 summit conference in Paris. But on 1 May, Soviet rocket forces shot down a CIA U-2 reconnaissance plane conducting a secret flight over the Soviet Union in the final months before the first U.S. spy satellites were scheduled to become operational.

(Eisenhower had only reluctantly agreed to the flight, the last in a series, trusting CIA assurances that the U-2 operated above the range of Soviet antiaircraft rockets and was rigged to be blown up if intercepted.) The pilot, Francis Gary Powers, choosing not to commit suicide, survived and confessed. Khrushchev walked out of the summit meeting in protest and the test-ban treaty went unsigned.

In June 1963, Kennedy proposed a more limited treaty banning weapons tests everywhere except underground. Eight years of prior discussions had cleared the way, and when the three powers met in mid-July they needed only ten days to negotiate an agreement. The Limited Test Ban Treaty entered into force on 10 October 1963. Since it allowed underground testing, it did little to limit the superpower nuclear arms race, but it contributed to slowing proliferation by making weapons tests much more expensive.

A more comprehensive international agreement addressing nuclear proliferation originated in a resolution that Ireland proposed to the United Nations General Assembly in 1961, which the General Assembly unanimously approved. It appealed to all nations to forego transferring or acquiring nuclear weapons. Negotiations to limit the transfer or acquisition of nuclear weapons went forward on several fronts in the years that followed. A major barrier was a program under development within NATO to field a multilateral nuclear force that would integrate U.S. nuclear weapons into NATO battalions in Europe; the Soviet Union considered such an arrangement equivalent to proliferation. The United States and the Soviet Union were able to agree on a draft treaty only in 1967, when the failure of the multilateral force concept allowed the United States to give assurances that it would retain final control of its nuclear arsenal in Europe.

Nonnuclear states had other concerns about the treaty draft. They wanted the nuclear industries of the five nuclear powers to be subject to International Atomic Energy Agency safeguards just as theirs would be, so that they would not be put at a commercial disadvantage. The United States agreed to such an arrangement in December 1967, as did Britain; over the next two decades, France, the Soviet Union, and China also complied. The nonnuclear states wanted guarantees that the nuclear powers would come to their aid if they were threatened with nuclear attack and would not attack them with nuclear weapons. The United States, Britain, and the Soviet Union offered the positive guarantee in 1968 and the negative guarantee a decade later. Finally, according to the arms-control expert and former U.S. ambassador Thomas Graham, Jr., the nonnuclear states wanted the nuclear powers to agree "to negotiate in good faith to achieve cessation of the nuclear arms race, nuclear disarmament, and general and complete disarmament. This, in effect, meant that the [treaty] included a basic bargain whereby the non-nuclear weapon states agreed to foreswear nuclear weapons in exchange for unfettered access to the peaceful benefits of nuclear energy and a pledge from the nuclear weapon states to eventually eliminate their nuclear arsenals."

The Nuclear Non-Proliferation Treaty (NPT) opened for signature on 1 July 1968 and entered into force on 5 March 1970. It provided that no nuclear-weapon state would transfer nuclear weapons to any other entity or assist any nonnuclear-weapon state in developing such weapons, while non-nuclear states pledged not to receive or try to develop nuclear weapons. It provided for safeguards of nuclear materials and verification of compliance. It specified that all the parties to the treaty had the right to develop nuclear energy for peaceful purposes, and that the parties would share knowledge of peaceful technologies to the fullest extent possible. It specified Graham's "basic bargain." But because states such as Sweden, West Germany, and Italy were skeptical that the nuclear powers would voluntarily disarm, the treaty also provided that a state could withdraw if it felt its "supreme interests" were being jeopardized, and that twenty-five years after the treaty entered into force—that is, in 1995—a conference would be convened to decide by major-ity vote, up and down, whether the treaty should continue in force indefi-nitely, or should only be extended for a fixed period or periods of time. In this regard it differed from all other multilateral arms-control treaties, which became permanent upon ratification.

The NPT curbed the nuclear proliferation that Kennedy had regarded in 1963 as "the greatest possible danger and hazard." It also put the five nuclear powers on notice that the rest of the world would not tolerate the presence of their menacing nuclear arsenals forever. In return for foregoing nuclear weapons, the nonnuclear states expected the nuclear powers to make good-faith efforts to limit, reduce, and finally eliminate those arsenals. They would not have to do so overnight; they would have a generous twenty-five years to work out their differences. If they were unable or unwilling to do so, the nonnuclear powers reserved the right to allow the treaty to lapse or to limit its extension.

Other international and bilateral efforts prior to the time Gorbachev took office in 1985 also sought to limit the proliferation of nuclear states and nuclear weapons and to reduce the risk of nuclear war: the Antarctic Treaty (1959); the hotline agreements (1963); the Outer Space Treaty (1967); the Seabed Arms Control Treaty (1971); the Anti-Ballistic Missile Treaty (1972); the Strategic Arms Limitation Talks (SALT I) Interim Agreement (1972); the

Threshold Test Ban Treaty (1974); and the first of several treaties establishing nuclear-weapon-free zones, the Treaty of Tlatelolco (1967), which demarcated Latin American and the Caribbean. But the Limited Test Ban Treaty and the Nuclear Non-Proliferation Treaty were the most effective in preventing rampant nuclear proliferation. Graham has called the NPT "the central document of world peace and security" after the United Nations Charter itself. "In a sense," he adds, "it is the club of civilization."

YET FOR ALL THEIR CONSIDERABLE VIRTUES, none of these agreements significantly limited the arms race between the two nuclear superpowers in the years before Gorbachev took office. That arms race began with the Anglo-American program itself—the Manhattan Project—because the United States and Britain had chosen not to share knowledge of the secret program (not of how to build atomic bombs—no one proposed to do that—but simply of the fact that the United States and Britain were developing them) with the Soviet Union even though it was an ally in the fight against Nazi Germany. Since the Soviets had recruited several high-level espionage agents within the Manhattan Project, they were fully aware that they were being excluded.

Stalin drew the logical conclusion that the Americans intended to use their unique weapon to intimidate him after the war. Once the evidence of Hiroshima and Nagasaki overcame his doubts about the authenticity of the bomb plans his spies had delivered, he made the full resources of the state available to the Soviet effort. By 1948, Soviet scientists under the charismatic physicist Igor Kurchatov had not only replicated the American plutonium implosion bomb ("Fat Man") but had also developed an improved design of half the weight and twice the yield. Lavrenty Beria, the brutal KGB chief whom Stalin had appointed to oversee the bomb program, was unwilling to risk the possible failure of an indigenous, untested design and ordered Kurchatov to copy the American design, which the atomic bombing of Nagasaki had proven would work. The Soviet copy, RDS-1 (Joe 1 in U.S. nomenclature), was tested on 29 August 1949 on a tower on the Kazak steppe lands at Semipalatinsk, yielding twenty-two kilotons, matching the yield of the Nagasaki bomb. A pilot series of five RDS-1 bombs inaugurated the Soviet nuclear arsenal in March 1950. Serial production of RDS-1s began in December 1951.

With its four-year lead, the United States was well ahead of the Soviet Union in nuclear-weapons development and production by the end of 1951.

Until 1948, the United States had stockpiled slightly improved Fat Man bombs and a few uranium bombs that were ruggedized for attacks on hardened targets such as submarine pens and command bunkers. In its first series of weapons-design tests, Operation Sandstone, which was conducted in the Marshall Islands in 1948, it had proved the principle of core levitation—suspending the nuclear core within its natural uranium tamper so that the tamper material had a gap across which to accelerate before imploding the core—and tested both a composite plutonium-uranium core and cores of highly enriched uranium (HEU) alone. These and other evolutionary improvements resulted in yields of up to forty-nine kilotons, effectively increasing the total yield of the U.S. stockpile by 75 percent. In 1951, that stockpile held 438 weapons; by then the Soviet Union had manufactured twenty-five.

Before 1949, the United States had considered its nuclear monopoly to be roughly the equivalent of the superior numbers of Soviet forces occupying the eastern half of Europe, a finding that had allowed President Harry S. Truman to bring U.S. troops home while cutting the defense budget drastically from its wartime highs. From Washington's point of view, adding atomic bombs to Soviet ground-force superiority deprived the United States of a unique capability and tilted the balance decisively in the Soviet Union's favor.

Truman responded in the autumn of 1949 by requesting advice from within his administration on whether or not to accelerate development of a thermonuclear or hydrogen fusion bomb, a new, unique weapon of potentially unlimited yield. The Hungarian-born theoretical physicist Edward Teller had been promoting a design for such a weapon, nicknamed the Super, that he had devised during and immediately after the war. Other Manhattan Project scientists who had studied the design and were now advisers to the U.S. Atomic Energy Commission were skeptical that the Super would work. They anticipated that it would require large quantities of tritium, but breeding tritium in the production reactors that bred plutonium for fission weapons would mean seriously slowing fission-bomb production with no guarantee that a workable thermonuclear weapon would emerge.

Since several fission bombs (which the United States knew how to make) would deliver damage equivalent to that of one thermonuclear bomb (which existed as yet as nothing more than an unproven design concept), the scientific advisory committee to the Atomic Energy Commission recommended in October 1949 that fission-weapon production, not hydrogen-bomb development, be accelerated. Two physicists on the committee, I. I. Rabi and Enrico Fermi, one a liberal and the other a conservative, both experienced in weapons work and both Nobel laureates, added to the recommendation their blunt judgment that "such a weapon goes far beyond any military objective and enters the range of very great natural catastrophes. By its very nature it cannot be confined to a military objective but becomes a weapon which in practical effect is almost one of genocide. . . . It is necessarily an evil thing considered in any light."

Robert Oppenheimer, the American theoretical physicist who had directed the design and construction of the first atomic bombs at the secret Manhattan Project laboratory at Los Alamos, New Mexico, and who was the chairman of the advisory committee, explained the committee's strategic reasoning in later testimony without moralizing:

> The notion that the thermonuclear arms race was something that was in the interests of this country to avoid if it could was very clear to us in 1949. We may have been wrong. We thought it was something to avoid even if we could jump the gun [on the Soviets] by a couple of years, or even if we could outproduce the enemy, because we were infinitely more vulnerable [because more of the U.S. population lives in large cities than does the Soviet population] and infinitely less likely to initiate the use of these weapons.

The U.S. military, which had not even heard of the idea of a thermonuclear weapon of potentially unlimited yield until the debate began in Washington in late 1949, had other ideas. The Joint Chiefs of Staff expressed them in a memorandum to the secretary of defense that the secretary, Louis Johnson, passed on to Truman in January 1950. The Joint Chiefs judged that it was "necessary to have within the arsenal of the United States a weapon of the greatest capability, in this case the super bomb. Such a weapon would improve our defense in its broadest sense, as a potential offensive weapon, a possible deterrent to war, a potential retaliatory weapon, as well as a defensive weapon against enemy forces." The chiefs were sensitive to the charge that a bomb with yields equivalent to millions of tons of high explosives might be considered, as Rabi and Fermi had considered it, almost a weapon of genocide. They demurred that they did "not intend to destroy large cities *per se* [with hydrogen bombs]; rather, only to attack such targets as are necessary in war in order to impose the national objectives of the United States upon the enemy." (The distinction between military and civilian targets had already become a distinction without a difference in the Second World War. In the 1930s and early 1940s, Japan and Germany had initiated terror bombing against cities such as Shanghai, Warsaw, and London, deliberately targeting civilians. When British and American attempts at precision bombing of the German and Japanese war industries failed, the two allies had begun area bombing and then firebombing German and Japanese cities in turn, and the atomic bombings had overwhelmed all distinctions: Whether an individual lived or died at Hiroshima or Nagasaki depended not on his status, military or civilian, newborn infant or factory worker, but simply on his distance from the bomb's hypocenter.) In conclusion, the Joint Chiefs ran off into unsupported and somewhat hysterical speculation. Although fission bombs were more than sufficient to destroy entire cities, as Hiroshima and Nagasaki had demonstrated, and should therefore be an effective deterrent against nuclear blackmail, the chiefs claimed that the nation would be put in "an intolerable position" if "a possible enemy possessed the [hydrogen] bomb and the United States did not." Worse, they argued, if the United States publicly renounced development of the hydrogen bomb, such renunciation "might be interpreted as the first step in unilateral renunciation of the use of all atomic weapons, a course which would inevitably be followed by major international alignments to the disadvantage of the United States. Thus, the peace of the world generally and, specifically, the security of the entire Western Hemisphere would be jeopardized."

No one within the U.S. government had suggested unilateral renunciation—bomb production had actually been greatly expanded in the autumn of 1949 on the advice of the scientific advisory committee—but the Joint Chiefs, who had endorsed surprise attack as the necessary strategy of the atomic age even before the first atomic bombings, had no intention of giving up a powerful new weapon if such a weapon could be invented, even if its advantages cut both ways. "Offense," they had written in 1947, "recognized in the past as the best means of defense, in atomic warfare will be the only general means of defense." And if a first-strike policy—which is what the Joint Chiefs were advocating—made sense with fission bombs, how much more sense would it make with the thermonuclear?

The opinion of the Joint Chiefs was all that Truman needed. "What the hell are we waiting for?" he asked his advisers. "Let's get on with it." On 31 January 1950, he announced that he was directing the AEC "to continue its work on all forms of atomic weapons, including the so-called hydrogen or super-bomb." Privately, the following month, Truman told his assistant press secretary Eben Ayers of his decision to build the thermonuclear bomb that "we had to do it" but that "no one wants to use it." We had to do it, he added, "if only for bargaining purposes with the Russians." Thus the United States announced to the world that it intended to make a potentially genocidal new weapon of mass destruction that it did not know how to make, did not want to use, but might need for political leverage in international negotiations. Even so, it took the Soviet Union, which had barely begun manufacturing atomic bombs, another full year to follow suit: Stalin formally approved a full-scale thermonuclear development program on 26 February 1951. By the late 1950s, more or less simultaneously, both sides were preparing to field deliverable megaton-yield weapons.

AMERICAN PLANNING FOR HOW TO USE its accumulating stockpile proceeded ad hoc during the years of the Truman administration (1945–1953). Truman had been shaken by the extent of civilian casualties at Hiroshima and Nagasaki. A third Fat Man had been ready for assembly and delivery in the final days before the Japanese surrender on 15 August 1945, but Truman had ordered atomic bombing stopped after the first two bombs were used. At a cabinet meeting, Henry Wallace, the secretary of commerce, recorded the president's reasoning: "He said the thought of wiping out another 100,000 people was too horrible. He didn't like the idea of killing, as he said, 'all those kids.'" After the war, Truman disguised his aversion to using nuclear weapons with public bluster, but his policies as well as private comments reveal his qualms. An artillery officer in the First World War, he hesitated to put atomic bombs into the hands of the military; he told James Forrestal, his first secretary of defense, that he did not propose "to have some dashing lieutenant colonel decide when would be the proper time to drop one." Through the Atomic Energy Act of 1946, the historian David Alan Rosenberg writes, Truman imposed "a system that made atomic weapons a separate part of the nation's arsenal, with the President of the United States the sole authority over their use. . . . His official policy initiatives through 1948 focused exclusively on the goals of establishing civilian control over American nuclear resources . . . and seeking international control of atomic energy in the United Nations. . . . International control remained the only official policy enunciated by the U.S. government relative to atomic weapons through the summer of 1948."

Truman changed his mind a year later when it became clear that international control of atomic energy was unacceptable to the Soviet Union so long as the United States alone knew how to build nuclear weapons. "Since we can't obtain international control," he decided, "we must be strongest in atomic weapons." The shock of the North Korean surprise attack on South

Korea on 25 June 1950 "led President Truman to take the lid off" nuclear-weapons production, a State Department official, Robert Bowie, remembers. The Atomic Energy Commission's eight sites and 55,000 employees in 1950 expanded to twenty sites and 142,000 employees by 1953, and the expansion continued. By the mid-1950s, the nuclear production complex consumed 6.7 percent of total U.S. electrical power and exceeded in capital investment the combined capitalization of Bethlehem Steel, U.S. Steel, Alcoa, DuPont, Goodyear, and General Motors. Between 1953 and 1955, the U.S. strategic stockpile doubled, from 878 weapons to 1,756, while its total yield increased almost forty times, from seventy-three megatons (4,867 Hiroshimas) to 2,880 megatons (192,000 Hiroshimas). Yet Truman wrote a critic during his last year in office, 1953, that the atomic bomb "is far worse than gas and biological warfare because it affects the civilian population and murders them by wholesale." In his farewell address, equally bluntly, he warned against trying to fight a war with nuclear weapons:

> The war of the future would be one in which man could extinguish millions of lives at one blow, demolish the great cities of the world, wipe out the cultural achievements of the past—and destroy the very structure of a civilization that has been slowly and painfully built up through hundreds of generations. Such a war is not a possible policy for rational men.

Truman assigned planning for the use of the new weapons to the Joint Chiefs of Staff, who turned over the preparation of target lists to the Air Force, the only service branch that could deliver the massive early-model bombs—the Mark 3 production model Fat Man, for example, was six feet in diameter and weighed ten thousand pounds. The target lists that the Air Force produced, David Alan Rosenberg notes, reflected the experience of planners who "were all veterans of the bombing campaigns against Germany and Japan," which is to say, they had experienced the failure of so-called precision bombing and the seeming success of mass bombings and firebombings using conventional explosives and incendiaries. A study presented to the National Security Council in 1950 estimated "that just sixteen atomic weapons, if properly targeted, could 'most seriously disrupt' the U.S. government." General Curtis LeMay, the commander in chief, as of October 1948, of the Strategic Air Command (SAC), who had overseen the firebombings of Japan and who would oversee the devastating but little-known strategic bombing of North Korea during the Korean War, was "firmly convinced that 30 days is long enough to conclude World War III."

Despite such vivid evidence that nuclear war would be completely different from conventional war, that it would be a destructive blitzkrieg providing no time to mobilize industry and workers for what had formerly been a long haul, Air Force and SAC planners nevertheless targeted cities, "with the primary objective," according to a classified Air Force history that Rosenberg cites, "of the annihilation of population, with industrial targets incidental." Thirty-day war or not, LeMay continued to believe that the right targets for atomic bombing were industrial complexes within urban areas, so that bombs that missed their aiming points would produce what he called "bonus damage," meaning massive destruction and civilian casualties. "What was a city," the planners asked each other, "besides a collection of industry?" Truman might have advised them that a city is also human beings, not to be "murdered . . . by wholesale" even if they were enemy subjects.

LeMay may have been ruthlessly rational in the tradition of Ulysses S. Grant, believing that it is better to wage total war from the first hour of a conflict than to allow it to drag on and consume more lives. His protégés were not necessarily so detached. Robert Gates, the director of the CIA under President George H. W. Bush, remembers an encounter at SAC with a general when Gates was a young Air Force officer and had the task of briefing commanders on the SAC targeting plan. Gates mentioned that most U.S. warheads were targeted on Soviet ICBMs (intercontinental ballistic missiles). "The general," he writes, "a LeMay 'wannabe' smoking a huge cigar, went ballistic. He jumped up and shouted that it was a 'goddamn outrage' to be targeting what would in war be empty missile silos. He demanded that I— a second lieutenant—change the targeting strategy, proclaiming that 'when the balloon goes up, I want to kill some fucking Russians, not dig up dirt.' "

But LeMay understood what his wannabes evidently did not: the impossibility of defending a nation against nuclear attack. Stanley Baldwin, the British prime minister in the years after the First World War, had formulated the essential dilemma of strategic bombing as long ago as 1932, telling the House of Commons, "The bomber will always get through." The only defense against an attack from the air is in offense, Baldwin argued, adding, in a phrase that shocked the country, "which means that you have to kill more women and children more quickly than the enemy if you want to save yourselves." He went on prophetically: "Fear is a very dangerous thing. It is quite true that it may act as a deterrent in people's minds against war, but it is much more likely to act to make them want to increase armaments to protect them against the terrors that they know may be launched against them." LeMay had paraphrased Baldwin's stark formula not long after he returned from Japan at the end of the Second World War: "No air attack," he told the Ohio Society of New York in November 1945, "once it is launched, can be completely stopped." He hoped that if the United States had a force in being that was prepared to retaliate, "it may never come. It is not immediately conceivable that any nation will dare to attack us if we are prepared."

He was whistling in the dark and he knew it. Even as he built SAC into the most devastating war machine in history, capable of visiting utter destruction upon any enemy anywhere in the world at the cost of millions upon millions of noncombatant lives, he knew that the bomber, the land-based missile, the submarine-launched missile, the low-flying cruise missile, would always get through, and now not merely carrying high explosives, which might destroy a block of houses, but carrying atomic or hydrogen bombs, which could destroy an entire city or region and take at least hundreds of thousands of lives. "In general," an Air Force evaluator briefed the Joint Chiefs of Staff in 1955 on the current nuclear targeting plan, "the destruction of Soviet aircraft and airfields has an important degrading effect on Soviet atomic capabilities, but even under the improbable assumption that only 5 percent of the aircraft survived, seventy-five [nuclear] weapons could [still] be lifted against the U.S." Not even preventive war could guarantee safety. Piling up armaments for massive preemption or retaliation might deter, but would invite disaster if deterrence failed.

Both sides took the point. McGeorge Bundy, the national security adviser to Presidents John F. Kennedy and Lyndon Johnson, stated it succinctly for the American side in an essay published in the journal *Foreign Affairs* in 1969:

> In light of the certain prospect of retaliation, there has been literally no chance at all that any sane political authority, in either the United States or the Soviet Union, would consciously choose to start a nuclear war. This proposition is true for the past, the present and the foreseeable future. . . . In the real world of real political leaders . . . a decision that would bring even one hydrogen bomb on one city of one's own country would be recognized in advance as a catastrophic blunder; ten bombs on ten cities would be a disaster beyond history; and a hundred bombs on a hundred cities are unthinkable.

On the Soviet side, Nikita Khrushchev recalled in retirement that his first nuclear-weapons briefing after he took power in 1953 had shaken him. "I couldn't sleep for several days," he said. "Then I became convinced that we could never possibly use these weapons, and when I realized that, I was able to sleep again." At least one member of the Soviet general staff, Vladimir Slipchenko, concurs. "The retaliatory strike of even one nuclear warhead," Slipchenko told a post–Cold War conference, "would cause unacceptable damage to a country."

Slipchenko's formulation notwithstanding, both military leaderships thought in military terms, as their training and experience predisposed them to do: A threat should be met with a more powerful counterthreat, and nuclear war, if it came to that, could be won or lost. The experience of the Second World War loomed large, not only for the military leaderships and the target planners but also for the heads of state. Truman, with military experience in the First World War, became president during the Second, upon Franklin Roosevelt's death. Eisenhower had been supreme allied commander. Kennedy had been a young naval officer commanding a patrol boat who saw action and was wounded in the Pacific. All the Soviet leaders between Stalin and Gorbachev had fought in the war. Nikolai Detinov, a lieutenant general who worked on arms control in the Soviet Ministry of Defense, remembers his response to a speech given in Moscow in the 1960s by the American arms strategist Herman Kahn:

> He said that the problem with the Soviet Union and the United States is that they are led by people who lived through the Second World War and are still thinking in the categories of World War II. And that explanation completely applied to the Soviet Union. If we think about Khrushchev or Brezhnev, these are people who went through all the hardships of World War II. They witnessed the early defeat of the Soviet army because we didn't have enough arms, they saw the cities and towns burning, they saw our divisions marching toward the east in retreat. And so they sought certain things, the promise of security.

That everything had changed with the advent of nuclear weapons was not immediately apparent after the war, since the first bombs were not more destructive in scale than the firebombings that had preceded them: The ruins of Hiroshima and Nagasaki looked like the ruins of Dresden and Tokyo, because all four cities had been burned out by mass fires, the primary mechanism of destruction. "These weapons were simply looked upon as larger conventional weapons," confirms Todd White, a SAC historian. No one seems to have done the numbers, multiplied each bomber carrying a single atomic bomb times the thousand bombers that it replaced and understood that the scale of war had changed, that bombing with even a single nuclear weapon, as Rabi and Fermi had understood, went "far beyond any military objective and [entered] the range of very great natural catastrophes," while a thousand bombers loaded with atomic and especially with thermonuclear bombs—though evidently not unthinkable—would be at least Bundy's "disaster beyond history."

With the memory of vast destruction and near-defeat at the hands of the Nazis burned into the Russian soul, and the shock tearing at the American spirit that the United States was for the first time vulnerable to such catastrophe delivered by Soviet bombers and, later, missiles, it hardly seemed possible to accumulate too many weapons, too many delivery systems, just as Baldwin had predicted. In an official oral history of U.S. strategic nuclear policy produced by Sandia National Laboratories, the historian Douglas Lawson of Sandia comments that "the large growth that we saw [in nuclear-weapons production] in the 1950s and 1960s was primarily driven by the capacity of the [production] complex and not truly by [military] requirements." A designer at Sandia, Leon Smith, notes that "it was our policy at that time not to wait for requirements from the military but to find out from the technologies that were available what the art of the possible would be." The former director of the Lawrence Livermore Laboratory, John S. Foster, Jr., adds, "We were making it up as we went along." So the bombs multiplied, while every national leader whispered to himself under his breath that he would never use them.

FIVE

"THE BOMBER WILL ALWAYS GET THROUGH" (II)

IN THE 1950S, U.S. PLANNERS FOR nuclear war with the Soviet Union and its Eastern European and Chinese allies defined three categories of targets: targets such as airfields directly involved in delivering nuclear weapons, which had to be "blunted"; targets such as roads and railroad yards that facilitated further military deployment, which had to be "retarded"; and targets such as industry and urban centers, which had to be "destroyed." Official SAC policy weighted targeting to reflect these categories, particularly blunting, but such distinctions, writes the historian David Alan Rosenberg, "all but disappeared at the operational level" because targets overlapped and the SAC commander Curtis LeMay intended to throw everything he had into the initial attack, which he called his "Sunday punch."

According to a Navy officer, Captain William B. Moore, who attended a briefing at SAC headquarters in Omaha in 1954, SAC had by then identified some 1,700 enemy designated ground zeros (DGZs), which included 409 airfields. At that time SAC had 2,400 ready flight crews, a mix of medium- and long-range bombers, including the huge B-36, with a range of eight thousand miles, the smaller but jet-powered and aerial-refueled B-47, and B-52s coming on line with an aerial-refueled range of nine thousand miles. Using these resources, Moore reported, SAC planned to

> lay down an attack . . . of 600–750 bombs by approaching Russia from many directions so as to hit their [radar] early warning screen simultaneously. It would require about 2 hours from this moment until bombs had been dropped by using the bomb-as-you-go system in which both [blunting] and [destruction] targets would be hit as they reached them [opening up corridors for the bombers that followed]. . . . The final impression was that virtually all of Russia would be nothing but a smoking, radiating ruin at the end of two hours.

As far as SAC was concerned, the more bombs the better. More bombs meant a more devastating first strike and a greater likelihood of effective retaliation if the United States was attacked by surprise and some of its strategic assets were destroyed. More bombs also meant more bombers to carry them and, not incidentally, a larger share of the defense budget for the Air Force. Between 1954 and 1957, for example, the Air Force's share of defense appropriations averaged 47 percent annually compared with the Navy's 29 percent and the Army's 22 percent.

The Soviet Union had produced two hundred bombs by 1955, most of them twenty-kiloton, ten-thousand-pound RDS-1s, but its bomber fleet was embryonic. The first Soviet postwar bomber, the Tu-4, was a copy of the U.S. B-29, with all of that Second World War aircraft's limitations. The round-trip from Moscow to New York to Moscow is fifteen thousand kilometers (ninety-four hundred miles); Moscow–London–Moscow is five thousand kilometers (three thousand miles). The Tu-4's three-thousand-mile maximum range thus made it suitable only for regional air strikes—on London at the outside—without refueling, while the real threat, U.S. strategic nuclear forces, remained based safely out of range.

A Soviet intercontinental bomber, the Bison A* turbojet, entered service in 1954, but its maximum range was only five thousand miles and it could only carry a 5,000-kilogram (11,000-pound) bomb load—that is, one RDS-1. An improved model, the Bison B, had a 7,500-mile range, and by 1960 about sixty Bison Bs had joined Soviet Long-Range Aviation. The larger Bear turboprop bomber entered service beginning in 1956. It could carry a heavier bomb load (nine thousand kilograms: 19,800 pounds) and had a range of more than eight thousand miles, but it was slow and vulnerable. Sixty Bears had reinforced the sixty Bison Bs in Long-Range Aviation by 1960, "deployed on airfields deep within the territory of the USSR and . . . on permanent alert" according to the best post–Cold War authority, the Stanford University scholar Pavel Podvig. The Soviets were working on aerial refueling by then (SAC had begun developing it a decade earlier). In the interim, they practiced refueling stops on ice airstrips in the Arctic. "Such action would greatly jeopardize their chance of surprising us," McNamara dryly concluded.

By 1960, the U.S. arsenal had increased to 18,638 bombs and warheads yielding 20,500 megatons (1.4 million Hiroshimas), of which 3,127 were strategic weapons deployed on B-47 and B-52 bombers, large first-generation Atlas and Titan liquid-fueled ballistic missiles and Polaris nuclear submarines. American megatonnage peaked in 1960. In those years, SAC favored massive ten- to twenty-five-megaton behemoths to maximize its delivery

---

* For simplicity I will use NATO nomenclature; for Soviet designations see Podvig (2001).

capacity and destroy multiple DGZs simultaneously, but as ballistic missiles came into prominence, the total yield of the U.S. stockpile declined to reflect the missiles' more critical weight requirements and greater accuracy. ("The rule of thumb," write the weapons historians Robert S. Norris and William Arkin, "is that making a weapon twice as accurate allows an eightfold reduction in yield while achieving the same level of destruction.")

Most Soviet nuclear weapons were tactical, designed for crushing NATO if a conflict arose with Warsaw Pact forces in Europe; the total Soviet arsenal in 1960 of seventeen hundred bombs and warheads included only about 350 strategic weapons. The small Soviet bomber force had been supplemented by late 1960 with only four intercontinental ballistic missiles and a limited and primitive force of submarines carrying short-range missiles. The Soviet bombers were slow and vulnerable; the KGB kept missile warheads separate from the missiles, which required up to twenty-four hours to assemble, warm up, and fuel; and the submarines, which were normally kept in port, would have to cross the Atlantic or Pacific to within about two hundred miles of North America and surface to launch their missiles. "The Soviets had paltry forces," comments the former secretary of defense James Schlesinger— "hardly enough to stage an attack on the United States."

Coordination of multiplying U.S. nuclear strike forces had become an obvious problem by the mid-1950s. "It became possible for fighter-bombers to carry megaton weapons," the chairman of the Joint Chiefs would explain. In consequence, the tactical air forces, the Navy, and the Army added nuclear weapons to their ordnance. SAC controlled about half the arsenal; commanders in Europe, the Atlantic, and the Pacific controlled the other half. Targets frequently overlapped, wasting weapons and threatening fratricide. The Joint Chiefs first tried to solve the problem by ordering annual World-Wide Coordination Conferences convened at the Pentagon where commanders could get together to swap and coordinate their targets and try to resolve what an official SAC history calls "the complex problems of generation, launch, mutual support and maximum bombing involved in preparing a single command's strike plan." But targeting duplications and triplications were not significantly reduced, the history notes. Exercises between 1958 and 1960 by the successors to these conferences, Joint Coordination Centers in Britain and Hawaii that were supposed to handle actual operational coordination, turned up more than two hundred "time over target" conflicts during which the aircraft or missiles delivering the weapons would probably inadvertently blow each other up.

The solution to the problem, the Joint Chiefs concluded in 1959 after prodding from the secretary of defense, was that "atomic operations must be pre-planned for automatic execution to the maximum extent possible." Thus was inaugurated the Single Integrated Operational Plan (SIOP), developed initially under the direction of Air Force Lieutenant General Thomas Power, who succeeded Curtis LeMay as commander in chief of SAC from 1957 to 1964.

John F. Kennedy was briefed on the first plan, SIOP-62, by the chairman of the Joint Chiefs, General Lyman L. Lemnitzer, on 13 September 1961. SIOP-62, Lemnitzer told the president, was designed to work either preemptively or in retaliation for a Soviet nuclear strike on the United States. Like SAC's earlier plan, it targeted not only the Soviet Union but also the People's Republic of China and allies of the two countries in Eastern Europe and elsewhere, all to be hit at the outset of hostilities with a massive simultaneous attack from all sides at once, bomb as you go. The PRC and Eastern Europe would be hit even if they had not initiated hostilities. (When Kennedy's secretary of defense, Robert McNamara, learned of SAC's targeting priorities, he was appalled. "We essentially blasted our way through the Warsaw Pact countries in order to get to the Soviet Union," he told the Sandia oral-history project, "and I remember thinking, 'My God, what are we going to do to Poland?' ")

The number of U.S. strategic nuclear weapons available to be delivered had increased slightly by 1961 to 3,153, but megatonnage had declined by almost half with the phasing out of SAC's largest bombs. Four-fifths of the SIOP-62 designated ground zeros were military. Lemnitzer explained, however, that "because of fallout from attack of military targets and co-location of many military targets with urban-industrial targets, the casualties would be many millions in number. Thus, limiting attack to military targets has little practical meaning as a humanitarian measure." Contemporary estimates of the consequences of an all-out SIOP attack put the death toll at 285 million Soviet and Chinese citizens and millions more dead in Eastern Europe— more than twice the dead of all the wars of the twentieth century. The journalist Fred Kaplan reports that General David Shoup, the Marine Corps commandant, asked Thomas Power at a similar SIOP briefing in 1960 if the United States had any options to avoid bombing China if that country happened not to be involved in the conflict that had led to nuclear war. "Well, yeah, we *could* do that," Kaplan reports Power replying, "but I hope nobody thinks of it because it would really screw up the plan." Back in Washington, Kaplan writes, other U.S. military leaders endorsed SIOP-62 to the secretary of defense. "David Shoup stood and said, 'Sir, any plan that kills millions of

Chinese when it isn't even their war is not a good plan. This is not the American way.'"

As if such deliberate democide were not horrific enough, one SIOP reviewer after another discovered its damage calculations were based only on the blast effects of nuclear weapons, when the primary mode of destruction of weapons with yields greater than one hundred kilotons—most U.S. strategic weapons—is fire. Admiral Harry Felt, the commander in chief of the Pacific fleet, cabled the Joint Chiefs in January 1961 after reviewing the SIOP, "ONLY BLAST EFFECTS WERE CONSIDERED. . . . OTHER EFFECTS SUCH AS HEAT, FIRE AND RADIATION SHOULD BE USED WHEN DRAWING UP DAMAGE CRITERIA FOR THE SIOP." A Ukrainian explosives expert and Manhattan Project veteran named George Kistiakowsky, President Eisenhower's astute science adviser, who was sent out to Omaha in late 1960 to review the work of the Joint Strategic Target Planning Staff, reported back, "The JSTPS used blast effect as the only criterion of damage and neglected thermal radiation, fires which will be caused by it, and fall-out. The question may be raised as to whether the resultant damage criteria are unnecessarily conservative, whether they result in overkill and will create unjustified additional 'force requirements.' "

Why should it matter whether people were killed by fire or blast? The answer began to emerge only in the 1980s, when a few independent scientists looked into the neglected subject of mass fires from nuclear weapons. As one of them, Theodore Postol, found, even a very limited attack on enemy industry "might actually result in about two to three times more fatalities than that predicted by the government for the [all-out] anti-population attack" if mass fires were included in casualty predictions. Two to three times the 285 million Soviet and Chinese dead that SIOP-62 predicted based on blast damage alone would raise that number close to 1 billion.

Until recently, the official explanation for why fire was left out of targeting calculations was that the extent of mass fire in an incendiary attack depends on weather conditions. Such had been true of the firebombings of the Second World War, but according to the preeminent expert on the subject today, the Stanford University scholar Lynn Eden, mass fires started by strategic nuclear weapons create their own environment:

> The extraordinarily high air temperatures and wind speeds characteristic of a mass fire are the inevitable physical consequence of many simultaneous ignitions occurring over a vast area. The vacuum created by buoyantly rising air follows from the basic physics of combustion and fluid flow. . . . As the area of

the fire increases, so does the volume of rising air over the fire zone, causing even more air to be sucked in from the periphery of the fire at increasingly higher speeds.

Using as an example a single three-hundred-kiloton airburst over the Pentagon, which by blast effects alone would hardly knock down buildings of heavy construction beyond Capitol Hill, Eden estimates that fire effects would generate "ground winds of hurricane force with average air temperatures well above the boiling point of water. . . . Within tens of minutes, the entire area, approximately 40 to 65 square miles—everything within 3.5 or 4.6 miles of the Pentagon—would be engulfed in a mass fire. The fire would extinguish all life and destroy almost everything else," south beyond Alexandria, Virginia, in one direction and north to Chevy Chase, Maryland, in the other. The intense light of a nuclear fireball, the equivalent at three miles of six hundred desert suns at noon, ignites fires simultaneously and instantly over a large area, with the fireball's shock wave, its blast, arriving long seconds later to break up, spread, and feed the flames. "A nuclear weapon could be considered the nearly ideal example of an incendiary weapon," Postol summarizes, because it delivers its entire yield in an instant—"about 300 trillion calories," Eden estimates, "within about a millionth of a second." Nor is one bomb over the Pentagon even remotely a realistic scenario. A former SAC commander told Eden, "We must have targeted Moscow with 400 weapons. . . . I would be comfortable saying that there would be several dozens of weapons aimed at D.C."

In her book *Whole World on Fire,* Eden finds organizational traditions and prejudices central to the neglect of mass fire in targeting calculations. Targeting planners and military leaders drew on their experiences in the Second World War to frame their priorities. At that time, strategic targeting had been focused on precision bombing—"tossing it right in the pickle barrel"—and only when that effort failed had the Air Force turned to area bombing and then firebombing. Though more successful, these practices were also a reminder of failure; the bureaucratic focus on precision bombing continued and renewed after the war. Precision bombing targeted specific structures that could be accumulated into target lists, so that destroying the structures would quantify destroying the enemy's capacity to make war. It also evoked a tradition of marksmanship with hand weapons that extends back through two centuries of American exploration and pioneering.

Targeting atomic and hydrogen bombs as if they were precision weapons is something like using a large meteor to drive a nail, and it depopulates the target zone. "The world of nuclear weapons damage," Eden writes, "is generally an unpeopled one of physical objects—structures, installations, and equipment." Rendering invisible the people who occupy the structures and installations and operate the equipment being targeted has obvious benefits of emotional relief for the planners. Interviewing a recent vice director of the JSTPS, Navy Vice Admiral Michael Colley, Eden heard of larger benefits as well:

> We don't like hitting cities [Colley told her], we don't like killing people. So we have a philosophy of mass destruction, yes, but aimed at military targets. So it's politically comfortable and morally comforting for political leaders of our country to espouse "urban polygons" or "city withholds," so we can tell the world, hey, we don't hit cities. So I put this in the realm of political policy, not military effects. Because there are military targets all over the world that are in or near cities. . . . The emotion, the politics, is very, very important.

Eden comments:

> Admiral Colley had just taken me through the self-contradictory world of nuclear strategy and operations, a world in which potential horror, political nostrums, and mundane organizational problem solving are all mixed together. In Colley's words, "Nuclear war is irrational and unthinkable. *But,* if you're going to believe in deterrence, you have to have a war plan which makes sense, is executable—and devastating." The logic of nuclear strategy requires a fully executable and devastating plan, but politicians generally do not like to acknowledge the extent of the devastation. Thus, they espouse "limited" mass destruction in executable plans that would be irrational and unthinkable to carry out. What many comfortingly call the "paradox" of nuclear strategy is perhaps better understood as the "nonsense" of nuclear strategy—literally, that which does not make sense.

Nor was mass fire the only nuclear-weapons effect that targeting planners neglected. Among others, Eden lists radiation, smoke, ash, dust, noxious gases, fireball anomalies, electromagnetic pulse (EMP, which burns out electronic circuits such as microchips and transformers), crater ejecta, and blast-driven debris. These would add their further lethalities to the results of a nuclear attack by either side, the United States or the Soviet Union—or both.

AS SAC ATE ITS WAY THROUGH the U.S. defense budget in the 1950s, the Navy, increasingly concerned that it would shrink to a vestigial service in a nuclear world, challenged and criticized the SAC program's obvious excesses while energetically looking for a strategic role of its own. It found that role—to become what it called the "ultimate national deterrent"—in the ballistic-missile nuclear submarine. The first SSBN,* the U.S.S. *George Washington,* was ordered hastily in December 1957, two months after the Soviet Union launched the world's first man-made earth-orbiting satellite, *Sputnik,* as the payload of its first intercontinental-range ballistic missile, the cryogenic liquid-fueled SS-6. Electric Boat, in Groton, Connecticut, built the top-priority *George Washington* by cutting apart a Skipjack fast-attack nuclear submarine already under construction and welding in a 130-foot compartment for sixteen missiles between the sub's navigation end and nuclear-reactor compartment. The *George Washington,* launched on patrol on 15 November 1960, carried Polaris A1 solid-fueled missiles with ranges of about thirteen hundred nautical miles, each carrying a Livermore-designed W47 thermonuclear warhead with a six-hundred-kiloton yield (forty Hiroshimas). Four more Polaris submarines entered service by March 1961, the five-boat fleet carrying a total of eighty missiles.

Around the ballistic-missile nuclear submarine the Navy elaborated an alternative concept of finite deterrence. A sea-based deterrent, Admiral Arleigh Burke told the Joint Chiefs in September 1959, hidden in the vastness and the depths of the world's oceans, would not invite preemption as land-based bombers and missiles did. And if the United States was attacked, a sea-based retaliatory capacity would remain viable and should therefore serve as a more robust deterrent than land-based systems that might be destroyed in a Soviet first strike. The first generations of submarine-launched ballistic missiles (SLBMs) might be less accurate than land-based missiles or bombers, but accuracy would be of little importance in a retaliatory attack, when Soviet bombers and missiles would already have departed from their bases and their launchpads, leaving cities hostage. Following these assumptions, David Alan Rosenberg reveals:

> The Navy projected that a fleet of 45 submarines, with 29 deployed at all times, could destroy 232 Soviet targets, "which was sufficient to destroy all of Russia. The total cost of such a program would be 7 to 8 billion dollars, and annual operating costs would be $350 million." This proposal, [Eisenhower administration] Budget Director Maurice Stans remarked, raised the obvious question as to why the U.S. needed "other IRBMs [intermediate-range ballistic missiles] or ICBMs, SAC aircraft, and overseas bases." Navy leaders agreed, but were in

---

* SSBN: "Submarine, submersible, ballistic-missile, nuclear-powered."

no position to propose the virtual elimination of SAC. That, they told Stans, "was somebody else's problem."

The Air Force fought back, of course, and won its argument to the extent at least that U.S. strategic nuclear forces came to be multiplied into a triad: ballistic-missile submarines, bombers, and land-based ICBMs. This triad, which has since been sanctified as a prudent redundancy vital to effective deterrence, was nothing of the kind; it was an artifact of interservice rivalries. The Navy's "finite deterrence" alone would have deterred the Soviet Union, unless one believes that the Soviet leadership would have been willing to accept, in return for gambling a first strike against the United States, the complete destruction of all its major cities and the violent death of most of its population.

Eisenhower didn't believe it, but his disillusion with massive retaliation came too late. By 1959, Rosenberg writes, Eisenhower judged "that military statements of nuclear weapons requirements were grossly inflated: 'They are trying to get themselves into an incredible position of having enough to destroy every conceivable target all over the world, plus a three-fold reserve.'" At a meeting of the National Security Council in November 1958, Eisenhower told the assembled Cabinet officers and military leaders (as the meeting notes paraphrase) "that in today's presentation of the U.S. retaliatory attack on the Soviet Union, the U.S. had as targets every city in the U.S.S.R. with a population of over 25,000 people.... Turning to General Twining and addressing him and other members of the Joint Chiefs of Staff, the President said that he could remember well when the military used to have no more than 70 targets in the Soviet Union and believed that destruction of these 70 targets would be sufficient."

Although the United States had little information about Soviet strategic assets before the advent of reconnaissance satellites and communications intelligence in 1960, Soviet strategic policy during this era revealed itself by its actions to have been cautious, conventional, and to some extent budget-driven. The only Soviet system capable of attacking the United States with nuclear weapons until the early 1960s was the small fleet of sixty Bison and one hundred Bear bombers. Since they were based deep within the Soviet Union, they would have to be staged forward before flying intercontinentally, which would give away their intention and make them vulnerable to preemptive attack.

Lacking access to bomber bases close to the United States, the Soviet military limited its inventory of bombers to concentrate more resources on ballistic-missile development. It focused on arming its forces in Europe first of all, developing intermediate-range "theater" nuclear missiles such as the SS-3, the first Soviet missile to carry a nuclear warhead, and the SS-4. Diesel-electric and nuclear-powered attack submarines armed with nuclear torpe-does, short-range missiles, and cruise missiles offered tactical and limited strategic force projection as well.

The Soviet Union began developing intercontinental ballistic and cruise missiles in 1954. The SS-6, the missile that carried *Sputnik* into orbit, was ready for flight testing in 1957, and the first two Soviet satellites were launched in November as part of those flight tests, the second with a dog aboard. The *Sputnik*s greatly impressed the Kremlin along with the rest of the world, Podvig writes, turning the Soviet leadership's attention to the missile-development program. The Strategic Rocket Forces emerged as a separate service in December 1959 to receive the new SS-6 ICBMs, but "the level of readiness of [the] missiles was extremely low," Podvig says—the cryogenic liquid-fueled missile required twenty-four hours to ready for launch—and "the high cost of launch complexes predetermined the very limited scale of their deployment."

At the time of the Cuban Missile Crisis, according to Podvig, the Soviet bomber fleet "could deliver about 270 nuclear weapons to U.S. territory." But fear of the SAC commander Thomas Power's bomber fleet, which he main-tained on airborne alert throughout the week of the crisis, flying orbits over the Mediterranean and northern Canada, landing only long enough to change crews, led the Soviets to keep their bombers grounded; the Soviet Union was nearly as defenseless against nuclear attack that week as Japan had been at the end of the Second World War, although Soviet submarines in the Caribbean could have launched their missiles against U.S. targets in retaliation. American nuclear assets consisted of several thousand bombs on 1,576 SAC bombers, 183 Atlas and Titan ICBMs, 144 Polaris missiles on nine nuclear submarines, and the first squadron of ten Minuteman I missiles car-rying W59 one-megaton warheads, brought to full alert for the first time at the height of the crisis on Friday, 26 October 1962.

The United States had discovered the vast discrepancy between U.S. and Soviet strategic forces when its first generation of Corona photographic reconnaissance satellites began returning film in August 1960. Kennedy had communicated the discovery to the Soviet leadership to call Khrushchev's bluff about barring the West from Berlin. American exposure of Soviet strategic weakness was one reason Khrushchev had attempted to install medium- and intermediate-range missiles—SS-4s and SS-5s—in Cuba. The weapons were intended primarily to protect Cuba from a U.S. invasion, but an additional purpose was certainly to boost Soviet deterrence capabilities through forward basing. The United States, after all, had Jupiter missiles with 1.4-megaton W49 warheads pointed at the Warsaw Pact countries and the Soviet Union from bases in Italy and Turkey.

While it is true, as Podvig writes, that "the U.S. superiority in capabilities and number of strategic nuclear weapons was one of the most decisive factors that shaped the evolution of the conflict and the positions taken by both countries during the crisis," it is also true that Kennedy and his advisers did everything possible to avoid provoking a Soviet attack—even if such an attack had culminated in no more than Bundy's "one . . . bomb on one city of one's own country." One bomb was always enough.

That the United States could force the leaders of the Soviet Union to remove their missiles from Cuba frightened and deeply humiliated them. "The results were very painful and they were taken very painfully by our leadership," the Soviet lieutenant general Nikolai Detinov remembers. "Because of the strategic [imbalance] between the United States and the Soviet Union, the Soviet Union had to accept everything that the United States dictated to it and this had a painful effect on our country and our government." As a result, says Detinov, "all our economic resources were mobilized [afterward] to solve this problem." The Soviet diplomat who negotiated the crisis settlement, Vasily Kuznetsov, had implicitly threatened such a response. "Well, Mr. McCloy," he challenged his American counterpart, John J. McCloy, "we will honor this agreement. But I want to tell you something. You will never do this to us again."

"Humiliation in Cuba," writes Robert Gates, "galvanized the Soviets into action. The USSR proceeded to undertake the largest military buildup in history over a twenty-five-year period, with profound consequences for the international balance of power, for the United States, and ultimately, and fatefully, for the Soviet economy and state." Detinov concurs:

> During the 1960s, the Soviet government mobilized the economy to the point that all industrial facilities were turned to military production. All factories were included. . . . The rate of growth of our national economy went down in all branches. While before the Caribbean crisis we had a very steady rate of production, after the Caribbean crisis all production in other areas started going down thanks to the fact that all factories were mobilized in the name of military technology. Turning the national economy around later on was very hard.

Work on what Podvig calls "a simple and relatively inexpensive missile that could be used to increase the number of missiles in the Soviet ICBM force and provide quantitative parity with that of the United States" was authorized in March 1963, just five months after the resolution of the Cuban Missile Crisis; the light SS-11 would carry a 1.1-megaton warhead to compensate for its inaccuracy. The following September, the Soviets tested a heavier missile already in development, the SS-9, with a 10-megaton warhead. SS-11 flight tests began in 1965, and by 1966 both missiles were being deployed. Soviet Yankee-class nuclear-missile submarines, each carrying sixteen missiles with 1-megaton warheads, began patrolling the coasts of the United States in 1967.

One casualty of the Soviet buildup of missile forces was the nation's program to put men on the moon. Soviet dreams of beating the United States to the moon "were quietly abandoned" in the late 1960s, writes the former Air Force secretary Thomas Reed, "in favor of a massive ICBM buildup."

Both sides were also investigating missile defense systems; the Soviets had built a primitive antiballistic-missile system (ABM) of sixty-four interceptors around Moscow beginning in 1962. To contribute to defeating a U.S. ABM system, Podvig reports, Soviet designers developed a fractional-orbital version of the SS-9 that could attack from any azimuth, a number of which were deployed in 1969.

"The Soviets increased the number of their ICBMs from fewer than a hundred to more than 850 by 1968 and to more than 1,500 by 1972," Gates writes, summarizing the Soviet buildup, "while the U.S. number remained constant at 1,054. They began a vast expansion of their submarine ballistic missile force and laid the foundations for qualitative improvements to their strategic forces . . . as well." Gates's enumeration omits the U.S. contribution to the doomsday contest. The American stockpile reached its historic high of about 32,200 bombs and warheads in 1966. The number of U.S. land-based missiles "remained constant at 1,054" because Kennedy and McNamara had decided in 1962 that a thousand Minuteman ICBMs were enough, added to the fifty-four Titan II ICBMs already in service. (The number reveals the political, as opposed to the strategic, basis of the decision. SAC had wanted ten thousand Minutemen. The Air Force leadership cut that request to three thousand. Kennedy and McNamara had come to favor a force of only six hundred, because the U.S. inventory already counted 656 Polaris missiles on forty-one nuclear submarines. But since Kennedy had made a supposed "missile gap" a major issue of his presidential campaign, a thousand Minutemen to fill the illusory gap was the least he thought he could order to save face.)

In addition, both sides began studying the possibility of MIRVing their missiles: clustering multiple warheads—as many as ten or more—on a platform called a "bus" that would carry them together into space, where they would then be sprung free on individual trajectories leading down to different targets; "MIRV" stood for "multiple independently targetable reentry vehicle." In 1969, when the two sides began the SALT I arms-control talks, the United States was five years ahead of the Soviet Union in mastering the destabilizing technology. Soviet missiles were larger and more powerful than their U.S. counterparts, however, primarily because they were designed to carry heavier and more powerful warheads to compensate for their inferior accuracy. When the Soviets mastered MIRVing, that greater "throw-weight"—effective payload—would be an advantage, but surprisingly few American experts challenged the wisdom of developing a force multiplier that could only benefit the Soviet Union when that nation caught up. Alfred Lieberman, a senior operations analyst at the Pentagon at that time, recalls demonstrating the consequences of MIRVing statistically using the large computer model of a Soviet–U.S. nuclear exchange that the Pentagon's Operations Analysis Office maintained to examine arms-control positions to make sure they were advantageous to the United States:

> One of the key issues was whether or not we should abolish the MIRVing of ballistic missiles. . . . The problem was that at the time we were way ahead of the Russians in MIRV technology. Some of our studies warned that they had larger missiles and some day might load more MIRVs on them than we had. We also showed that MIRVs created a destabilizing situation since one attacking missile could destroy several missile silos. It was however not possible at that time to convince the inter-agency that MIRVs should be limited because we were so far ahead of the Soviets. In the end the Soviets caught up and loaded many more MIRVs on their missiles than we did on ours.

"Other considerations," McGeorge Bundy comments on U.S. strategic nuclear decision making, "were always found more important at moments of choice." The Joint Chiefs wanted MIRVing because it would effectively (and cheaply) override McNamara's thousand-missile ceiling. McNamara himself, Bundy says, thought MIRVing "would be a powerful means of penetrating any Soviet ABM system." MIRVing eventually resulted in both U.S. and Soviet warhead numbers five to six times as high as they had been with single-warhead missiles. It also interfered with treaty verification, since identifying a MIRVed warhead from space was difficult. "The inadequacy of verification," wrote the Russian security analyst Alexei Arbatov, Georgi's son, "was used as an excuse to do what both sides intended to do anyway."

FROM THE BEGINNING, AND THROUGHOUT all the years of the Cold War, the United States led the Soviet Union in total numbers of strategic nuclear bombs and warheads. The bitter U.S. political debates of the 1970s and early 1980s about nuclear strategy, nuclear force levels, supposed Soviet first-strike capabilities, and strategic defense hinged on arguments as divorced from reality as the debates of medieval scholars about the characteristics of seraphim and cherubim.

To cite one example among far too many: Paul Nitze, the American arms-control negotiator, arguing in 1976 against the SALT II treaty then under discussion, which would set a limit of 2,400 launchers on each side's collection of ICBMs, SLBMs, and bombers, pointed to the superior throw-weight of Soviet launchers and a supposed Soviet "massive and meticulously planned civil defense effort" as reasons why the United States should be wary of limiting its arsenal to parity. Though he was well aware that the United States had concluded in the early 1960s, after thorough study, that it was better off with lighter but more accurate land-based missiles and fewer rather than more of those (since they would eventually be vulnerable to destruction by Soviet ICBMs), he nevertheless found it politically useful to argue that the Soviet march toward a greater number of missiles of greater throw-weight betokened an aim of establishing "a nuclear-war-winning capability on the Soviet side."

Jan M. Lodal, a deputy to Secretary of State Henry Kissinger, responded to Nitze's argument by pointing out what Nitze must have known that, "unless accuracies are better than about 0.2 nautical miles, no reasonable MIRV system can have much of a counterforce capability [that is, capability to destroy enemy missile silos]; once accuracies are better than 0.1 nautical miles, essentially any size missile, even those of relatively low throw-weight, can destroy silos." In the case of the new Trident I missile, then being developed for U.S. nuclear submarines, Lodal added, "the United States could have just as well increased the throw-weight, had it been thought important to do so. Nonetheless, our military planners—correctly in my opinion—chose to emphasize the survivability of our submarines, and thus to use the additional capability of the missile to extend its range [rather than increase its effective payload]; this extra range gives our submarines a much greater operating area and reduces dramatically any possibility that the Soviets could determine their location and attack them."

Of Soviet efforts at civil defense, Nitze cited the *Soviet Civil Defense Manual,* of all suspect authorities, as estimating "that implementation of the prescribed evacuation and civil defense procedures would limit the civilian casualties to five to eight percent of urban population or three to four percent of the total population—even after a direct U.S. attack on Soviet cities." Acknowledging that "the Soviets may well overestimate the effectiveness of their civil defense program," Nitze argued that the *Manual* demonstrated that they assumed "that nuclear war could happen, and that the Soviet Union could survive." One of Nitze's early protégés, the Reagan-era deputy secretary of defense Richard Perle, carried on this Soviet civil-defense argument for years. But Alfred Lieberman, the Pentagon's operations analysis expert, remembers clearly his office's investigation of the Soviet civil-defense program:

> We did a very large study which showed that the Russians' civil defense would not save them from disaster in a nuclear war. We got some data from the CIA; we also got a lot of data from the Defense Department and the [military] services. But the essence was that we ran our nuclear exchange model with many variables and showed what would occur under a variety of different conditions. Our studies showed what disasters would occur in case of nuclear war even with the most sophisticated civil defense. . . . Our offensive forces would create horrendous damage against even the most advanced civil defense program.

These two examples of one prominent nuclear strategist's threat inflation are not in any way unique; on both sides, during the years of the high Cold War, there was always political capital to be earned from exaggerating the dangers or benefits of any particular nuclear strategy or weapons system. But even for those within the two governments with the best of intentions, trying to find security among the shifting and partly obscured maps of both sides' evolving force structures led to convoluted and sometimes absurd conclusions.

Robert McNamara, for example, visited the Omaha offices of the Joint Strategic Target Planning Staff for a briefing about the U.S. nuclear target list in February 1961, shortly after he became secretary of defense. McNamara was curious to compare the targeting-system criteria to a target known to have been destroyed, Hiroshima, burned out by a mass fire after a fifteen-kiloton bomb, Little Boy, exploded 1,900 feet above the city center on 6 August 1945. This dialogue ensued:

> Q.—McNamara—Have you applied your procedures to Hiroshima?
> A.—Smith—Yes. 3 DGZs of 80 KT each.

That is, were Hiroshima still a target, the JSTPS would have identified three designated ground zeros within the city and would have assigned three nuclear weapons, each equivalent to eighty kilotons of TNT, to destroy them. Such overkill gives meaning to Winston Churchill's notorious 1954 comment, "If you go on with this nuclear arms race, all you are going to do is make the rubble bounce." In the real world, one bomb of fifteen kilotons had been more than sufficient.

I asked McNamara, who has come to believe that nuclear weapons should be abolished, why the United States built so many more than it realistically needed during the Cold War. "Each individual decision along the way seemed rational at the time," he told me. "But the result was insane." His explanation echoed something he wrote in 1986, that "each of the decisions, taken by itself, appeared rational or inescapable. But the fact is that they were made without reference to any overall master plan or long-term objective. They have led to nuclear arsenals and nuclear war plans that few of the participants either anticipated or would, in retrospect, wish to support."

Among the reasons the decisions appeared rational or inescapable were difficult, threatening, and sometimes appalling political conflicts between the two sides which I have deliberately avoided discussing in this chapter and the last: from Soviet attempts to cut Berlin off from the West, to the Korean War, to brutal suppressions of dissent in Hungary, Czechoslovakia, and Poland, to the secret attempt to install missiles in Cuba and much more. Leaving these events out of the narrative must seem to some readers to severely bias my discussion of the progressive buildup of weapons on both sides, but none of these crises was resolved or resolvable with nuclear weapons.

However compromised the Soviet leadership felt afterward by the disparity between U.S. and Soviet strategic forces at the time of the Cuban Missile Crisis, for example, and contrary to Kennedy's public statements, there was never any question on the U.S. side of initiating a nuclear attack, McNamara reveals: "Despite an advantage of seventeen to one in our favor, President Kennedy and I were deterred from even considering a nuclear attack on the USSR by the knowledge that, although such a strike would destroy the Soviet Union, tens of their weapons would survive to be launched against the United States. These would kill millions of Americans. No responsible political leader would expose his nation to such a catastrophe." Kennedy's sanity was confirmed years later, after the end of the Cold War, and much to McNamara's surprise and shock, when Russian participants in the Cuban crisis revealed that no fewer than 162 nuclear weapons (warheads, submarine-launched missiles, and bombs) had already been deployed to the Caribbean and to Cuba before the crisis began. The missile warheads, McNamara learned, were "moved from their storage sites to positions closer to their delivery vehicles in anticipation of a U.S. invasion" at the height of the crisis on Friday, 26 October 1962. Khrushchev personally approved the move, which increased the risk, writes McNamara, that in the event of a U.S. invasion "the Soviet forces in Cuba would have decided to use their nuclear weapons rather than lose them. We need not speculate about what would have happened in that event. We can predict the results with certainty."

The conservative, seemingly prudent tendency on both sides was to pile destruction upon destruction with the hope that enough would eventually be enough. "We are piling up these armaments," Eisenhower said in 1956, "because we do not know what else to do to provide for our security." But the buildup itself added to the mutual fear, confirming to each side that the other must have nuclear-war-fighting plans, whatever its stated intentions. Worse, both sides' plans were regularly revised upward not to meet actual military needs but to justify the ongoing production of nuclear weapons. The operative concept in the United States was called the "greater than expected threat," which was based on the Soviet Union's potential weapons production capacity regardless of whether or not such production was actually budgeted. As a former assistant secretary of defense for systems analysis explained to two inquiring scholars, "We begin with the National Intelligence Estimate. We then use a planning and analytic device called the greater than expected threat. What we do is develop a substantially larger threat than the National Intelligence Estimate shows. This is developed by consulting various of the experts around the government . . . and approved by the Joint Chiefs of Staff." Since the threat is inflated, the two scholars point out, and the corresponding numbers of proposed weapons is therefore larger than the Joint Chiefs could have justified based on the National Intelligence Estimate alone, there is seldom any difficulty in winning their approval.

If actual needs were the basis of procurement, then the "assured destruction" criteria that McNamara's experts worked out at his request would have been sufficient. The Soviets would be deterred, McNamara advised President Lyndon Johnson in December 1963, if the United States possessed a survivable arsenal of four hundred one-megaton warheads, sufficient to kill 30 percent of the Soviet population, demolish 50 percent of Soviet industry, and destroy 150 Soviet cities.

Nuclear weapons were not simply larger conventional weapons. Their destructive force was orders of magnitude greater, producing mass fire and lethal fallout as well as blast damage. "We had maps of the United States," Alfred Lieberman recalls, "showing how a major Soviet attack would create fallout over most of the country. . . . In general, our study illustrated what would really happen in a major nuclear war. Not just the human casualties but also the massive destruction of the infrastructure of both the U.S. and the Soviet Union."

So much confusion, so much paranoia, so many good intentions, so much hard work, technical genius, cynicism, manipulation, buckpassing, buck-pocketing, argument, grandstanding, risk-taking, calculation, theorizing, goodwill and bad, rhetoric and hypocrisy, so much *desperation,* all point to something intractable behind the problem of how to deploy sufficient and appropriate nuclear arms to protect one's nation from a nuclear-armed opponent. There was such a beast. It was quite simply the fundamental phys-ical fact of nuclear energy: that such energy is relatively cheap to generate and essentially illimitable. Nuclear warheads cost the United States about $250,000 each: less than a fighter-bomber, less than a missile, less than a patrol boat, less than a tank. Each one can destroy a city and kill hundreds of thousands of people. "You can't have this kind of war," Eisenhower con-cluded. "There just aren't enough bulldozers to scrape the bodies off the streets." It followed, and follows, that there is no military solution to safety in the nuclear age: There are only political solutions. As the Danish physicist and philosopher Niels Bohr summarized the dilemma succinctly for a friend in 1948, "We are in an entirely new situation that cannot be resolved by war." The impossibility of resolving militarily the new situation that knowledge of how to release nuclear energy imposes on the world is the reason the efforts on both sides look so desperate and irrational: They are built on what philos-ophy calls a category mistake, an assumption that nuclear explosives are mil-itary weapons in any meaningful sense of the term, and that a sufficient quantity of such weapons can make us secure. They are not, and they cannot.

Mikhail Gorbachev came to that conclusion. But before he did so, one final, major crisis intervened. Unfortunately for the policy of détente that Richard Nixon and Henry Kissinger pursued during Nixon's years in the presidency (1969–1974), the desperate, all-out Soviet effort of the 1960s and 1970s to achieve nuclear parity with the United States looked to one group of American ideologues like an attempt to dominate the superpower competi-tion—or so its spokespersons argued. When one member of the group, a former professional actor and governor—Ronald Reagan—won election in 1980 as president of the United States, thirty-one other members moved into positions of federal authority and proceeded to act on their convictions.

SIX **THE SORCERER'S APPRENTICES (I)**

ACCURATE THREAT ASSESSMENT, ALWAYS AN IMPORTANT responsibility of government, became critical with the advent of nuclear weapons. Partly because the Soviet Union was a closed society, difficult to read, partly because measuring a threat requires judging intent as well as counting warheads, U.S. national-security studies were vulnerable to ideological bias. Since assessments often influenced policy decisions, those who wrote them and framed their conclusions could use them to ambush opponents and win bureaucratic battles.

No one was better at influencing policy by writing reports than Paul Nitze, a handsome, imperious patrician of German descent whose involvement in U.S. security strategy and arms diplomacy spanned five decades. Nitze's grandfather had been a banker, his father a professor of Romance languages at the University of Chicago, his mother an outspoken liberal and proto-feminist. Having made himself wealthy through marriage to a Standard Oil heiress and with Wall Street dealings during the Great Depression, Nitze had moved on to Washington as a dollar-a-year man managing wartime materials procurement. In 1944, he joined the fledgling U.S. Strategic Bombing Survey, an investigation critical to shaping his views of nuclear strategy. "I became interested in strategic concepts when I was with the USSBS," he acknowledged later. Interviewing captured Nazi leaders in Germany after its May 1945 surrender, he identified what he called "the essential requirement" for winning the air war in Europe: the necessity of first destroying the German air defense forces to open up the country to area bombing. Had the air defense forces not been destroyed first, too many Allied bombers would have been lost to sustain the campaign.

Moving on to Japan after its surrender in August 1945, Nitze made a thorough study of the atomic bombings, which impressed him perhaps less than they should have. He commented in 1989 that they "were not the most devastating air attacks that Japan had suffered," which was true but misleading.

The firebombings of Tokyo were more devastating, but by later standards Little Boy at fifteen kilotons and Fat Man at twenty-two kilotons were low-yield weapons. Nitze's judgment of the atomic bomb's significance, that it "compressed the explosive power of many conventional bombs into one," minimizes the potential impact of future bombs' more devastating fire and fallout effects and signals an early conviction that nuclear weapons not only could be used to fight wars but would not necessarily be decisive.

Nitze's "essential requirement" conclusion about the air war in Europe confirmed that conviction. If, as he believed, nuclear weapons simply improved the efficiency of strategic bombing, it followed that the conventional strategy of attacking military targets to clear the way for area bombing would be essential in an air war with nuclear weapons as well. "This experience and the concepts derived therefrom," he told a colleague in 1966, "go to the roots of the counterforce concept." That is, from the necessity of suppressing German air defenses to open the way to strategic bombing, Nitze extrapolated a strategy for fighting a nuclear war that involved attacking military targets first—called a "counterforce" strategy—rather than attacking industry and urban populations at the outset of a conflict—a "countervalue" strategy—as Curtis LeMay had programmed SAC to do.

Back home in 1946, Nitze worked as principal author with a small team of colleagues to write the Strategic Bombing Survey's final *Summary Report on the Pacific War.* He contributed importantly to the development and administration of the Marshall Plan, which underwrote the rebuilding of Europe. By 1949, he was deputy to George Kennan on the State Department Policy Planning Staff and then Kennan's successor when the originator of the U.S.'s Soviet-containment policy resigned at the end of the year.

President Truman announced his decision to proceed with the development of the hydrogen bomb on 31 January 1950. In his decision directive he asked his secretaries of state and defense, Dean Acheson and Louis Johnson, "to undertake a reexamination of our objectives in peace and war . . . in the light of the probable fission bomb capability and possible thermonuclear bomb capability of the Soviet Union." Acheson turned over the work of research and writing to Nitze.

Both men believed that Europe was vulnerable—two world wars had begun there—and that the Soviet leadership was fanatic beyond any possibility of negotiation. They also intended to prevent Germany from rearming. Acheson and Nitze were therefore committed to a major expansion of U.S. military forces and armaments to stabilize Europe, and the report that Nitze and his staff prepared between February and April 1950, "NSC-68: United

States Objectives and Programs for National Security," tendentiously constructed that case. "The purpose of NSC-68," Acheson would admit later, "was to so bludgeon the mass mind of 'top government' that not only could the President make a decision but that the decision could be carried out." Nitze, according to a scholar of the report who interviewed him on the subject, "wanted to sacrifice a degree of rationality in the analysis of NSC-68 in order to exaggerate the [Soviet] threat, with the hope that the reaction of opinion leaders would be commensurate with the threat." Which is to say, the bludgeon Nitze chose to use was threat inflation.

Although Nitze and his staff consulted no experts on the Soviet Union, and were neither experts themselves nor even fluent in Russian, NSC-68 is weighted with rhetorical absolutes. The Soviet Union, it claims, was "animated by a new fanatic faith, antithetical to our own, and seeks to impose its absolute authority over the rest of the world." Not only America but "civilization itself" confronted either "fulfillment or destruction" in the "endemic" conflict with the Soviet Union; and "every individual" faced "the ever-present possibility of annihilation" should the conflict enlarge to total war.

The United States had "purpose" in this Manichaean struggle; the Kremlin had "design":

> The design . . . calls for the complete subversion or forcible destruction of the machinery of government and structure of society in the countries of the non-Soviet world and their replacement by an apparatus and structure subservient to and controlled from the Kremlin. To that end Soviet efforts are now directed toward the domination of the Eurasian land mass. The United States, as the principal center of power in the non-Soviet world and the bulwark of opposition to Soviet expansion, is the principal enemy whose integrity and vitality must be subverted or destroyed by one means or another if the Kremlin is to achieve its fundamental design.
>
> . . . Thus unwillingly our free society finds itself mortally challenged by the Soviet system. No other value system is so wholly irreconcilable with ours, so implacable in its purpose to destroy ours, so capable of turning to its own uses the most dangerous and divisive trends in our own society, no other so skillfully and powerfully evokes the elements of irrationality in human nature everywhere, and no other has the support of a great and growing center of military power.

The "degree of reality" that Nitze sacrificed to this portrait of implacable evil was considerable. Just five years earlier, the Soviet Union had emerged from a brutal war to count its losses: at least twenty-five million people killed, one-tenth of its population; millions more invalided and twenty-five million made homeless; half its industry destroyed; coal production as of 1945 down 33 percent compared to 1941, oil production down 46 percent, steel 48 percent, meat 40 percent, dairy 55 percent, electricity 33 percent. Yet NSC-68 was asserting that the war-battered nation had recovered sufficiently five years later to muster the energy and resources for an implacable campaign to destroy the United States and rule the world.

The most egregious exaggeration of NSC-68 was its assessment of the Soviet Union's 1950 war-fighting capability. It was certainly true that Stalin had added two million more men to the three million kept under arms facing the West at the end of the war—his counterpoise to the American nuclear monopoly—and then had tested an atomic bomb as well. Nitze, however, citing the Joint Chiefs as his authority, claimed that if a major war should occur that year, 1950, the Soviet Union would be capable not only of immediately overrunning Western Europe, but also of "driv[ing] toward the oil-bearing areas of the Near and Middle East," consolidating "Communist gains" in the Far East, launching air attacks against Britain and air and sea attacks against the shipping lanes of both the Atlantic and the Pacific, and attacking "selected targets with atomic weapons, now including the likelihood of such attacks against targets in Alaska, Canada and the United States." (With only five atomic bombs in its arsenal that year, the Soviets would have had to be selective indeed in choosing targets.)

Further, Nitze judged that 1954 would be "a critical date for the United States," estimating (with CIA, military services, and Atomic Energy Commission concurrence) that by then the Soviets would have stockpiled about two hundred atomic bombs, enough to "seriously damage this country." The actual number in 1954 was about 150, so the estimate is not far off. But Nitze chose not to mention the rapidly enlarging U.S. stockpile: By 1954, the United States would have deployed more than fourteen hundred strategic nuclear weapons of a total yield of more than three hundred megatons, a powerful deterrent that would make any attempted attack by the Soviets suicidal and therefore highly unlikely. Nitze underplayed the American deterrent because he wanted his country not simply to deter a theoretical Soviet attack but also "to check and to roll back the Kremlin's drive for world domination." He, Acheson, and the military services thus called for "a rapid build-up of political, economic and military strength in the free world."

Truman, on the other hand, concerned about the federal budget, was skeptical of NSC-68 at first. Following the outbreak of the Korean War, which the president believed to be a Soviet feint into South Asia in preparation for war in Europe, he endorsed it. He had imposed a limit of $14.4 billion on the 1949 defense budget, and beginning in 1950 it was supposed to be cut further to $13 billion. After Truman endorsed NSC-68, he allowed the defense budget to increase almost fourfold; defense outlays in 1953 totaled more than $52 billion.

Even more significantly, NSC-68 began the historic uncoupling of the U.S. defense budget from fiscal policy. Truman and his predecessors had first determined a total budget number, based on available resources, and had then allotted part of that total to defense. Such prudence now became politically dangerous. Most administrations after Truman's determined the defense requirements first and then either allocated what was left to domestic needs or added to the deficit (or, more rarely, raised taxes) to sustain both guns and butter. Determining defense requirements first was the way it worked in the Soviet Union as well, with the significant difference that the far larger U.S. economy cushioned the impact of increasing diversions of federal income to the military. As the assistant secretary of the Army Karl R. Bendetsen summarized, "Once the President, upon recommendation of the National Security Council members, approved the recommendations" of NSC-68, "the foundation had then been laid for U.S. rearmament, for the reestablishment of an industrial mobilization base, for the generation of new, modern weapon systems and for NATO and the several follow-on mutual security pacts."

We have fear for things, Thomas Hobbes wrote in *Leviathan*, "not only which we know have hurt us, but also that we do not know whether they will hurt us or not." This latter "dimension of unknowable harm," writes the political scientist Corey Robin, "can make fear ripe for abuse. . . . Since the future is 'but a fiction of the mind' [in Hobbes's words], whoever defines the objects of our fear necessarily traffics in the realm of imagination. This makes the fear of unknowable harm a kind of rational fiction, a hypothetical speculation about the future, based upon experience and inference." Nitze's best-known hypothetical speculation about the future, NSC-68, characterized the United States as vulnerable to as few as one hundred Soviet atomic bombs but the Soviet Union as implacable despite America's thousands. On what experiences and inferences did he base this "rational fiction," if rational it was?

Nitze was specific about the basis for his argument. NSC-68, he wrote in his memoirs, "addressed what I have considered throughout my career to be the fundamental question of national security: How do we get from where we are to where we want to be without being struck by disaster along the way?" Even the title of his memoirs, *From Hiroshima to Glasnost,* reflected his sense that life is a dangerous journey. Curiously, of the very few incidents from his childhood that Nitze mentioned in his memoirs and in interviews, the two that stand out as formative concern dangerous journeys. The first, to which he attributed his interest in influencing world affairs, began in the Austrian Alps in 1914:

> At the beginning of the war I was seven and we were in Austria, climbing mountains in 1914, when the Austrian archduke was murdered at Sarajevo. And that is what set off the powder chain that led to the outbreak of World War I. We saw it happen, we saw the mountaineers in Austria being mobilized for war. My father decided it had become dangerous in Austria, decided to go to a safe country. So he took us all off to Germany, and we arrived in Munich on the day that Germany declared war on Russia. Bombs were thrown in the railroad station. Then we lived through the early days of the war when the Germans were marching to the Western Front. Most of them were eventually killed in that war. We saw the wounded come back, so the horror of that war—I had a second cousin who was killed on the Eastern Front by the Russians at the battle of Königsberg, where the Russians were defeated. He lost his life in that. We finally got out through Holland and came back to the United States, but that memory of what happened during World War I stuck with me. It still sticks with me. It's one of the most moving, dreadful events that I lived through.

His second dangerous journey, a little later in childhood, Nitze also associated with his diplomatic career, calling it his "first lesson in power politics":

> We lived on Fifty-sixth Street [in Chicago]. On Fifty-fifth, just one block away, lived and operated some of South Side Chicago's toughest gangs. My mother insisted on dressing me in a Buster Brown outfit, complete with flowing tie. In this attire, I walked the gauntlet to and from school every day.
>
> I soon received my first lesson in power politics. The gang on the block bounded by Fifty-fifth Street, Woodlawn and Kimbark avenues, would waylay and soundly beat me up every day on my way home from school. For protection, I joined the Scotti brothers' gang on the neighboring block run by the sons of an Italian family. The eldest brother was a charismatic leader, a blue-eyed, blond Italian, full of courage and paternal kindness to his gang. He inspired great loyalty in me; I did whatever he asked, without concern for the fine distinction between legal and illegal activities.
>
> Of course, a good part of this admiration came from intense gratitude, for from the moment I joined the gang, they defended me. Thereafter I was able to live in relative peace in that part of Chicago's jungle.

Among the activities the charismatic leader asked of Nitze was theft: "One time he gave me a directive to rob the construction site across the way from our house, where a whole row of houses were being built, and liberate the work tools for the use of the gang. And I liberated them, and turned them over to the gang."

So Nitze's memorable lesson in power politics, still recalled near the end of his life, was that the way to get from where you are to where you want to be without being struck by disaster is to surround yourself with overwhelming force. "To have the advantage at the utmost level of violence helps at every lesser level," he argued chillingly in 1978, calling the point "a copybook principle in strategy." (It has been a fundamental principle of U.S. nuclear strategy across more than six decades.) What Nitze only barely acknowledges in his story—in the phrase "relative peace"—is the protected ten-year-old's concomitant fearfulness, caught as he is between two rival violent gangs over which he has no control. The man the ten-year-old became spent most of his life exaggerating the Soviet threat and scolding his countrymen for what he believed to be their feeble and naïvely insufficient commitment to maintaining "the utmost level of violence." A free society is vulnerable, he wrote oddly in NSC-68, "in that it is easy for people to lapse into excesses—the excesses of a permanently open mind wishfully waiting for evidence that evil design may become noble purpose, the excess of faith becoming prejudice, the excess of tolerance degenerating into indulgence of conspiracy." In his own lapse into "excess," Nitze transformed the crude and deeply insecure men in the Kremlin into masters of evil—a small boy's view of a menacing gang.

NITZE'S NEXT IMPORTANT OPPORTUNITY to influence defense policy came in 1957, when President Eisenhower appointed a large panel of private citizens headed by the former Ford Foundation president H. Rowan Gaither, Jr., to assess a Civil Defense Administration proposal to build a $40 billion system of fallout shelters to protect the U.S. population in the event of nuclear war. Unknown to Eisenhower, the Gaither panel went rogue, enlarging its mandate to include the same range of policy issues that NSC-68 had covered. Nitze's name is buried in the back of the Gaither report—because he was a Democrat helping out a Republican administration, he said—but McGeorge Bundy confirms that he was "a principal draftsman."

By 1957, a series of events and confrontations had raised the specter of Communism on the march. Herbert York, a physicist and the first director of the Lawrence Livermore Laboratory, was a consultant to the Gaither panel, and remembers being concerned. "You have to recall that in 1948 there was the Berlin Blockade," he told an interviewer, "in 1948 there was the coup in Czechoslovakia, and the expansion that these things represented seemed quite real. And then there was the fall of China, as we put it, to the Communists [in 1949,] the creation of the Sino-Soviet Bloc, the Korean War in the early fifties. So looking back from the late fifties, what we saw was a lot of successes or what seemed to be successes on the part of the Russians, including territorial expansion." In retrospect, York adds ruefully, "that was the high-water mark, but we didn't know it at the time."

But whether or not the advances of Sino-Soviet Communism were real or only apparent by 1957, Nitze and his colleagues on the Gaither panel chose to exaggerate the dimensions of the threat. Nineteen-fifty-four had been NSC-68's year of maximum danger. That year having passed without attack, the Gaither report moved the threat forward to 1959, much as frustrated prophets revise their estimates of the end of the world. By 1959, it seemed, "the USSR may be able to launch an attack with ICBMs carrying megaton warheads, against which SAC will be almost completely vulnerable under present programs." Although the Gaither report itself mentions no specific number of Soviet ICBMs, Eisenhower's science adviser George Kistiakowsky wrote later that the Gaither panel "predicted a catastrophic 'missile gap'—claiming that by 1959 as many as 150 Soviet ICBMs would be aimed at the U.S." The columnist and Washington insider Joseph Alsop confirmed having heard the number in private briefings, adding that U.S. strategic forces presented "no more than about 50 targets" according to the Gaither panel, and therefore "the Soviets were expected to be able to wipe out American strategic striking power by 1961." (In fact, the Soviets had deployed no operational ICBMs at all by 1959.)

If such a preemption were successful, the report continued, "manned bombers could then deliver a decisive attack against the U.S." (The Soviet Union had fielded a total of 115 strategic bombers by 1959, carrying 210 strategic weapons. Few would be likely to penetrate U.S. defenses, especially if no Soviet ICBM blunting attack had prepared the way.) Already, according to the report, the Soviets had developed "a spectrum of A- and H-bombs and produced fissionable material sufficient for at least 1500 nuclear weapons." (If so, they were behind in production, because the actual number of nuclear weapons in the Soviet arsenal in 1959 was about 1,050, of which only 283 were strategic weapons. They had built three thousand short-range jet bombers, the report claimed, "and probably surpassed us in ICBM development."

To counter these dangers, the Gaither report proposed increasing U.S.

intermediate-range ballistic-missile numbers "from 60 to 240" and Atlas and Titan ICBM numbers "from 80 to 600." It proposed augmenting the alert status of SAC bombers and developing "a nationwide fallout shelter program to protect the civilian population."

Eisenhower was not impressed, nor did he believe the panel's inflated threats. Given the president's years of military experience, McGeorge Bundy notes, "he knew . . . that in essence the gloomier predictions were based mainly on what estimators believed about what the Soviets would decide to do and not on activities of which anyone had significant direct experience." The U-2 overflights Eisenhower authorized, while not covering the entire Soviet Union, gave him information about "the most likely [missile] sites," Bundy says, which were "along railroad lines . . . and to a man with a long experience of estimating the enemy, the absence of any positive confirmation was significant." Impressed or not, Eisenhower and his vice president, Richard Nixon, had to challenge John F. Kennedy's assertions of a "missile gap" during the 1960 Nixon-Kennedy presidential campaign, and in the end, by the smallest of margins, Kennedy won the presidency. Threat inflation—appealing to fear for political advantage—worked.

IF NITZE'S PENCHANT FOR threat inflation was driven by his own deep-seated fears as well as his ambitions, it also followed from his conviction that the American people and too many of their leaders lacked what he called "moral fiber" and needed to be frightened into action. Eisenhower did not embrace the conclusions of the Gaither report, Nitze alleged in his memoirs, not because the former supreme allied commander thought they were aberrant but because "he was anxious to maintain his image as a man of peace" and "fell into that broad category of people who believed that nuclear war was 'unthinkable,' and therefore the effort to achieve a reliable deterrent capability was not urgent." Similarly, Nitze believed that those who judged that "defense against nuclear war was futile" were not judging on technical grounds but cravenly endorsing "what can only be described as a policy of preemptive surrender." In the late 1960s, amid the political turmoil generated by the Vietnam War, Nitze cast resistance to the development of an ABM system—which was strong among experts who doubted the technical feasibility and strategic benefit of such a system—as the response of "prominent members of the scientific-academic community who had become disgruntled with defense policy in general and Vietnam in particular."

To counter this anti-ABM campaign, Nitze decided to set up a committee to lobby in favor of the ABM. In doing so, he unleashed a team of sorcerer's apprentices whose trail of wreckage extends well into the present century. In 1969 he, Dean Acheson, and a University of Chicago professor and nuclear strategist with the RAND Corporation named Albert Wohlstetter formed the Committee to Maintain a Prudent Defense Policy; "lacking funds to hire a full-time staff for research and writing, we recruited three young but exceptionally talented graduate students who agreed to work for expenses— Peter Wilson, Paul Wolfowitz and Richard Perle." Wilson went on to serve in the Carter State Department. Wolfowitz, born in 1943, a graduate student of Wohlstetter's at the University of Chicago, returned there after his CMPDP summer to finish his Ph.D., went on to teach at Yale, and then moved permanently to Washington in 1973 to work at the Arms Control and Disarmament Agency under the conservative former RAND analyst Fred Iklé.

Perle, a night owl with characteristic dark circles around his eyes even as a young man, was an informal Wohlstetter protégé. Born in 1941, the son of a self-made textile merchant of Russian Jewish ancestry, he had dated Wohlstetter's daughter Joanie in high school in Hollywood, where he grew up, and seems to have modeled himself on her prominent father while moving through his later education: college at the University of Southern California, graduate study at the London School of Economics, and then work toward a Ph.D. at Princeton. "Wohlstetter was flamboyant and eccentric, worldly and suave," an admiring Perle biographer writes, "and spoke as easily about food and wine as he did [about] the threat of Russian bombers and missiles." Perle came to share Wohlstetter's style, if not his substance. Returning to graduate school to finish his doctorate looked pallid after a summer working for a former secretary of state, a leading strategist, and a legendary Cold Warrior; instead, Perle won a position on the congressional staff of Democratic senator Henry "Scoop" Jackson of Washington, whose specialty was defense. Perle—bright and bashful, a young man on the make—learned the game of defense politics from Jackson himself and from Jackson's hawkish staff director for the Senate Permanent Subcommittee on Investigations, Dorothy Fosdick, a daughter of the Reverend Harry Emerson Fosdick who also happened to be Adlai Stevenson's mistress. Congressional staff members siphon authority from their high-octane bosses. Perle discovered a gift for bureaucratic infighting and rapidly accrued power.

Nixon and his national security adviser, Henry Kissinger, moved toward détente with the Soviet Union at the beginning of the 1970s with the expectation that the Soviets in return would help the United States extricate itself from Vietnam. Simultaneously they normalized relations with the People's

Republic of China, hoping to take advantage of the increasing conflict between the two Communist powers. (By 1977, Robert Gates writes, Leonid Brezhnev was telling people that China was now "the number one enemy.' ")

Nixon and Brezhnev signed an ABM treaty in Moscow on 26 May 1972 as well as an Interim Agreement (SALT I) temporarily capping the numbers of strategic arms. The Interim Agreement was limited to a life span of five years to allow for further negotiation of unresolved issues. Because it recognized the United States's preponderance of heavy bombers (the United States, with an estimated 450, had 300 percent more than the U.S.S.R. with 150) it allowed the Soviet Union about 50 percent more ICBMs and 30 percent more SLBMs, sensibly decoupling warhead parity from parity in delivery systems. (In fact, since the United States was five years ahead of the Soviet Union in MIRVing its missiles, the United States's total delivery capability was superior to the Soviets' especially since bombers could carry more than one bomb each.)

Scoop Jackson was outraged at the agreement's appearance of ballistic-missile inequality. "A longtime anti-Communist," writes the defense analyst Anne Cahn, "supporter of Israel, and defender of the defense industry ('the senator from Boeing' some said derisively), Jackson, whom John F. Kennedy passed over as his choice for vice-president in 1960, still harbored serious presidential ambitions. By identifying himself with the attack on détente, Jackson hoped to broaden his political base and to tap into the wide ideological diversity present in the strange bedfellows' coalition." When SALT I came up for Senate ratification, Jackson introduced an amendment to the resolution of ratification asking the president "to seek a future treaty that, *inter alia* [i.e., among other things], would not limit the United States to levels of intercontinental strategic forces inferior to the limits provided for the Soviet Union."

Even among those like Jackson who demanded it, strategic equality answered to perceptions rather than reality, as the clinical psychologist Steven Kull discovered when he interviewed a range of defense policymakers for a study of how they coped with the counterintuitives of nuclear strategy. Kull's sample of eighty-one men and three women included two former secretaries of defense, two Joint Chiefs, two senators, two representatives, five high-level current and former members of the State Department, five presidential advisers, six "key nuclear strategists from the 1950s and 1960s," and fourteen current and former RAND Corporation employees as well other influentials. When traditional rationales drawn from conventional strategy failed under Kull's polite but relentless questioning, the men and women he was interviewing typically invoked the perceptions of third parties (such as Japan and Germany) and of the American people themselves to justify the nuclear-arms race. One respondent had this to say:

> The game between the United States and the Soviet Union tended to be two frogs in a pond, each one of them blowing one's self up larger than the other and wanting to be more impressive. And the impression that was made was not only on the other frog but on third audiences—particularly so in the case of the United States because we had acquired, one way or another, the responsibility of holding a nuclear umbrella over the heads of other people.

A RAND analyst attributed the need to maintain numerical equality with the Soviets to political pressure:

> If you had a strong president, a strong secretary of defense, they could temporarily, if you will, go to Congress and say, "We're only going to build what we need, and we're not going to spend a penny more on it, we're going to cancel this, we're going to cancel that, and if the Russians build twice as many, tough!" . . . But I personally think that that kind of situation is unstable politically, and that five years hence—maybe less—there would be a political scandal. . . . And it's therefore better for our own domestic stability, as well as international perceptions . . . to insist that we remain good competitors, even if the objective significance of the competition is—uh—dubious.

A "prominent strategic analyst" concurred:

> Strategic weapons are political artifacts first. And when they cease to be political artifacts, then they're entirely irrelevant, entirely without a purpose. . . . The only existence that these weapons have that has any meaning is in political terms. And perceptions is the only relevant category.

Another strategic analyst—from the context, possibly Nitze or Wohlstetter—told Kull with uncharacteristic candor, "Let's put it this way, in more understandable terms. All roads in the strategic equation lead to MAD"—that is, mutual assured destruction, McNamara's four hundred megatons. "All the other ones . . . are games, are window dressings, and they are window dressings for upmanship. . . . But when you take away all these layers of cloth, at the bottom of the thing, basically, is MAD, and no one likes it."

Leaders may default to perception in nuclear matters because they lack direct experience with weapons effects, find confronting the brutalities of war disconcerting, or are accustomed to manipulating political issues for their advantage, to list only a few of many possible reasons. The veteran journalist Robert Scheer, who followed Jackson around for *Esquire* in 1975, when the senator was exploring the possibility of running for president, noticed Jackson's proprietorship in this area:

> He pushes MIRVs and Polarises and atomic bombs with the detachment of a delicatessen owner summarizing his collection of cold cuts. He has never witnessed war except from a guided tour and thinks of it more in terms of points to be scored against the Russians, or even the Secretary of State, than of pain to be suffered by people. His concern is an abstraction called national security, a science that he feels he has mastered.

Jackson's butcher shop was Richard Perle's postgraduate school. Whatever Perle's fundamental convictions, he learned from mentors like Nitze, Wohlstetter, and Jackson that politics, even the politics of mass destruction, was sausage-making. Gates reports his similar enlightenment while serving as a CIA representative to the SALT talks:

> Participation in SALT both in Washington and overseas was a real education for me. I saw that the internal negotiations in both our government and the Soviets' were probably tougher and dirtier than between the two countries. The more complicated the issues became, the more senior officials—especially Presidents—found themselves deferring to the experts. Four of the five Presidents I worked for were bored to tears by the details of arms control.*

"Because fear is a pliable emotion," Corey Robin paraphrases Thomas Hobbes, "shaped and reshaped by moral instruction and ideology, the sovereign has great power to define its objects. No sovereign automatically possesses such power; indeed, he often competes with 'private' men attempting to persuade people to fear objects he has not authorized them to fear." When presidents, from distraction or distaste, avoid thinking about arms control in any detail, they leave unclaimed a space of power where other politicians such as Jackson, bureaucrats such as Nitze or Perle, or ideology-driven groups of private citizens can battle for dominance.

AN OPPORTUNITY FOR SUCH A COMPETITION opened up in the mid-1970s when Americans, impressed with détente, had begun to feel more favorable toward the Soviet Union even as the Soviets, continuing their post–Cuban Missile Crisis buildup, started MIRVing their missiles while

---

* Gates doesn't say which president was exceptional—probably Jimmy Carter.

introducing several new models as well. "Most threatening of all," writes Thomas Graham, Jr., "was the replacement of the SS-9 with the very large SS-18 ICBM with ten MIRVs, each containing a warhead of around half a megaton. Now Minuteman was really threatened—the 308 SS-18s alone could lay over 3,000 large warheads on the [1,000-Minuteman] U.S. ICBM force, 50 percent more than would be needed to destroy the force." Graham understood that the United States had ample retaliatory capacity in the other legs of its triad, but also understood that "private men" are eager to persuade people to fear if such fear can be turned to political advantage: "Whether a first strike on Minuteman could ever realistically be considered anything other than an act of complete madness—with the SLBM force out there, not to mention the bomber force—is beside the point. After 1975, the theoretical capability existed to threaten Minuteman and this had significant political repercussions."

The ongoing SALT talks were a key battleground and Henry Kissinger a primary target. At a press conference in Moscow in July 1974, confronted about giving away nuclear superiority after the talks had stalled, Kissinger had responded in exasperation, " 'One of the questions which we have to ask ourselves as a country is what in the name of God is strategic superiority? What is the significance of it, politically, militarily, operationally, at these levels of numbers? What do you do with it?' " Revealing in public what Kull's nuclear policymakers would acknowledge at length in private—the uselessness of overkill—made the secretary of state few friends among the policy elite, Cahn writes. One of them told her, "Those were remarks that he would always regret." Telling the truth about the cynicism of the nuclear arms race was politically dangerous.

"The critics of détente," Cahn notes, "were certain that the Cold War was far from over and were determined that American hegemony should not disappear." On the evening before a conference on strategic doctrine in Beverly Hills in June 1974, some of them, including Wohlstetter and Nitze, assembled for dinner and discussion at a private home in Santa Monica. Forty more joined the conference the next day to hear Wohlstetter present a long paper that was about to appear in the journal *Foreign Policy*: "Is There a Strategic Arms Race?" Drawing on newly declassified data, Wohlstetter argued that the Department of Defense had consistently underestimated the buildup of Soviet strategic nuclear forces. At the same time, Wohlstetter asserted, U.S. strategic forces and the budgets to sustain them were decreasing, not increasing, and thus "the United States had not been running a quantitative strategic race" at all. By implication, inadequate methods of intelligence estimating had played into the hands of those such as Henry Kissinger who believed the Soviets could be trusted to keep the bargains they had made in the name of détente. The ideology that underlay Wohlstetter's argument was the same Manichaean division between the two nuclear superpowers that Nitze had been preaching since the late 1940s.

At least one conference participant was not taken in by Wohlstetter's numerical razzle-dazzle. Sidney Drell, a Stanford physicist and government adviser, told Cahn that Wohlstetter's "conclusions were the result of his choosing the right year for starting his comparisons." The graph of U.S. warhead deployments that Wohlstetter displayed, Cahn explains, "stopped with 1972, but a substantial number of warheads were coming into the American force in 1974, and Wohlstetter and many in the audience had known that for several years. The Soviet inventory of intercontinental ballistic missiles reached its peak of 1,600 in 1975 and dipped to 1,400 by 1979. Their submarine fleet declined from 370 to 257 during the decade as they retired many of their diesel subs."

A year after the Beverly Hills conference, an expert at Harvard, Michael Nacht, published a rebuttal to Wohlstetter's article. By 1974, Nacht pointed out, the United States had 6,318 total ballistic missile warheads compared to the Soviet Union's 2,319. And although the Soviets led the United States in total megatonnage, 3,618 to 2,144, "for the vast majority of targets, any warhead in the strategic arsenal is capable of producing untold damage and destruction. . . . High-yield warheads are militarily significant only against hardened targets [such as missile silos], and even against these targets they are substantially less important than high accuracy and the number of deliverable warheads." Wohlstetter's work, Nacht concluded damningly, had "not lived up to his own previously established high standards. . . . When advocacy is portrayed as analysis . . . no one's cause is served."

Drell told me something similar when I asked him about Paul Nitze. "His problem was that he believed in numbers," Drell said, "way beyond their actual value or reliability. He thought he was smarter than everyone else." Apparently the same was true of Wohlstetter, and, like Nitze, he was not above manipulating the numbers to political advantage. "Wohlstetter's charges," Cahn concludes, "were the opening salvo of a movement determined to destroy détente and to steer U.S. foreign policy back to a more militant stance vis-à-vis the Soviet Union."

Ironically, the anti-détente campaign was launched just as détente was succeeding, and serving as political cover for a U.S. military buildup as well. Nixon and Kissinger, Robert Gates points out, used it "to defend a number of strategic-weapons programs from the budget knife on the Hill—from ABM to Trident [missile submarines], cruise missiles, and the B-1 bomber." The new generation of weapons systems that Jimmy Carter stalled in 1976 and then restarted in 1979 and that Ronald Reagan greatly expanded in the 1980s "amid applause from conservatives," says Gates, "could not have been started or sustained politically in the Nixon years without détente. During the 1970s, on defense programs, the conservatives were never able to put congressional votes where their mouths were." Meanwhile, the growth in Soviet military spending, Cahn adds, "declined sharply" in 1975, "from 4–5 to 2 percent, and procurement of weapons was flat."

The conservatives responsible for this burgeoning exercise in threat inflation, many of them Democrats allied with Scoop Jackson, fought détente through the inglorious conclusion of the Nixon administration—the humiliated president resigning his office and flying home to California in August 1974, and a new president, Gerald Ford, taking the reins. These conservatives discerned a nation in decline, reeling from a war lost in Vietnam, dangerously misled by détente—and themselves ignored and out of power. "Soviet policy never changes," the former undersecretary of state Eugene Rostow, one of the most outspoken, scolded Henry Kissinger at the time. Kissinger responded sharply that "a balance of mutual interest" was a better guide to policy than "ideological dogma." But "the Democratic Party didn't want to hear us," Rostow complained, "and we weren't getting any general publicity" because Americans were sick of domino theories and war-derived domestic conflict.

ORGANIZING HIS PRESIDENCY IN AUGUST 1974, Gerald Ford called in Richard Nixon's forty-three-year-old ambassador to NATO and former presidential counselor, Donald Rumsfeld, to serve as his White House chief of staff. Rumsfeld brought along his longtime protégé and factotum, thirty-four-year-old Richard B. Cheney, to be his second-in-command. Ford's senior speechwriter and trusted adviser Robert Hartmann worked with Rumsfeld and Cheney and observed them closely throughout the brief Ford administration; his portrait of the pair, published in 1980, is uncontaminated by post-2000 events:

> Cheney was a serious student of political power and derived both his employment and his enjoyment from it. Whenever his private ideology was exposed, he appeared somewhat to the right of Ford, Rumsfeld or, for that matter, Genghis Khan.
>
> Rumsfeld and Cheney were a rare match. Their differences reinforced the team. Rummy was darkly handsome, like Tyrone Power. Cheney was a presentable young man who could easily be lost in a gaggle of Jaycee executives. His most distinguishing features were snake-cold eyes, like a Cheyenne gambler's. Rummy was expansive and, when it suited him, all smiles; Cheney's demeanor was low-key and even dour. He was tough, tireless, book-smart, with a touch of sarcasm occasionally overcoming studied subordination. Rumsfeld was more secure, more sensitive to others' feelings, more sophisticated and, when crossed, more passionate. But Don had some class; he was ruthless within the rules.

Rumsfeld had been on Ford's list of candidates to appoint as vice president. Ford thought Nelson Rockefeller better qualified and chose him instead. Rumsfeld harbored presidential ambitions in those days, however, and when pressure from the Ronald Reagan end of the Republican Party made Rockefeller a liability, Rumsfeld and Cheney helped convince Ford to dump him from the 1976 presidential election ticket. At a private meeting with Ford on 28 October 1975, Rockefeller agreed to announce his withdrawal from candidacy whenever the president asked him to, which turned out to be 3 November, in the wake of a 31 October reorganization of Ford's cabinet so extensive that the press came to call it the Halloween Massacre. Besides dumping Rockefeller from the ticket (he continued as vice president until the end of the term), Ford relieved Kissinger of his White House position as national security adviser, replacing him with Brent Scowcroft but leaving him as secretary of state; removed William Colby as director of the CIA, replacing him with George H. W. Bush; removed James Schlesinger as secretary of defense, replacing him with Rumsfeld; and appointed Cheney as White House chief of staff.

"Rumsfeld and Cheney were the right wing of the Ford administration," writes the journalist Sidney Blumenthal, "opposed to the policy of détente with the Soviet Union, and they operated by stealthy internal maneuver." Once Rumsfeld became secretary of defense, he attempted to sabotage Kissinger's SALT II negotiations. An important reason for Colby's replacement with the more pliable George H. W. Bush, Blumenthal says, was the CIA's unwillingness to cooperate with the Rumsfeld-Cheney effort. "Instead of producing intelligence reports simply showing an urgent Soviet military buildup, the CIA issued complex analyses that were filled with qualifications. Its National Intelligence Estimate on the Soviet threat contained numerous caveats, dissents and contradictory opinions. From the conservative point of view, the CIA was guilty of groupthink, unwilling to challenge its own premises and hostile to conservative ideas."

The nuclear-weapons establishment fed into this moil of manipulation in the person of John S. Foster, Jr., a lean, wary California physicist and nuclear-weapons designer who had been the director of the Lawrence Livermore Laboratory from 1961 to 1965 and then for the next eight years director of the Pentagon's Department of Defense Research and Engineering, DDR&E. In that capacity, in 1969, Foster had promoted the view that the Soviet heavy SS-9 ICBM, which in one configuration carried three two-megaton warheads, was a MIRV. He did so, it seems, to promote the Nixon administration's Safeguard ABM system then under fire in Congress: "If the public and Congress could be made to see the SS-9 missiles as threatening Minuteman silos," Anne Cahn explains, "it would be easier to sell the ABM system" to protect them. A single MIRVed SS-9 might threaten three Minuteman silos, while an SS-9 with three un-MIRVed warheads would only indicate that the missile needed to shotgun three large warheads on each Minuteman silo simply to compensate for its poor accuracy—and in fact its maximum error was no less than five kilometers.

The CIA disagreed with Foster's and the Nixon administration's assessment of the SS-9's capability. Nor did CIA analysts believe, as Foster did, that the Soviets were building toward a first-strike capability. The agency underlined its arguments in an update of one of its 1968 National Intelligence Estimates and held its ground against not only Foster and the defense secretary, Melvin Laird, but also against Henry Kissinger. Foster never forgot. In 1973, now out of government, he joined the President's Foreign Intelligence Advisory Board (PFIAB*), an elephant's graveyard of influentials including such fellow conservatives as Edward Teller; the future director of Central Intelligence (DCI) under Reagan, William Casey; Polaroid's founder, Edwin Land; a former governor of Texas, John Connally; the former army secretary Gordon Gray; George Shultz; and Clare Boothe Luce. Finding that their suspicions of Soviet intentions and fears of Soviet dominance matched his, Foster began organizing a revolt. He consulted with Teller and the influential RAND and Livermore physicist Richard Latter. Latter told Cahn he suggested to Foster "that what was needed was a second CIA, an alternative source of information." Though Teller had used that approach to institutionalize his disagreements with Los Alamos, lobbying successfully for a second weapons lab established on an old Air Force base in Livermore, California—the Lawrence Livermore National Laboratory—he balked at the idea of a second CIA. "Foster . . . liked the concept but thought it would be too difficult bureaucratically, and came up with a less grandiose notion—a small group of outside experts should perform an alternative threat assessment. Teller agreed with this plan."

After Foster convinced the chairman of PFIAB of his idea, Cahn writes,

> Teller quickly prepared a draft "alternative NIE" and gave it to State Department counselor Helmut Sonnenfeldt to pass on to Secretary of State Kissinger. Teller explained to Sonnenfeldt that current NIEs didn't deal with worst-case scenarios but his draft did. Teller introduced three propositions: Soviet missile accuracies might be better than estimated [by the CIA] and would continue to improve [thus threatening U.S. missile silos and ICBMs]; U.S. submarines would become increasingly vulnerable due to breakthroughs in Soviet antisubmarine warfare; and U.S. bombers might be destroyed before reaching the Soviet Union [by improved Soviet air defenses]. Sonnenfeldt effectively discounted Teller's NIE by commenting, "Teller's technique is to take propositions that can neither be proved nor disproved at this time. Nevertheless, his consis-

* Pronounced "piffy-ab."

tent suggestion that every proposition will unfold in a worst case situation for the U.S. undermines the overall credibility of his 'alternative' NIE."

Stonewalled at the State Department, Teller and Foster next took their worst-case scenarios to the CIA, which not surprisingly found them unconvincing, since they were unsupported by evidence. By November 1975, the CIA's director, William Colby, had won the endorsement of the U.S. Intelligence Board (the formal body of the U.S. intelligence community) of a letter to President Ford that opposed setting up an outside team. "It is hard for me to envisage," Colby wrote, "how an ad hoc 'independent' group of government and non-government analysts could prepare a more thorough, comprehensive assessment of Soviet strategic capabilities . . . than the Intelligence Community can prepare."

Colby was a lame duck by then, however; he was only able to send the letter because he had remained as CIA director until George H. W. Bush could be confirmed, early in 1976. The two Livermore physicists continued to agitate. "Foster and Teller believe intelligence officers should deliberately try to shape policy," a Bush deputy wrote the new director, "by calling attention to the worst things the Soviets could do in order to stimulate appropriate countermeasure responses by the U.S. Government. This, they believe, is the path of prudence; but is not the view of intelligence held by your predecessors." The Foster-Teller worst-case approach recalls Acheson and Nitze's bludgeon approach to NSC-68. The physicists and their fellow PFIAB members soon renewed the issue formally with Bush. "Bush was more compliant in the political winds than his predecessor," Blumenthal comments. Bush agreed to experiment with intelligence assessment by appointing three outside panels, "B teams" that would review the data and conclusions of the "A teams" within the CIA that were preparing the 1976 NIE, after which a panel of senior military and civilian "consumers" would critique the results.

One B team examined Soviet air defenses, a second examined the accuracy of Soviet ICBMs. The third—the one that concerns us here—examined the larger question of Soviet strategic objectives. The Team B project benefited from White House Chief of Staff Cheney's instrumental support, Blumenthal writes. This aid was the origin of Cheney's alliance with the loose association of blusterous Manichaean Democratic and Republican radicals who came to be called the neoconservatives. Rumsfeld put up Paul Wolfowitz to represent his interests, Blumenthal adds; the young special assistant to the Arms Control and Disarmament Agency would coauthor the team's final report.

The Team B Strategic Objectives Panel was led by a Polish-born, waspish

Harvard historian named Richard Pipes. A Richard Perle discovery, Pipes was a former director of the Harvard Russian Research Center, "imported to Washington" originally, according to Blumenthal, "as a consultant to [Scoop] Jackson." Other Team B members and advisers included Lieutenant General Daniel Graham, the chief of defense intelligence who would soon become the main proponent within the Pentagon of strategic missile defense; Nitze; and, informally, Teller, Foster, and Albert Wohlstetter, whose *Foreign Policy* essays served as a starting point for deliberations. Although their bias was a fundamental basis for their appointment—"Members of Team 'B,' " their report would explain, "were deliberately selected from among experienced political and military analysts of Soviet affairs known to take a more somber view of the Soviet strategic threat than that accepted as the intelligence community consensus"—they were given unprecedented access to the nation's intelligence secrets. No comparable "Team C" from the liberal political community contributed balance; as Team B saw it, the CIA professionals represented that community.

In Pipe's paranoid formulation, revealed in a *Commentary* essay a decade later, the vast U.S. intelligence community was merely the handmaiden of a naïve and arrogant body of natural and social scientists who had "acquired a dominant voice in the formulation of U.S. nuclear strategy" under Dwight Eisenhower and had "used this voice to lead U.S. strategy away from traditional ways of military thinking and toward arms-control negotiations." They scorned history, claimed this conventional historian:

> So persuaded are many scientists of the incontrovertible and universal validity of their [scientific] method that in their public capacity they readily succumb to a fanaticism that is quite impervious to both argument and experience. They are no more prepared to take seriously the proposition that nuclear weapons might be effective instruments of warfare than to waste time proving that the earth is not flat.

The "fanaticism" Pipes had in mind, as he went on to explain, was McNamara's Mutual Assured Destruction, which he labeled sarcastically "the only scientifically sound strategy." The public at large, he wrote, "was not initiated into the complexities of Mutual Assured Destruction," implying a cover-up by the fanatical scientists and their intelligence-community devotees. "It was told simply that there was 'overkill,' that nuclear build-ups beyond the figures set by McNamara constituted 'madness,' and that henceforth security lay not in unilaterally arming but in mutually disarming." Such logic was anathema to Pipes, whose argument recalls Edward Teller's timorous, unremitting insistence across his long career that there was no such thing as enough nuclear weapons when it came to dissuading an implacable Kremlin from attack. Pipes credits Teller (a scientist, but one with "a great deal of civic courage") with leadership of the group that advocated "deterrence through strength," contrasting it with scientists such as Hans Bethe, a Manhattan Project veteran and Nobel laureate in physics who supposedly advocated "deterrence through agreement" and who "believed that nuclear weapons were so destructive that they could deter at a low level."

Were they, and could they? Jerome Wiesner, science adviser to President Kennedy and president of MIT, argued the case in a speech at Stanford in 1984:

> I will give you a simple piece of calculus. For most cities it is reasonable to equate one bomb and one city. It would take a bigger bomb for Los Angeles or New York. If you are a weapons expert you know you should probably use several, "pepper 'em down"; you would get a better effect. In any event, it does not take many. And if you ask yourself: "Where would you put 300 large nuclear weapons to be most destructive?" you run out of vital cities and towns and railroad junctions and power plants before you get to 300. The same thing is true in the United States and the Soviet Union. If I was not trying to be conservative I would say 50 bombs, properly placed, would probably put a society out of business, and 300 in each of the two countries leading the arms race would destroy their civilizations. That is a pretty clear-cut fact.

However clear-cut, it was not a fact that Pipes, Teller, Perle, Wolfowitz, Rumsfeld, Cheney, Nitze, Wohlstetter, and their comrades-in-arms, each perhaps for his own reasons, were prepared to accept. In their own eyes tougher and more realistic, they shared that disagreement with experts on the Soviet side, as Pipes wrote nastily, who "simply ignored the doctrine of Mutual Assured Destruction which Soviet disinformation agents were ladling out at their convivial encounters to science professors from Harvard, MIT and Stanford." (Pipes had been excluded from the prestigious Pugwash and Dartmouth Conferences organized between Western and Soviet scientists and resented it.) The Team B report accuses the CIA's experts of "mirror-imaging," which Pipes defines as attributing to others—in this case the Soviet leadership—"one's own motives and intentions on the unspoken assumption that these alone are 'normal' or 'rational.' " According to Pipes, the CIA analysts and the fanatic scientists he believed to be behind them assumed that the Soviets thought the same way about the perils of nuclear weapons as they did: believed in MAD, believed in détente, believed a nuclear war must be too destructive to fight. But in aligning themselves with purported "Soviet experts" as hard-eyed realists, it was Pipes, Wolfowitz, and their team who were mirror-imaging; their argument was with the American arms-control community, not with the Soviets. The Soviets had demonstrated by their caution and their desperate race to catch up with a technologically and economically superior adversary that they would follow our lead wherever we led them, evidently believing we knew where we were going. They had even sacrificed their cherished goal of putting men on the moon to turn their science and industry to missile building in the years after the Cuban Missile Crisis. The "scientific" view that Pipes despised, based as it was on the fundamental physical reality that nuclear weapons were devastating instruments of terror and mass fire, so destructive that one or two per city would deliver chaos and suffering enough to terminate any war, needed no one's insight or approval. Pipes told the American physicist and government adviser Richard Garwin that his argument was based on "his deep knowledge of the Russian soul." But nuclear reality was never a matter of opinion, however soulful. It was a matter of fact, as political leaders facing the brink seem repeatedly to have understood.

Once again, as with Nitze's earlier policy papers, the Team B report suffered from its authors' underestimate of the destructiveness of the weapons they were manipulating. The political scientist Hans Morgenthau identified the problem in an essay published that same year, 1976:

> We have a disjunction between the conventional ways we think and act about nuclear weapons and the objective conditions under which the availability of nuclear weapons forces us to live. . . . We have tried . . . instead of adapting our modes of thought and action to the objective conditions of the nuclear age, to conventionalize nuclear war. . . . The idea that a nuclear war should necessarily end in a stalemate or in the mutual destruction of the belligerents is simply unacceptable to people who have made it their business to prepare for victorious wars.

Team B, reflecting the conventionalized consensus about nuclear war that united nuclear conservatives like Nitze and Pipes with neoconservatives like Paul Wolfowitz and Richard Perle, gave its beliefs urgency and authority by discovering them to be Soviet policy. Mirror-imaging with a vengeance, it found that the CIA's national intelligence estimates "ignore the possibility that the Russians seriously believe that if, for whatever reason, deterrence were to fail, they could resort to the use of nuclear weapons to fight and win a war." The NIEs misunderstood Russian history, the Team B report argued—here Pipes inserted a long Harvardian disquisition—and it emphasized in italics that the NIEs lacked "*a realistic overall conception of Soviet motives and intentions.*" They "*consistently underestimate the significance of the Soviet strategic effort.*" The Soviets were building more bombs, more bombers, more missiles, more submarines. If they had devoted "a substantial portion of [their] strategic defensive budget" to anti-submarine-warfare research but seemed to have nothing to show for it, "the implication could be that the Soviets have, in fact, deployed some operational non-acoustic systems and will deploy more in the next few years." That is, it's probably out there, but it's so good it's invisible. ("Yes, that's important," Pipes would tell an interviewer mysteriously. "If something is not there, that's significant. But the CIA was not aware of that.") Nitze's signature threat, of a menacing window of vulnerability a few years down the road, turns up once again in the Team B report, perfunctorily, like a bone thrown to an old dog; the report proposes "the possibility of a relatively short term threat cresting, say, in 1980 to 1983, as well as the more obvious long range threat."

The conclusion of the Team B report pulled out all the stops:

An intensified military effort has been under way designed to provide the Soviet Union with *nuclear as well as conventional superiority both in strategic forces for intercontinental conflict and theater or regional forces.* While hoping to crush the "capitalist" realm by other than military means, *the Soviet Union is nevertheless preparing for a Third World War as if it were unavoidable.* The pace of the Soviet armament effort in all fields is staggering; *it certainly exceeds any requirement for mutual deterrence. . . .* So does the high proportion of the national budget devoted to direct military expenditures. The intensity and scope of the current Soviet military effort in peacetime is without parallel in twentieth century history, its only counterpart being Nazi remilitarization of the 1930's. . . .

In Soviet perceptions the gap between long-term aspirations and short-term objectives is closing. This probably means that the Soviet leaders believe that their ultimate objectives are closer to realization today than they have ever been before. *Within the ten year period of the National Estimate the Soviets may well expect to achieve a degree of military superiority which would permit a dramatically more aggressive pursuit of their hegemonial objectives,* including direct military challenges to Western vital interests, in the belief that such superior military force can pressure the West to acquiesce or, if not, can be used to win a military contest at any level.

"All of it was fantasy," Anne Cahn said later. "They looked at a facility at the nuclear test range in Semipalatinsk and said, This is a facility for tests of nuclear-powered laser beam weapons, when in fact it was nothing of the sort—it was used to test nuclear-powered rocket engines [for space flight]. They even took a Russian military manual, the correct translation of which is *The Art of Winning,* and translated it as *The Art of Conquest.* If you go through most of Team B's specific allegations about weapons systems and you just examine them one by one, they were *all* wrong. All of them."

IF THE SOVIET MILITARY wasn't preparing for World War III in building up its forces to match and sometimes to exceed (at least in numbers) the forces of the United States, what was it preparing for? The clinical psychologist Steven Kull, wishing to know if Soviet defense policymakers struggled with the same cognitive dissonance about nuclear weapons as U.S. policymakers, managed to interview a small number of such men in the early 1980s. "Several [Soviet] respondents used the term *inferiority complex* to describe the Soviet psychology," he writes. "This stemmed from the traumatic experience of being in a unilaterally vulnerable position [compared to the United States], particularly in the 1950s. Several respondents became very emotional as they explained how frightful this period was, and seemed to be imploring me to be more understanding of Soviet policies that may have come out of an effort to 'compensate.' "

No doubt nuclear conservatives such as Richard Pipes would dismiss Kull's respondents (without evidence) as deliberate plants, sent by the KGB to disinform a naïve American. The same can hardly be said of Andrei Sakharov, however, who reported in his memoirs similar motives for working on atomic and thermonuclear weapons:

> What was most important for me at the time, and also, I believe, for [Igor] Tamm and the other members of the group, was the conviction that our work was *essential.*
>
> I understood, of course, the terrifying, inhuman nature of the weapons we were building. But the recent [Second World] war had also been an exercise in barbarity; and although I hadn't fought in that conflict, I regarded myself as a soldier in this new scientific war. . . .
>
> Our initial zeal . . . was inspired more by emotion than by intellect. The monstrous destructive force, the scale of our enterprise and the price paid for it by our poor, hungry, war-torn country, the casualties resulting from the neglect of safety standards and the use of forced labor . . . all these things inflamed our sense of drama and inspired us to make a maximum effort so that the sacrifices—which we accepted as inevitable—would not be in vain. We were

possessed by a true war psychology, which became still more overpowering after our transfer to the Installation.

In Soviet and other journals as well, Kull found an explanation for what American analysts such as Pipes took to be an effort to develop a war-fighting capability. A Soviet colonel, Viktor Girshfeld, an analyst at a Soviet institute, sought to explain that effort in an anonymous interview with the magazine *Détente,* for example:

> *Col. X:* All of us, more or less, know that nuclear war would be the end. All our theoreticians say that there is no way of preventing nuclear war from escalating to the global level, that you cannot win a nuclear war. That is our *general theoretical* position.
>
> But from a *professional military* point of view, such a position is impossible. Can a professional military man say that nuclear war is inconceivable? No, because some fool of an American president may really start a nuclear war. A professional military man must consider what to do in that event.
>
> *D: What difference does it make what you do in that event?*
>
> *Col. X:* Ah, *you* can say that. Mr. General cannot say that.
>
> *D: I am still confused.*
>
> *Col. X:* Consider the point of view of another professional, the doctor who knows that his patient is suffering from an incurable disease. He cannot for that reason abandon further efforts.... To make no plans for [a nuclear war] ... would be openly to proclaim our helplessness. It would be *psychologically* wrong.

So this Soviet analyst, at least, attributed to the arms race the sole value of disguising from the Soviet people their utter helplessness in the face of nuclear attack, just as Kull had found American policymakers did when he pushed them into a logical corner. The difference for the Soviets was that they felt they had come from an even more terrifying place—far behind the United States—and were finally, at the end of the 1970s, catching up, which changed the nature of the confrontation. "There was an expressed optimism," Kull summarizes, "that the Soviets were gaining more confidence and would soon be less preoccupied with the balance. One respondent explained, 'It is easier to arrive at a more sophisticated understanding when we are strong. . . . Now we're more secure.'"

Lieutenant General Nikolai Detinov spoke more bluntly at the 1998 conference at Brown University of the terrifying place where the Soviets had found themselves during the Cold War. "There was not a year and not a moment," he told his fellow American and Russian panelists impatiently, "when the Soviet Union, in the actual number of nuclear warheads that delivery vehicles could deliver, exceeded the United States. Quite the contrary, the United States was always ahead by 20, 30 percent. . . . In other words, the Soviet Union was always catching up with the United States on strategic arms. Therefore, accusing Russia of perpetuating the arms race and of having certain advantages is absolutely and totally incorrect." Detinov added perspicaciously, "We always viewed these kinds of statements by U.S. leaders as an attempt to knock some extra money out of their own Congress for their own military programs." The American ambassador Jack Matlock, Jr., responded to Detinov's assessment by explaining why U.S. hardliners had believed that their nation was lagging behind: "We did not believe that either bombers or submarine-launched ballistic missiles would ever be considered credible first-strike weapons. Obviously the picture looks different depending on how you define it, but I think that perception on our part was quite genuine." Since the Soviets would be on the receiving end of those bombs and SLBMs, the picture did indeed look different to them.

What the Team B analysts and their supporters never seemed to grasp, or chose not to take into account, was how surrounded the leaders of the Soviet Union felt. Though they had achieved what they considered to be parity with the United States by around 1970, they were far from finished protecting themselves from their increasing numbers of enemies, according to a former deputy chief of the Soviet general staff, A. A. Danilevich:

> There is another factor which explains why we created such a huge quantity of weapons. We perceived our main opponent to be the United States, and the second one to be the European NATO countries, in particular [West] Germany. As a result of our political mistakes we began also to be in conflict with China. This was a serious threat. If one considers Brezhnev and [defense chief] Andrei Grechko, then in the 1970s they were not so much afraid of the United States as of China. Our strongest conventional forces were stationed in the east. We considered that Western politicians and military leaders were more sober and rational than was the case in China. With China anything was possible.
>
> In the 1960s and 1970s, twenty-three countries were categorized as our potential enemies. Among our main allies, we counted the six countries of the Warsaw Pact and seven other countries. Forty countries were considered basically neutral, but their orientation, especially in case of war, was uncertain. It is often said that the USSR squandered its resources by helping all these countries, including extending them military aid. However, just consider the global balance of power—we had to do something about this lopsided situation. If the

forty countries regarded as neutral joined the enemy, we would have to face sixty-three rather than twenty-three countries. So we had to try to convince these countries, or at least some of them, to come on our side. . . .

Some threats were simply concocted by our short-sighted policy. These alleged threats were grounded in pure ideology, fueled by the simplistic logic of global confrontation, the quest for an "iron shield" around our borders. . . . I recall a 1987 meeting of the Defense Council at which our military doctrine was discussed. [General Sergei] Akhromeyev spoke about the likely scenario in case of global military conflict. His attitude enraged Shevardnadze, who said: "Is this the basis for our defense strategy? You want to fight practically the entire world!"

The most authoritative statement of the Soviet mentality during the later years of the Cold War comes from Anatoly Chernyaev, one of Mikhail Gorbachev's two most intimate advisers (other than Raisa), also speaking at the Brown conference:

There were two layers in our political life: ideology and real politics—*realpolitikom.* You mentioned [Soviet support of] Angola and Cuba. Those were ideological issues. We had to maintain our image as an ideological superpower. This was important to us. However, it did not mean that we were planning to organize or begin a nuclear war. Among our elders [i.e., the aging members of the Politburo], there was not a single person who believed that one day we were going to take over the United States or that we could defeat the United States, or that we were seriously preparing for a nuclear war with the United States. No one, as far as I know, had this absurd notion.

I listened to their speeches. I was present at every one of the Politburo meetings beginning with the time when I became the assistant to the General Secretary. Look at détente, look at the situation in the 1970s with Nixon, and Brezhnev who hugged Nixon in Washington, and everything that happened as a result of détente. You cannot think that this was just Pharisaical and hypocritical games—acting, role-playing to fog up the vision of the United States, to get out of the current moment and then to become more and more aggressive and build up more and more muscles and defense. No, détente was a sincere policy. We wanted détente, we wanted peace, we craved it. . . .

Look at [Central Committee Secretary Yegor] Ligachev, he was a conservative, right? A reactionary, even, and yet he . . . would stand up, right in front of Gorbachev, and he would scream, "How long will our military-industrial complex keep devouring our economy, our agriculture and our consumer goods? How long are we going to take this ogre, how long are we going to throw into its mouth the food of our children?" Even [the Soviet premier Nikolai] Ryzhkov,

[and] all who were located on the conservative side, everybody was against the arms race. They were against the fact that the military-industrial complex was depressing not only the whole economy but also the psychology. We did not want to feel like a fortress under siege. We needed to unchain and liberate our brains from this military-psychological setup which, you are right, does come from the Great Patriotic War, from World War II, where we lost 27 million [people].

"Apes on a treadmill," the American arms negotiator Paul Warnke famously characterized both sides in a 1975 essay in *Foreign Policy* responding to Albert Wohlstetter's question if the United States could even be said to be racing the Soviet Union for advantage in strategic arms. "We couldn't ignore the Soviet Union as an international power," Warnke wrote, "in the many years when we dwarfed its strategic nuclear forces. Today both countries know, and the rest of the world knows too, that we dare not fight one another. The respective strategic nuclear forces serve only as offsets [i.e., they cancel each other out], not as exploitable resources. They are not translatable into sound political currency." What was needed, Warnke believed, was "not a conceptual breakthrough but a decision to take advantage of the stability of the present strategic balance. It's futile to buy things we don't need in the hope that this will make the Soviet Union more amenable. The Soviets are far more apt to emulate than to capitulate. We should, instead, try a policy of restraint, while calling for matching restraint from the Soviet Union."

AT FIRST THE TEAM B REPORT seemed to go nowhere. It was secret, and CIA Director George H. W. Bush, who believed in loyalty, agonized over what to do with it, since it criticized the shop of which he had just become proprietor. Someone on Team B leaked its story to the *Boston Globe* on 20 October 1976, before the report was even finished (it was completed in December), but the national press failed to take it up. The *New York Times* had noticed, however, gained CIA access by promising not to go public until the report was approved and finally ran an account the day after Christmas. The *Washington Post* followed up a week later, describing "one source on the Pipes panel" as gloating, " 'We just licked [the CIA analysts] on a great number of points.' " Ray Cline, a former CIA deputy director, offered the *Post* a more accurate assessment. "It means, Cline said, that the process of making national security estimates 'has been subverted,' by employing 'a kangaroo court of outside critics all picked from one point of view.' " Shortly before leaving office, early in 1977, Henry Kissinger dismissed Team B as a scheme to "sabotage SALT II." No American president, he told the National Press Club, "would ever allow the Soviet Union to gain superiority over the United States."

Writing a decade before Vice President Richard Cheney, Secretary of Defense Donald Rumsfeld, and their associates in the administration of George W. Bush pushed the CIA to inflate the threat of Iraqi weapons of mass destruction to make a case for war, a Nitze biographer, David Callahan, identified a similar modus operandi in the Team B episode:

> To critics in Congress, the Team B episode was a blatant attempt to undermine the objectivity of intelligence and twist CIA estimates to fit an ideological agenda. Nor did the timing of [George H. W.] Bush's undertaking—during the last months of the Ford administration—seem coincidental. Democrats suspected that Team B was aimed at saddling any incoming administration with a preordained, anti-Soviet pessimism. Three congressional committees began investigations into the affair. Summing up the sentiments of many who looked into the matter, Senator Gary Hart would write that " 'competitive analysis' and use of selected outside experts was little more than a camouflage for a political effort to force the National Intelligence Estimate to take a more bleak view of the Soviet threat."

(The deeper flaws in the report, which were common to the A team analysis as well, awaited later reexamination. Arthur Macy Cox, who had been an assistant to George Kennan at the State Department and a CIA officer, identified one important misunderstanding: The A team's realization that Soviet defense spending as a percentage of Soviet GNP was twice as high as the CIA had previously estimated meant not that Soviet spending had dramatically increased, as the Team B report alleged, but, to the contrary, "that Soviet defense production, in fact, was not very efficient. . . . Soviet defense industries . . . all experts now agree, produce weapons at a much higher cost than ours." And a thorough 1993 CIA-sponsored reexamination by a team of outside reviewers noted, "If the objective is to provide the best evidence regarding the military threat . . . the most appropriate subjects of comparison should have been NATO and the Warsaw Pact," not the United States and the U.S.S.R. alone. "The main reason is that, in our strategy for meeting the Soviet military threat, it was not U.S. military forces alone on which we counted but also the substantial forces of our NATO allies. . . . In seeking to understand Soviet strategy, the U.S.S.R. should have been seen as facing not only U.S. military forces but those of Germany, Britain, and the other allies, including France in most circumstances. . . . Had greater attention been directed toward NATO-Warsaw Pact comparisons, the magnitude of the Soviet military threat would not have appeared as large as it appeared from the U.S.S.R.-U.S. comparisons alone.")

A newly elected Jimmy Carter summarily rejected the Team B report and abolished PFIAB for good measure, which might have quelled the debate, but by then the nuclear conservatives' threat-inflation project had found a new home. Former undersecretary of state Eugene Rostow, his effort to influence Kissinger in the autumn of 1974 having been rejected out of hand, had cast about for the next year for an effective vehicle to block détente and influence domestic politics. He settled on the idea of a bipartisan citizens' committee—a lobby—to communicate the conservative defense perspective to the American public and the world, discussed his idea at length with Defense Secretary James Schlesinger, and recruited Paul Nitze, who reached out in turn to his wide circle of influential friends. Schlesinger's recent dismissal by Gerald Ford, and "a couple of bloody Marys before lunch" on Thanksgiving Day 1975, inspired Rostow, he said, to propose to Nitze and another colleague, "by God, why don't we just do it?"

The organization that resulted borrowed a name out of the Cold War past: the Committee on the Present Danger. The first CPD, long defunct, had been formed by James Bryant Conant, a Harvard president and Manhattan Project overseer, at the time of the Korean War to promote a beefier defense program and universal conscription; Nitze had been a member. It had taken its name from Supreme Court Justice Oliver Wendell Holmes's famous 1919 opinion that "the most stringent protection of free speech would not protect a man in falsely shouting fire in a theater and causing a panic." Ironically, the phrase "a clear and present danger" appears in the Holmes opinion in the context of just such a false act: "The question in every case is whether the words used are used in such circumstances and are of such a nature as to create a clear and present danger that they will bring about the substantive evils that Congress has a right to prevent." The Committee on the Present Danger, the old one and the new, did indeed shout fire and cause panic erroneously, if not falsely, and to the great detriment of the very cause—the security and prosperity of the American people—that each committee believed itself to be patriotically defending.

The new CPD attracted a large membership from both political parties, including Rostow; Nitze; Pipes; Hewlett-Packard's cofounder David Packard; the AFL-CIO treasurer Lane Kirkland; the former secretary of state Dean Rusk; the former chief of naval operations Elmo Zumwalt, Jr.; the future

Reagan administration national security adviser Richard Allen; Reagan's campaign manager and a future DCI William Casey; the former DCI William Colby; Eisenhower's aides Gordon Gray and Andrew Goodpaster; a scholar and future U.N. ambassador under Reagan, Jeane Kirkpatrick; Clare Boothe Luce; Richard Perle; the neoconservative journalists Norman Podhoretz and Midge Decter; the civil-rights leader Bayard Rustin; the right-wing Republican billionaire Richard Scaife; Edward Teller; and even the writer Saul Bellow. Ronald Reagan joined the organization in the spring of 1976, before its formation was announced publicly. "He needed credentials," his campaign manager explained.

When the CPD went public, on 11 November 1976 (nine days after Jimmy Carter's election), before a large audience of journalists at the National Press Club, it used the occasion to release its first policy statement, a Pipes creation titled "Common Sense and Common Danger." Three CPD founders read it aloud, purporting to find "the principal threat to our nation" to be "the Soviet drive for dominance based upon an unparalleled military build-up." The solution was "higher [American] levels of defense spending"; otherwise, "we shall become second best to the Soviet Union in overall military strength . . . isolated in a hostile world, facing the unremitting pressures of Soviet policy backed by an overwhelming preponderance of power."

Despite the large Press Club audience and the new CPD's grand ambitions, none of the national media bothered to announce its founding. Of fifty-three CPD members recommended for positions in the Carter administration, the new president chose not one, not even Nitze, who had offended Carter the previous July by trying to bully him at a defense policy seminar the Democratic candidate had organized at his home in Plains, Georgia. "Nitze was typically know-it-all," Carter said later. "He was arrogant and inflexible. His own ideas were sacred to him. He didn't seem to listen to others, and he had a doomsday approach." When eight CPD members met with Carter at the White House early in 1977, Rostow recalled, "we were stunned, just stunned. The notion that that fellow was president was just frightening."

What frightened the CPD was Carter's initial program, as he described it later, "to try to put forward to the Soviet Union a much more dramatic reduction in the total quantity and effectiveness of the nuclear weapons in our arsenals, and to bring about a comprehensive test ban to eliminate the explosion of any nuclear devices, either underground or in the air." By March, Carter had dispatched his secretary of state, Cyrus Vance, to Moscow "with what I thought was a very good proposal for dramatic cuts [in the two sides' nuclear arsenals]," Carter said. At that point the CPD declared all-out war, opposing Carter and his "frightening" notions of nuclear sufficiency with a full arsenal of op-eds, talk-show appearances, position papers, and congressional testimony. CPD resistance was all the more odd since the proposal had been drafted by Zbigniew Brzezinski, Carter's anti-Soviet national security adviser, with substantial input from Richard Perle, and was designed to be unacceptable to the Soviet Union.

In the meantime, Albert Wohlstetter had organized a low-profile alliance of U.S. and NATO defense strategists, the European-American Workshop. German participants in the workshop counseled the West German chancellor, Helmut Schmidt, no friend of Carter's in any case, that he should pursue adding cruise missiles to the NATO nuclear arsenal to counter the Soviet deployment within the Soviet Union, facing Europe, of a sophisticated new intermediate-range, solid-fueled, mobile ballistic missile, the SS-20 (Pioneer). The missile had a five-thousand-kilometer (thirty-one-hundred-mile) range, sufficient to reach Europe, Britain, the Middle East, and parts of Asia, and carried three MIRVed 150-kiloton warheads that it could deliver within three hundred meters of its intended targets. "Owing to their limited range," Schmidt would write, "the SS-20s are directed not at the United States but practically only at countries which cannot reach the Soviet Union with similar weapons." Even though the SS-20s were clearly being installed to replace an earlier generation of Soviet liquid-fueled missiles that required hours to launch and were therefore useful only for a first strike, Schmidt's advisers convinced him, he wrote, that "the Soviet Union has upset the military balance in Europe."

Since Carter appeared to be more concerned with intercontinental strategic assets than European-theater assets, Schmidt agitated for a NATO response, and, in a 1977 speech, invoked for the first time a requirement of parity between Warsaw Pact and NATO strategic weapons. NATO had more than enough nuclear weapons aimed at the Soviet Union to cover any contingency: four hundred Poseidon 50-kiloton warheads on U.S. Polaris nuclear submarines allotted to European defense and 164 U.S. F-111 long-range fighter-bombers based in Britain carrying B-61 bombs with variable yields up to 340 kilotons, as well as thousands of tactical weapons. Several hundred British and French warheads and bombs added to Europe's defenses as well. Schmidt, however, worried that Carter might give some of the NATO arsenal away in the SALT II negotiations.

Carter eventually responded to European pressure for a more politically visible land-based deterrent, and in 1979 NATO announced that it would pursue a two-track strategy: "Arms control would be attempted for four years," Thomas Graham, Jr., summarizes, "to try to remove or contain the threat of the SS-20s. If after four years, in 1983, satisfactory results had not been achieved on the arms-control track, then NATO would proceed with the planned deployments" of 108 Pershing 2 medium-range ballistic missiles, each with a single maneuverable W85 fifty-kiloton warhead, and 464 Tomahawk ground-launched cruise missiles with W84 fifty-kiloton warheads. The seemingly precise numbers of these weapons followed not from any special deterrent requirements, the scholar Raymond Garthoff points out, but from a general decision to deploy a mix "in the range of 200–600 missiles. . . . More, it was deemed, would seem provocative; less, too weak." The 108 Pershing 2s would replace the U.S. Army's 108 Pershing 1As. The Tomahawks came in squadrons of sixteen, and "units of 48 were the minimum logical units per major deployment area. The Tomahawk total was set at 464 [i.e., 29 times 16] as the next to highest multiple of 16 keeping the . . . total (including the 108 Pershing 2s) under the 600 ceiling. . . . That level also was designed to allow some negotiating room for talks with the Soviet Union as well."

The new Euromissiles were not only a surprise to the Soviet leadership; they were also a grave new danger. The Pershing 1A's five-hundred-mile range had made it a tactical weapon. Moscow, one thousand miles from Berlin, was outside its perimeter. But the Pershing 2 had been reengineered with a Kevlar body and more powerful rockets to extend its range to beyond one thousand miles, which meant, given its forward position in Germany, that it was a strategic, first-strike weapon that could reach Moscow in less than ten minutes after launch. Tomahawks were slower—with turbofan engines, they flew close to the ground at subsonic speed, comparing the terrain to a stored digital map—but their maximum range was fifteen hundred miles with an accuracy of eighty feet. If the Soviets had introduced the SS-20 as a challenge and a provocation, they could have expected such an escalation, but in fact, writes Garthoff, they had thought the SS-20 deployment "was a normal modernization program. . . . There is no evidence to support the idea that the Soviet leaders saw a political option flowing from their decision on the SS-20 or that they even considered such a political purpose in making the decision. . . . They did not see this action as creating any gap [in theater nuclear forces] in their favor."

The event that finished off détente, even for Carter, was the Soviet invasion of Afghanistan in December 1979. He and Brezhnev had signed the SALT II treaty in Vienna on 18 June limiting strategic delivery vehicles; Carter had submitted the treaty to the U.S. Senate for ratification four days later. The CPD had then fanned out across the country agitating against its ratification. Scoop Jackson, speaking words Richard Perle had crafted for him, proposed that even Neville Chamberlain had been more realistic in 1938 once his "policy of appeasement lay in ruins." Carter, however, believes that the Soviet invasion, which came as a complete surprise, not the CPD assault, was the reason SALT II ratification stalled. "The Congress never did ratify this treaty," he told an interviewer, ". . . because that winter . . . the Soviet Union invaded Afghanistan, and at that time it would have been almost impossible to get the Congress and the American public to approve anything that related to commonality with the Soviet Union." What Carter failed to tell the interviewer was that he himself pulled the treaty from Senate consideration within days of the Soviet invasion.

Afghanistan seemed at first to reveal the Soviets on the march. "I could see that the Soviet movement into Afghanistan was not an end in itself, " Carter recalled. "The intelligence that I had from various sources, including within the Soviet Union, was that the Soviets' long-term goal was to penetrate into access to warm-water oceans from Afghanistan, either through Iran or through Pakistan. I saw this as a direct threat to global stability and to the security of my own nation." (Despite Carter's contemporary intelligence sources, the primary reason for the invasion, besides quelling a growing anti-Soviet insurgency, has turned out to be concern that the Afghan prime minister, Hafizullah Amin, who had recently had his predecessor murdered, was planning to defect from his country's alliance with the Soviet Union and align with the United States.)

Carter, who believed he and Brezhnev had gotten along well and felt personally betrayed, responded forcefully by threatening military action, not excluding nuclear weapons, should the Soviets invade either Pakistan or Iran. Besides that threat, Gorbachev wrote, "the USA and other nations took a number of measures against us. The Americans, in particular, stopped shipping even those consignments of grain that they had already contracted to send. The embargo resulted in our not receiving about 17 million tonnes" of grain, a shortage Gorbachev called "alarming." The White House and the State Department worked up a long list of possible sanctions, most of which were adopted. In his State of the Union address on 23 January 1980, Carter extended U.S. military protection (and implicit hegemony) over the Persian Gulf and proposed increasing the U.S. defense budget by 5 percent, which would amount to $20 billion in real growth in 1981 and 1982 (about $102 billion in 2006 dollars). "By the 1980 presidential election," Anne Cahn summarizes, "the choice in foreign and defense policy was between that of the Carter administration, which favored the [MIRVed, ten-warhead] MX missile, the Trident submarine, a Rapid Deployment Force, a 'stealth' bomber, cruise missiles, counterforce targeting leading to a first-strike capability, and a 5 percent increase in defense spending, and that of the Republicans under Ronald Reagan, who favored all of these *plus* the neutron bomb, antiballistic missiles, the B-1 bomber, civil defense, and an 8 percent increase in defense spending."

The official Soviet response to the Carter reversal was to reaffirm détente. Privately, however, Yuri Andropov, then still head of the KGB, began to suspect that the United States was preparing for nuclear war.

EIGHT **DECAPITATION**

FOR MANY AMERICANS, THE SOVIET INVASION of Afghanistan on 25 December 1979 confirmed the conclusions about the expansion of Soviet power that the Committee on the Present Danger had been proclaiming across the land. During the 1980 presidential election campaign, Ronald Reagan made the CPD agenda his own, even comparing Jimmy Carter directly to Neville Chamberlain (as Scoop Jackson had done as well). "Reagan openly disdained arms control in favor of an arms race with the Soviets," Sidney Blumenthal summarized. "America would seize the initiative, and Russia would be pushed into collapse."

Reagan at least understood that the Soviet system was vulnerable—he called it "some bizarre chapter in human history whose last pages are even now being written"—which is more than can be said of the CPD. Nitze, Perle, Rumsfeld, Wolfowitz, Pipes, and their associates believed their own exaggerations, or acted as if they did. "By virtue of the billboard effect of publicizing their views that the Soviet Union was stronger than the United States and getting stronger all the time," Anne Cahn concludes, "that it meant to achieve world domination, that it was the fount and origin of all radical movements around the world, that détente and arms control negotiations were a snare and a delusion, Team B and the CPD prevented the intelligence community and the public from correctly interpreting the many signs of the coming demise of the Soviet Union. That is the real legacy of Team B."

Were there such signs? Could the dissolution of the Soviet Union have been predicted? Would knowing it was failing have made a difference?

Cahn found evidence of public discussion of Soviet economic problems from as early as 1966, when "a study prepared for the Congressional Joint Economic Committee reported that 'both official Soviet data and Western estimates show a marked decline in the rate of growth of industrial production in the U.S.S.R.' " The same committee learned in the late 1960s that the rate of Soviet oil production was declining, resulting in fuel shortages, and that population demographics were worsening. This information went to the President's Foreign Intelligence Advisory Board (PFIAB), Cahn notes, and therefore was available to Nitze and other board members and thus to Team B. The near-collapse of Soviet agriculture was obvious to the whole world, of course, exposed by the Soviet Union's massive grain purchases. Cahn cites Melvin Laird, the secretary of defense during Nixon's first term— "surely no dovish liberal," she comments—enumerating Soviet economic problems in 1974:

> By any assessment the Soviet economy is in trouble. The growth rate of Soviet productivity has been declining. Her technological industries, so vital in today's world, have shown a marked incapacity to come up with economical, efficient and innovative products. The loss of the "moon race," which was felt very acutely by the Soviets, is but one indicator of this. The wheat deal . . . was forged to save the Soviets from the results of a disastrous agricultural program. The availability of consumer goods in the Soviet Union is still among the lowest of developing nations.

Andrei Sakharov diagnosed the real predicament of Soviet industry and society in the second of three celebrated memoranda that he sent to Leonid Brezhnev between 1968 and 1972. The first and best-known was his appeal for superpower cooperation, "Reflections on Progress, Peaceful Coexistence, and Intellectual Freedom," which was published in the *New York Times* in July 1968. In the second memorandum, sent to Brezhnev in 1970 after having circulated in *samizdat* and published in the United States in 1973, Sakharov wrote:

> The more novel and revolutionary the aspect of the economy, the wider becomes the rift between the USA and ourselves. We are ahead of the USA in the production of coal but behind them in the production of oil, gas, and electric power, ten times behind in chemistry and immeasurably behind in computer technology. The latter is especially essential, for the introduction of electronic computers into the national economy is of decisive importance which could radically change the face of the system of production and culture in general. This phenomenon has rightly been called "the second industrial revolution." Meanwhile the total capacity of our computers is hundreds of times less than in the USA, and as for the use of electronic computers in the national economy, here the rift is so enormous that it is impossible to measure. We are simply living in a different era.

These problems, Sakharov added, "cannot be resolved by one or two persons in positions of power and who claim to know everything. They demand the creative participation of millions of people at all levels of the economic system. They require a broad exchange of information and ideas." Otherwise, the Soviet Union could "gradually revert to the status of a second-rate provincial power."

Sakharov went further in a postscript to his third memorandum, which he gave to Western journalists in 1972, correctly diagnosing the basic Soviet economic problem as runaway militarization of the economy:

> In socialist countries it is also essential to reduce the militarization of the economy and the role of a messianic ideology. . . . Militarization of the economy leaves a deep imprint on international and domestic policy. . . . The role of the military-industrial complex in US policy has been thoroughly studied. The analogous role played by the same factors in the USSR and other socialist countries is less well known. It is, however, necessary to point out that in no country does the share of military expenditure with relation to national income reach such proportions as in the USSR (over 40 percent).

The boldest prediction of impending Soviet collapse during this period, however, was the work of a young and previously unknown French historical demographer named Emmanuel Todd, reported in a book titled *The Final Fall,* published in France in 1976 and in translation in the United States in 1979. (Demography is the branch of anthropology that concerns statistics of health and disease, birth and death; historical demography uses demographic tools to study the past—or, in Todd's case, to investigate a closed society that deliberately obfuscated its demographics.) Todd had written his remarkable book while still a graduate student. It was reviewed in English primarily in journals of Russian studies, exactly where it needed to be noticed to alert the community of experts on which the U.S. government relied for information about Soviet trends. Unfortunately, almost without exception, professional Sovietologists—Richard Pipes was a typical specimen—were the last to recognize the decline and fall of the political system on whose leviathan enigmas they had built their careers. The reviewers praised Todd's innovative approach, but his prediction of impending Soviet collapse was dismissed as a "penchant for dramatic prophesying."

"Internal pressures are pushing the Soviet system to the breaking point," Todd dramatically—but also accurately—prophesied on the opening page of his book. "In ten, twenty, or thirty years, an astonished world will be witness to the dissolution or the collapse of this, the first of the Communist systems." To explain how he came to such a radical conclusion in an era when the Committee on the Present Danger was claiming that the Soviet Union was growing in strength and malevolence, he demonstrated that Soviet statistics, otherwise "shabby and false," could still be mined for valuable information on the state of society. Even censored statistics, such as rates of birth and death missing from the charts for the Terror famine years 1931 to 1935, "indicate the abuses of Stalinism, especially when they succeed a period marked by a relatively large volume of data." Age pyramids, he pointed out—graphs in which stacked horizontal bars represent the percentage of the population in each age group—"have fixed for everyone to see the errors of Stalinism, Maoism, or any other totalitarian alternative which declares war upon a human community. . . . Rather belatedly, it is apparent that 30 to 60 million inhabitants in the USSR are missing. In 1975, it was clear that about 150 million were missing in China. Given population, the proportions are nearly the same."

Todd noted and moved past the zero growth of the Soviet economy, from which he predicted "there will be no recovery." The "sluggishness" of the centralized Soviet economy, he remarked, "appears to be natural, obvious, and inevitable. . . . The lack of common sense on the part of Stalinist economists remains a curious historical phenomenon. How is it possible for a central organization to coordinate the activity of 250 million Soviet inhabitants, distributed over 22 million square kilometers, by arbitrarily fixing prices and wages?" In fact, Todd argued, "the degree of polarization and level of economic development in the USSR today is most clearly reminiscent of the West in the 1860s. . . . In Communist countries the working class is frequently fired upon, as they were in Western Europe during the nineteenth century. They have personally witnessed what is a set piece of *Marxist* art and literature. . . . Real Communism has all the legendary vices of the capitalism condemned by Marx: misery, class conflict and alienation."

Soviet defense spending, Todd realized, was not simply a consequence of the Soviet Union trying to steal a march on the United States, as the neoconservatives believed. Had it been, the Soviets could have alleviated their economic problems merely by switching to minimal deterrence such as the Chinese have practiced since they first developed nuclear weapons. (As late as 2006, the People's Republic of China had fielded only about twenty ICBMs capable of reaching the United States.) As I hope I have demonstrated by now, there has never been a realistic military justification for accumulating large, expensive stockpiles of nuclear arms. In the United States the pressures to do so, seldom acknowledged publicly, have been primarily political, bureaucratic, economic, and palliative. In the Soviet Union, Todd discerned, the pressure to do so was dictated in part "by the logic of the economic system, which depends on central planning (i.e., strict control) and thus must only produce goods which are *held in common and impossible to consume individually.* Armaments is not the only dynamic sector of Soviet industry. All individually *nonconsumable* goods are given priority. This includes such things as ores and petroleum, of which there are *surpluses* that can be exploited."

Why only nonconsumable goods? The Soviet economy was a double system, Todd pointed out, half official and half black market or "free sector." The free sector, decentralized and robust, clandestinely produced some of the consumer goods that the official sector disdained:

> Consider that every advance in the production of consumable goods in the USSR encourages the parallel or free black market sector. *The Soviet system cannot take the path of a consumer society because this would automatically encourage the growth of the free sector at the expense of the centralized sector.* . . . Increasing decentralization would, in and of itself, lead to political awareness. Consumer culture develops from the market and is completely incompatible with a totalitarian system. . . . A highly developed consumer society is more and more individualized; *everyone does his own thing.* We readily perceive that this saying is more compatible with a "developed liberal society" than with the "dictatorship of the proletariat," a totalitarian system under the sway of a single party. Why limit the choice to a single party, if there is freedom to choose among different life-styles?

"In 1976," Todd added, "an enormous portion of national revenue was still devoted to arms production and the armed forces. This very high percentage is *necessary to prevent the transfer of productive forces to the consumer sector. Arms expenses* serve, among other things, *to maintain the preeminence of the centralized sector of the economy.*" (Todd was describing the Soviet Union, but of course the description also applied, and still applies, to the United States.)

Locating the origins of liberty in the heart of the marketplace may have made some of Todd's more socially conscious Western readers wince. Paralleling his mercantile model with an analogous model frequently invoked in those years—the "marketplace of ideas"—clarifies his point. The Soviet leadership tried to centralize control over thought directly as well as by centralizing economic power. It restrained its citizens' movements and communication and restricted and even criminalized discussion of unofficial (particularly liberal democratic) ideas; simultaneously it forced approved speech—official Marxist-Leninist speech—into a worn, cast-iron mold of orthodoxy. Todd took note of this phenomenon as well, although he did not draw its parallel with the Soviet economic system: "To transform Marxism into an empty, meaningless litany is absolutely crucial for the regime. The Soviets must speak, but not think, like 'Marxists.' The official ideology must transform Marx's texts into a collection of high-sounding but irrelevant rhetoric. If the Communist masses understood the true meaning of terms like 'exploitation,' 'alienation' and 'oppression,' the system that dominates them could not survive."

Arms production, Todd concluded, "is the chief element which keeps the Soviet economy functioning. These nonconsumable goods pose no threat to centralization." But since Soviet workers knew "that every increase in [their] productivity will eventually be absorbed by armaments expenditures," they had no reason to work harder; "they are a dispirited group whose only incentive is to lower productivity." No one who visited the Soviet Union at any time in its last twenty years missed hearing the disillusioned mantra of Soviet labor: "They pretend to pay us and we pretend to work."

For the Soviet system to function at all, the bureaucracy had to be bought off; thus the emergence of the *nomenclatura* class with access to higher-quality food and consumer goods at special stores, to better apartments, dachas, and medical services, to travel outside the country, and even to Western journals and books.

The most fundamental measure Todd found of the deep malaise affecting Soviet society was an increasing infant-mortality rate, which he believed marked "the beginning of a large-scale regressive cycle." The Soviet Union's worsening demographics, already revealing themselves a decade and a half *before* its dissolution in 1991, offer further evidence that the Communist society was imploding domestically before the Carter and Reagan arms buildup that Reagan partisans in particular have claimed to be the cause of the Soviet collapse. "No one dares even imagine," Todd commented, "the real extent of their problems. The relaxation of [totalitarian] pressure, accompanied by the simultaneous lowering of administrative and industrial productivity (not to mention the agricultural deficits) as a result of centralization is bringing about the *absolute regression* of the national wealth."

Yet the perspicacious young Frenchman doubted that the Soviet regime would "suffer a violent upheaval." Its organization protected it from mass uprisings, and the West was intervening with grain sales to protect it from famine. Astonishingly, he thought "the successive or simultaneous breaking away of the [East European] satellites should soon be accepted by the Kremlin without too much fuss." His imagination failed him where Afghanistan was concerned, however; he "could not imagine the Red Army in a situation like Viet Nam." As it happened, even the Soviet Union's war with Afghanistan did not detonate revolution. "Change in the USSR," Todd concluded, "might take the form of what happened in Czechoslovakia, when intellectual reformers took control of the state apparatus. . . . Soviet reform would have to be intelligently executed. The situation in which the USSR finds itself is so implausible and tangled that it would require perfect mastery on the part of a solidly established ruling class. The way elites are recruited assures that mediocrity will reign in precarious positions of power. This is because elites are selected by their peers and not by free elections. Let's pray for a uniformly intelligent Politburo in the years to come."

It mattered greatly whether the U.S. government believed the Soviet Union to be an expanding or a declining power. The Soviet government's decision to replace its first-generation missiles in Europe with threatening new SS-20s had already strained détente, as did the United States and NATO's decision in response to deploy Pershing 2s and Tomahawks in Europe late in 1983 if negotiations to remove the SS-20s failed. Carter and Brezhnev still signed the SALT II treaty in Vienna on 18 June 1979, limiting strategic nuclear-delivery vehicles, but Carter soon found himself forced to endorse a larger U.S. defense budget to improve the treaty's chances for Senate ratification. Then the Soviets invaded Afghanistan. Carter responded by increasing the defense budget even further, asking Congress in January 1980 for 5 percent real growth.

As early as November 1978, addressing Warsaw Pact leaders in Moscow, Leonid Brezhnev expressed serious concern about U.S. and NATO intentions. "Even the tentative parity in armaments and armed forces [between NATO and the Warsaw Pact]," he said, "is perceived quite nervously in the ruling imperialist circles. In those circles—especially in the USA and in the ruling leadership of NATO—they obviously do not want to let go of the hope of achieving some kind of breakthrough, of overturning the existing correlation of forces, and of gaining an opportunity to impose their will [and] their ways on the rest of the world." Washington's defense budget that year was $130 billion, Brezhnev pointed out. "They are working on new systems of weapons of mass destruction—we know this very well—in closed American engineering and construction offices." At the same time, he complained, the Americans were "pushing their allies toward the path of unrestrained growth of military expenditures. . . . In this atmosphere, one could anticipate a massive attack against détente, against the policies of the socialist states." Similarly, a German scholar notes that in secret discussions among Warsaw Pact defense ministers during this period, "the threat of a nuclear surprise attack appears as a constant theme in [their] threat perceptions."

Yuri Andropov confessed his concerns to Markus Wolf, the head of East German intelligence, during a meeting in February 1980. Wolf reports:

> [The KGB chief and I] began discussing the East-West conflict. I had never before seen Andropov so somber and dejected. He described a gloomy scenario in which a nuclear war might be a real threat. His sober analysis came to the conclusion that the US government was striving by all available means to establish nuclear superiority over the Soviet Union. He cited statements of President Carter, his adviser Zbigniew Brzezinski, and of Pentagon spokesmen, all of which included the assertion that under certain circumstances a nuclear first strike against the Soviet Union and its allies would be justified.

"When Carter announced a record defense budget of $157 billion," Wolf adds, ". . . the reaction in Moscow was one of barely controlled panic. 'We cannot fight them with funds,' a leading Soviet nuclear strategist confided to me. 'Thank God we are good at other things.' " Wolf tactfully chose not to speculate about what those "other things" might be.

The increasing misapprehension between the nuclear-armed superpowers produced its share of near disasters in 1980. "On at least three occasions" that year, writes Robert Gates, "there had been failures of the U.S. early warning computer system leading to combat alerts of U.S. strategic forces. CIA later learned that during the first half of June 1980, the KGB had sent a message to all of their residencies reporting these failures and saying that they were not the result of errors but were deliberately initiated by the Defense Department for training." Gates dismisses the KGB's response as "paranoid," and perhaps it was, but in the context of the Carter defense buildup and the proposed NATO deployments it might also be interpreted as an attempt by Andropov, a chess player, to think more than one move ahead. "The KGB circular," Gates concludes, "stated that the Soviet government believed that the United States was attempting to give the Soviet Union a false sense of security by giving the impression that such errors were possible, and thereby diminish Soviet concerns over future alerts—thus providing a cover for possible surprise attack."

Nor was the KGB the only entity that took the computer errors seriously, Gates reports:

> As he recounted to me, [Carter's national security adviser Zbigniew] Brzezinski was awakened at three in the morning by [his military assistant, William] Odom, who told him that some 220 Soviet missiles had been launched against the United States. Brzezinski knew that the President's decision time to order retaliation was from three to seven minutes after a Soviet launch. Thus he told

Odom he would stand by for a further call to confirm a Soviet launch and the intended targets before calling the President. Brzezinski was convinced we had to hit back and told Odom to confirm that the Strategic Air Command was launching its planes. When Odom called back, he reported that he had further confirmation, but that 2,200 missiles had been launched—it was an all-out attack. One minute before Brzezinski intended to telephone the President, Odom called a third time to say that other warning systems were not reporting Soviet launches. Sitting alone in the middle of the night, Brzezinski had not awakened his wife, reckoning that everyone would be dead in half an hour. It had been a false alarm. Someone had mistakenly put military exercise tapes into the computer system. When it was over, Zbig just went back to bed. I doubt he slept much, though.

Defense experts in the Soviet Union debated the question of the likelihood of war vigorously in 1979 and 1980, writes the CIA staff historian Benjamin Fischer, "and by June 1980 a CPSU Central Committee Plenum resolution expressed the official view that 'adventuristic actions of the United States and its accomplices have increased the danger of war.' "

On 25 July 1980, Carter added further to Soviet fears by promulgating a new presidential directive, PD-59, that included an argument for fighting extended nuclear wars rather than attacking at the outset with everything in the arsenal, the early LeMay strategy that was still enshrined in the SIOP. "If deterrence fails initially," PD-59 argued, "we must be capable of fighting successfully so that the adversary would not achieve his war aims and would suffer costs that are unacceptable, or in any event greater than his gains, from having initiated an attack." The Republican National Convention that had just nominated Ronald Reagan as its candidate for the presidency had also endorsed preparing to fight prolonged nuclear wars. The Republican platform and PD-59 together presented the Soviet Union with a solid front in favor of a new and more threatening U.S. nuclear posture.

To fight an extended nuclear war meant holding Soviet cities hostage by not attacking them first. Instead, PD-59 proposed attacking the Soviet leadership itself, a strategy that would soon win the grisly name "decapitation." Two conservative defense strategists, Colin Gray and Keith Payne, described the strategy in an essay published that summer under the provocative title "Victory Is Possible." "The most frightening threat to the Soviet Union," Gray and Payne wrote, "would be the destruction or serious impairment of its political system. Thus, the United States should be able to destroy key leadership cadres, their means of communication, and some of the instruments of domestic control. The USSR, with its gross overcentralization of authority, epitomized by its vast bureaucracy in Moscow, should be highly vulnerable to such an attack. The Soviet Union might cease to function if its security agency, the KGB, were severely crippled. If the Moscow bureaucracy could be eliminated, damaged, or isolated, the USSR might disintegrate into anarchy."

I remember hearing statements in those years that the United States would soon be capable of targeting the individual offices, apartments, and dachas of Politburo members—of delivering nuclear warheads through office windows on opposite corners of an intersection, a capacity that seemed incredible at the time, not to mention redundant, though it would find dramatic demonstration a decade later in the conventionally armed cruise-missile attacks on Baghdad at the beginning of the first Gulf War. And already in December 1980, in an early field test, a Tomahawk cruise missile flew six hundred miles out to sea and returned to impact within sixteen feet of its target; twelve hundred miles was a range more than adequate to deliver Tomahawks from West Germany to Moscow.

Specified among PD-59's targets were seven hundred so-called leadership relocation sites, meaning fortified underground bunkers, and fourteen hundred ICBM silos hardened against U.S. missile attacks. To that end, the U.S. Air Force's Minuteman II ICBMs and the U.S. Navy's Trident C4 SLBMs received higher-yield warheads and new terminal guidance systems that greatly improved their accuracy, which increased their kill probability to about 99 percent even against superhardened Soviet ICBM silos. The new Pershing 2s scheduled for European deployment in 1983 looked even more dangerous and destabilizing to the Soviet leadership: In their forward location they would be positioned outside the range of Soviet launch-detection satellites and early-warning radar, their flight time was ten minutes or less, and they were accurate to within one hundred feet. In their original configuration, intended to carry an earth-penetrating 340-kiloton W86 warhead, they had been planned for bunker-busting, but in September 1980, two months after PD-59 was announced, they were reconfigured with a lighter, 0.3- to 45-kiloton dial-a-yield W85 warhead that extended their range, allowing them to be targeted against Soviet mobile missiles or for low-yield precision decapitation strikes in central Moscow with limited collateral damage.

RONALD REAGAN WAS INAUGURATED as the fortieth president of the United States on 20 January 1981. Besides the president himself, no fewer than thirty-one appointees to his administration would be members of the Committee on the Present Danger, including the national security adviser,

Richard Allen; the CIA director, William Casey; the U.N. ambassador, Jeane Kirkpatrick; the Navy secretary, John Lehman; the Arms Control and Disarmament Agency (ACDA) director, Eugene Rostow; the ACDA adviser William Van Cleave; the undersecretary of defense Fred Iklé; the assistant secretary of defense Richard Perle; the National Security Council adviser Richard Pipes; and the arms negotiators Max Kampelman and Paul Nitze. Casey was sworn in on 28 January; two days later, at the first meeting of the new administration's National Security Principals Committee, he proposed mounting a covert program of deliberate intimidation against the Soviet Union by assaulting it from every side with military probes, feints, and surprises. The goal of the program, according to Peter Schweizer, an enthusiastic chronicler of the Reagan administration, was to make the Soviet leadership "less prone to take risks":

> "It was very sensitive," recalls former Undersecretary of Defense Fred Iklé. "Nothing was written down about it, so there would be no paper trail."
>
> "Sometimes we would send bombers over the North Pole, and [Soviet] radars would click on," recalls Gen. Jack Chain, the former Strategic Air Command commander. "Other times fighter-bombers would probe their Asian or European periphery." During peak times, the operation would include several maneuvers in a week. They would come at irregular intervals to make the effect all the more unsettling. Then, as quickly as the unannounced flights began, they would stop, only to begin again a few weeks later.
>
> "It really got to them," recalls Dr. William Schneider, undersecretary of state for military assistance and technology. . . . "They didn't know what it all meant. A squadron would fly straight at Soviet airspace and their radars would light up and units would go on alert. Then at the last minute the squadron would peel off and return home."

Why such threat displays would make a nuclear superpower known for its insecurity "less prone to take risks" is a question only Casey and his colleagues might have answered; the actual Soviet response was to judge the new American leadership to be dangerous and reckless and probably intent on starting a nuclear war. The probes began quickly, in mid-February, by which time the administration had gone public with its intention to greatly enlarge the already large increase in defense spending that Carter had authorized.

Carter's 5 percent increase in defense spending had been borrowed from a Reagan campaign proposal; Reagan's budget director, David Stockman, describes Carter's preemption of that figure as "a parting 'up yours' gesture at the new administration." Secretary of Defense Caspar Weinberger wanted an 8 or 9 percent increase for the Reagan defense budget. At a hasty meeting on 31 January, Stockman proposed a compromise interim real-growth increase of 7 percent and Weinberger signed on. Only later, going over the numbers several weeks after the meeting, did Stockman discover that by starting their calculations from 1982 forward, a point where Carter's increase and a preliminary Reagan increase had already been factored in, they had not added 2 percent more but had unintentionally doubled Carter's parting gesture. "We had taken an already-raised defense budget and raised that by 7 percent. Instead of starting from a defense budget of $142 billion, we'd started with one of $222 billion. And by raising that by 7 percent—and compounding it over five years—we had ended up increasing the real growth rate of the United States defense budget by *10 percent* per year between 1980 and 1986." Stockman "nearly had a heart attack. We'd laid out a plan for a five-year defense budget of *1.46 trillion dollars!*" But by then, he concludes, "the February 18 budget was out and they were squealing with delight throughout the military-industrial complex."

Never a detail man, Reagan seems not to have been disturbed by the magnitude of the defense buildup budgeted in his name, nor to have questioned budget numbers derived from such a late-night crap game. Few backroom episodes demonstrate so clearly the disconsonance between national-security politics and military necessity.

Reagan ended up spending almost as much on defense in the first five years of his presidency as had Ford, Nixon, and Carter combined, more than the cost of both the Korean and Vietnam wars—the largest peacetime buildup in American history. One purpose of the Reagan defense buildup, of course, was to starve the beast of government domestic spending, part of the conservative Republican agenda. As the political scientist Daniel Wirls notes, "for fiscal 1982, Reagan negotiated with Congress for about $35 billion in cuts in hundreds of domestic programs. . . . In budgetary terms, this change is . . . striking: from [fiscal year] 1981 to 1987 discretionary spending on domestic programs *decreased* by 21 percent in real terms while defense outlays *increased* by 45 percent." Reagan himself, however, was primarily interested in the United State's relationship with the Soviet Union—the CPD's bogus "window of vulnerability." His administration's "extraordinary surge in defense spending," Wirls writes, "was devoted to the modernization and expansion of the gamut of military programs, conventional and nuclear, but first and foremost to the nuclear weapons rearmament program."

"In all of their writings on foreign policy," the journalist Frances Fitzgerald writes, assessing what she calls the "warrior intellectuals" of the CPD and the Reagan administration, "they offer not one single constructive suggestion as to what the United States might do to, say, prevent widespread famine, stop the crazy lurches of the economic system, prevent ecological disaster or simply keep the peace and lessen the risk of nuclear war. The solution they have to all problems is confrontation and the threat, or use, of military force. Nowhere do they attempt to count the cost of keeping the Third World down by force, and nowhere do they consider in any serious fashion what risks this policy may pose to the physical security of the United States."

The Reagan rearmament program included more than $20 billion to improve and protect the most vulnerable part of the U.S. nuclear deterrent, its far-flung command, control, communications, and intelligence (C3I) systems, which had been given short shrift for years by contending military services more interested in buying new weapons systems than in hardening radars, satellites, and telecommunications systems. C3I was the greatest vulnerability of both the superpowers, writes the strategic analyst John D. Steinbruner, susceptible to destructive disconnection by "fewer than 100 judiciously targeted nuclear weapons. . . . Even 50 nuclear weapons are probably sufficient to eliminate the ability to direct U.S. [or Soviet] strategic forces to coherent purposes." But $20 billion was not nearly enough. The military services, across Democratic and Republican administrations alike, had chosen not to modernize the key systems that controlled the vast U.S. nuclear arsenal that was supposed to protect the nation, the better to limit the politicians' options to the only option the services ever believed to be realistic, which was firing first and preempting. "Command vulnerability," Steinbruner confirms, "has produced powerful incentives within the U.S. military planning system to conduct full-scale strategic operations at the outset of any serious nuclear engagement. This bias is very likely strong enough and deeply enough entrenched to defeat any attempt to utilize strategic forces in limited engagements of significant size." So one purpose of the Reagan C3I allocation was to push the U.S. military toward acceptance of its schemes of limited nuclear war.

If the massive Reagan administration arms buildup threatened what the Soviet leadership perceived to be rough nuclear parity between the two nations, the administration's decision to spend a significant share of its enlarged budget on C3I improvements sent an even more threatening message, Steinbruner concludes: "As seen from current Soviet perspective, an extensive U.S. program to prepare the command structure to support a nuclear campaign will be understood as a sign of increased willingness to initiate war."

And taken together with Reagan's hostile rhetoric and his arms buildup, it was. Yuri Andropov shocked a major KGB conference in Moscow in May 1981 with the news that the Reagan administration was preparing for a surprise nuclear first strike against the Soviet Union. In consequence, he instructed, both the KGB and its military intelligence counterpart, the GRU, for the first time in Soviet history, would combine their efforts in the largest intelligence-gathering program the Soviet services had ever mounted in peacetime, to be code-named Project RYAN, an acronym derived from the Russian words for a surprise missile attack, *raketno-yadernoye napadenie.* "Those in the KGB familiar with the United States," Gates writes, "thought this was 'alarmist' and suggested that Andropov's 'apocalyptic vision' originated with the Soviet military high command and, specifically, Andropov's close associate Defense Minister [Dmitri] Ustinov."

Donald Maclean thought so as well. The former British diplomat, who had been a Soviet spy in his own country and in Washington during and after the Second World War until he defected to the Soviet Union in 1951, had made himself useful in Moscow as an expert on British and U.S. foreign and domestic policy. As a committed Communist, he judged the Brezhnev regime to be biased toward military strategies, writing in a private memorandum in 1981: "What appears to have happened during the last five years is that at certain crucial turning points in policy-making the views of the military authorities with their natural professional interest in maximizing the armed strength of the country, have, with the support of the top leadership, prevailed over the views of those who are called upon to assess the overall influence of military policy upon the international interest of the country." Maclean was particularly concerned with the Soviet introduction of SS-20s into Europe, which he suspected the leadership had not understood would prompt a NATO response. "The next result . . . will be, unless the Soviet Union changes its policy, a rise in the level of nuclear confrontation in Europe with no compensating advantage to itself, indeed quite the reverse." Ustinov should not have been surprised at the NATO response, since he conceived his own SS-20s to be war-fighting weapons, writing secretly in September 1981 that the strategic goals for the system were "participation in the first and subsequent nuclear strikes by the strategic offensive forces of the Soviet Union . . . on the territory of all European NATO states and adjacent seas. . . . Currently, and in the coming years, the United States and other NATO states do not have a comparable missile system ready." (The SS-20s could not, of course, reach the United States.)

But if KGB residencies in the West thought Andropov was being alarmist, they were not prepared to challenge him. "RYAN," writes the Cambridge

University historian Christopher Andrew, "thus created a vicious circle of intelligence collection and assessment. Residencies were, in effect, ordered to search out alarming information. The Center was duly alarmed by what they supplied and demanded more."

RYAN was the KGB's top priority in 1982, and Andropov's elevation to general secretary on 10 November, Gates writes, "only added to the priority given RYAN." Reagan had seemed to confirm Soviet fears in his speech to the British Houses of Parliament assembled at Westminster on 8 June 1982, when he characterized the Soviet Union as a country "that runs against the tide of history by denying human freedom and human dignity to its citizens" and one that was also "in deep economic difficulty." He had pledged "to foster democratic change" in Eastern Europe and in the Soviet Union itself, to offer "open assistance to fraternal, political, and social institutions to bring about peaceful and democratic progress." According to Thomas Reed, who worked on Soviet policy in the White House at the time, Reagan's Westminster speech was a public version of National Security Decision Directive 32 (NSDD-32), which Reed says called for nothing less than seeking "the dissolution of the Soviet empire." The Cold War "was no longer to be viewed as some permanent condition. . . . We were not just going to *talk* about freedom anymore. One side in this Cold War was going to win and one was going to lose." Reagan's "open assistance" would also "include covert action," Reed noted: Neither the public speech nor the secret decision directive would have come as any surprise to Andropov.

"The president has publicly blamed the Soviet Union for all events abroad adverse to U.S. interests," Charles William Maynes, the longtime editor of *Foreign Policy,* wrote that year. "He has asserted that Soviet leaders will resort to any tactics to achieve their revolutionary goals. A senior national security council adviser [i.e., Richard Pipes] has stated that unless the Soviet internal system changes, war is inevitable." Today, Maynes went on, "some Soviet officials contend privately that the United States is increasing arms expenditures at the worst possible moment. They argue that having achieved nuclear parity, the Soviet Union was ready to level off its strategic programs but that the Reagan administration is now reopening the arms race with its massive defense programs. If so, the Soviets must ask themselves how any American administration can understand or believe in the benign intent of plans so buried in secrecy that they are never relayed until it is too late."

Defense Minister Ustinov's response to American threats, Benjamin Fischer reports, was "a spectacular Soviet military exercise on 18 June 1982 that simulated an all-out first strike against the US and Western Europe. The

Soviets dubbed it the 'seven-hour nuclear war' that demonstrated the 'might of the Soviet Space Troops to the West.' " The exercise opened with a submarine ballistic-missile launch. "Next, two ground-based SS-11 ICBMs and an SS-20 intermediate-range ballistic missile (IRBM) were fired off and then destroyed in flight by Soviet ABM-X-3 antiballistic missile interceptors. The simulated attack included the launch of a Kosmos-1379, a low-orbit 'combat' satellite; a practice 'destruction' of US reconnaissance satellites 'whose role was played by Kosmos-1379 and Kosmos-1375'; and the launch of two missiles carrying photo-reconnaissance and navigational satellites as a 'prompt replacement' for Soviet spacecraft 'destroyed by the enemy.' " Ustinov's deputy marshal Nikolai Ogarkov, who was also the Soviet chief of staff, underlined the Soviet military's mood three months later in a speech to Warsaw Pact chiefs of staff in Minsk. He compared the American challenge to the situation on the verge of the outbreak of the Second World War: "The Reagan administration has inaugurated open preparations for war. This can be seen every day in the political, economic, diplomatic and military fields. . . . The United States has, in effect, already declared war on us, the Soviet Union and some other states of the Warsaw Treaty. In several fields, the battle is already going on. . . . In the present stage, the risk of war is as high as ever before."

TO THE SOVIET GOVERNMENT, NOW NEWLY INVIGORATED by Yuri Andropov's leadership, the approaching year, 1983, appeared to mark a turning point. The American Pershing 2s were scheduled to be deployed in Europe beginning in late November if no agreement stood them down. For negotiating terms, Reagan had offered his zero option, a Richard Perle contrivance designed to look to the millions of Europeans and Americans in the burgeoning Nuclear Freeze movement like a reasonable bargain. It required the Soviet Union to give up all its intermediate-range ballistic missiles in Europe, including its new SS-20s, while the United States pledged merely to retire some older theater missiles it had planned to retire anyway and not to deploy the new Pershings and Tomahawks. Nor would British or French nuclear assets be reduced.

According to the diplomatic correspondent Strobe Talbott, the idea of such a *Null-Lösung,* a "zero solution," had originated with the West German Social Democratic Party. The Reagan administration national security adviser, Richard Allen, had rejected it as "illusory" until Perle resurrected it. Perle "intended [it] to be unacceptable," Thomas Graham, Jr., writes, an assertion supported by Douglas MacEachin, a Soviet specialist with the CIA: "I do know from firsthand knowledge that some of the people who designed our zero solution . . . designed it believing they had come up with a proposal which would not get a yes, which would therefore make it possible to deploy the missiles, and we could still say we're not being aggressive." Talbott also characterized Perle as someone opposed to arms control, "at least as it had traditionally been practiced. . . . Many Europeans were calling for the zero solution. So why not give it to them? Then, when it failed, they would be party to the failure, just as they had been party to what Perle saw as the folly of the December 1979 decision"—to negotiate withdrawal of the SS-20s, if possible, before deploying the Pershings and Tomahawks.

Perle himself evidently considered the zero option a cynical masterstroke.

Not long after he left government at the end of the Reagan years he published a novel, *Hard Line,* about a sophisticated, espresso-sipping assistant secretary of defense very much like Richard Perle, "compact and reserved"; ever at bureaucratic war with a State Department counterpart modeled on Perle's perennial adversary in the Reagan administration, Assistant Secretary of State Richard Burt, "convinced that only a hard line would produce a Western victory in the Cold War." With no help from the German Social Democrats, "Michael Waterman," Perle's fictional alter ego, invents a zero option, noting as he does so that it was "unlikely the Soviets will agree":

> Zero. That was it. Zero. Zero for both sides.
>
> *Get rid of all of them—SS-20s, Pershing IIs, ground-launched cruise missiles, the whole lot.*
>
> We will abandon our deployment if the Soviets give up theirs. Oh, it was perfect. It was fair. Balanced. Simple. Elegant. Obvious. Clean. Tidy. Neatly wrapped.
>
> How could they say no? How could *anyone* fail to say yes? Who would criticize it—and how? With what argument? The simple flawlessness of it. It was exquisite. It was fastidious. It was sublime. It was . . . *inevitable.*
>
> His fingers flew like Bach's at the harpsichord. The words were music to his ears.

"Urbane guerrillas in dark suits," Perle characterizes his sturdy breed of heroes, "they fought not with AK-47s but with memos, position papers, talking points, and news leaks." (A reviewer, Robin Winks, a Yale historian, came to a different conclusion. "What is intriguing," he wrote of Perle's novel, "is the sense of how bureaucrats deal with one another in Washington, how they devote inordinate time to silly activities, how they speak in a special kind of wise-guy jargon, and how they let their ambitions overcome their good sense. Waterman is not an attractive person. . . . He loves the perks of office, the limousines, the flights to Paris, the chance to eat in the best restaurants. He is unwilling to learn; he undermines colleagues; he is intent on the triumph of his will, his ideas, his solutions. In the end we are led to believe that this is a good thing, though some readers may simply stand aghast at the pettiness of so much of this activity.")

Perle's zero option did not inspire Andropov with the music of a Bach fugue. The new general secretary took missile threats seriously, and the approaching deployment of Pershing 2s was beginning to look to him like another Cuban Missile Crisis, with Reagan in the Khrushchev role. Speaking to the Warsaw Pact's Political Consultative Committee in January 1983,

Andropov was shockingly candid. "What has caused the sharp turn in U.S. and NATO policy, which produced the current flare-up of tensions, and how long will this aggravation last?" he asked. The Soviet achievement of "military-strategic parity with the West" was one cause, he asserted; so was its "dynamic policy of détente." But the United States and NATO had found opportunity as well "in the difficulties we have all been facing to one extent or another in our economic development. I have in mind the growth of foreign debts, the food situation, our technological lag in certain areas and a series of other bottlenecks. Internal political complications in some socialist countries have been appraised in a similar vein."

"Especially dangerous," Andropov continued, "is the military challenge thrown at us. . . . The new round of the arms race, imposed by the USA, has major, qualitative differences. Whereas before, the Americans, in speaking about their nuclear weaponry, preferred to accentuate the fact that it was above all a means of 'intimidation' and 'deterrence,' now, in creating modified missile systems, they do not hide the fact that they are really intended for a future war. From here spring the doctrines of 'rational' and 'limited' nuclear war; from here spring the statements about the possibility of surviving and winning a protracted nuclear conflict. It is hard to say what is blackmail and what is genuine readiness to take the fatal step."

A month later, following up Andropov's cautions, the KGB sent its residents in the capitals of Europe and North America imperative further instructions on Project RYAN. The first of two directives spoke of the "growing urgency of the task to uncover NATO preparations for a nuclear missile attack on the USSR" and suggested watching for activity at "the places where government officials and members of their families are evacuated," identifying "the location of specially equipped civil defense shelters," assessing "increased purchase of blood from donors and the prices paid for it," counting cars at defense offices in the day and in the evening, noting changes in the police administration system, and reporting regularly. A second directive explained that determining the launching of a missile from the United States "leaves roughly 20 minutes reaction time. This period will be considerably curtailed after deployment of the 'Pershing-2' missile in [West Germany], for which the flying time to reach long-range targets in the Soviet Union is calculated at 4–6 minutes." Since the United States had pledged to its NATO allies that it would not launch nuclear weapons against the Soviet Union without first consulting with them, the second KGB directive emphasized that the "most important problem for the information-gathering apparatus of Soviet intelligence" was "to ascertain in good time the moment when nuclear consultations begin inside NATO."

Reagan, not yet aware of the developing Soviet war scare, ratcheted his rhetoric higher in a March 1983 speech to the annual convention of the National Association of Evangelicals in Orlando, Florida. There he named the Soviet Union "the focus of evil in the modern world" and, famously, "an evil empire." The speech, built in part from paragraphs cut by more cautious advisers from his speech at Westminster, was meant to win the support of fundamentalist Christians against the Nuclear Freeze movement. It won the support as well of Vladimir Slipchenko, a member of the Soviet general staff:

> The military, the armed forces . . . used this [speech] as a reason to begin a very intense preparation inside the military for a state of war. . . . We started to run huge strategic exercises. . . . These were the first military exercises in which we really tested our mobilization. We didn't just exercise the ground forces but also the strategic [nuclear] arms. . . . For the military, the period when we were called the evil empire was actually very good and useful, because we achieved a very high military readiness. . . . We also rehearsed the situation when a non-nuclear war might turn into a nuclear war.

EVEN AS SOVIET FORCES WERE PREPARING their exercises, the U.S. Pacific Fleet began three weeks of maneuvers in the North Pacific. Doughty little John Lehman, Perle's former business partner, who was now Reagan's truculent secretary of the Navy, intended the maneuvers to demonstrate his "forward strategy" policy of dominating "high-threat" areas near the Soviet Union—in this case, the Kurile Islands, which the Soviet Union had wrested from the Japanese in the last days of the Second World War and, farther north, the vulnerable intelligence-collecting centers on the Kamchatka Peninsula. Making sure that Soviet intelligence was aware of the U.S. presence, the journalist Seymour Hersh writes, "was one of the basic purposes of such exercises . . . to show the Soviets who is boss." Reagan had just authorized U.S. warships to sail closer to Soviet borders, Hersh notes. Now "three aircraft carrier battle groups, part of a forty-ship armada accompanied by Air Force B-52 bombers . . . sailed defiantly in the icy waters off Alaska's Aleutian Islands, 450 miles from . . . Kamchatka. . . . American attack submarines and antisubmarine aircraft began operating for the first time inside the normal patrol area of the Soviet submarine fleet. In all, 23,000 American military men took part. . . . As one expert later said, 'They know we're there.' "

In the midst of these aggressive exercises, on 23 March 1983, Reagan announced to the world his unvetted, pristine new program to render nuclear weapons "impotent and obsolete," the program that would shortly be named the Strategic Defense Initiative (SDI) by the administration and Star Wars—from George Lucas's 1977 film of the same name—by the public:

> Let me share with you a vision of the future which offers hope. It is that we embark on a program to counter the awesome Soviet missile threat with measures that are defensive. Let us turn to the very strengths in technology that spawned our great industrial base and that have given us the quality of life we enjoy today.
>
> What if free people could live secure in the knowledge that their security did not rest upon the threat of instant U.S. retaliation to deter a Soviet attack, that we could intercept and destroy strategic ballistic missiles before they reached our own soil or that of our allies?
>
> I know this is a formidable technical task, one that may not be accomplished before the end of this century. . . . There will be failures and setbacks, just as there will be successes and breakthroughs. And as we proceed, we must remain constant in preserving the nuclear deterrent and maintaining a solid capability for flexible response. But isn't it worth every investment necessary to free the world from the threat of nuclear war? We know it is. . . .
>
> Tonight . . . I'm taking an important first step. I am directing a comprehensive and intensive effort to define a long-term research and development program to begin to achieve our ultimate goal of eliminating the threat posed by strategic nuclear missiles. This could pave the way for arms control measures to eliminate the weapons themselves.

Senator Barry Goldwater wrote Reagan the next day, "That was the best statement I have ever heard come from any President."

SDI was seemingly the last piece in a puzzle that Reagan had been trying for several years to solve, the puzzle of how to eliminate nuclear weapons from the world when one's main adversary, as Reagan had said at his first presidential press conference, reserved unto itself "the right to commit any crime, to lie, to cheat, in order to attain [world revolution]." The SDI proposal would lead to major debate and maneuvering between the two superpowers as well as debates within each government, but its immediate effect was more ominous.

A KGB spy working at the Soviet Embassy in Washington, Yuri Shvets, remembers with delight his relief from his onerous RYAN duties, which "took prodigious amounts of time and energy with negligible effect. And here President Reagan comes with the SDI! As far as the leaders of the KGB intelligence service were concerned, this program jibed beautifully with the RYAN concept, and could not have come at a more opportune time. There was no longer any need to peek into windows, count cars and cut facts out of whole cloth."

Though SDI was as yet only a twinkle in the president's eye, Christopher Andrew and the former KGB colonel Oleg Gordievsky note that "the rhetoric and television advertising with which the project was unveiled were interpreted by the Center as further evidence of the US administration's attempts to prepare its citizens for nuclear war." The British novelist James Buchan, at that time the Bonn correspondent for the *Financial Times,* recalls that he "paid a visit to Moscow in the summer of that year. . . . And every Soviet official one met was running around like a chicken without a head—sometimes talking in conciliatory terms and sometimes talking in the most ghastly and dire terms of real hot war—of fighting war, of nuclear war." Thomas Powers explains why: "Civilians debated whether anybody could afford such a system [as SDI] or whether it could ever work, but defense theorists all knew that space-based defenses were well-suited only to one job—mopping up the ragged retaliatory missiles that would be fired by strategic forces devastated by a first strike. The tough talk in Washington was actually aimed at rallying Congress to support politically difficult cuts in domestic spending to free up funds for Star Wars; but the Soviets did not appreciate such nuances." Andropov confirmed the point at a Moscow press conference on 26 March. He said SDI was meant to leave his military "unable to deal a retaliatory strike" and was thus "a bid to disarm the Soviet Union in the face of the U.S. nuclear threat."

APRIL BROUGHT FURTHER PROVOCATIONS as the U.S. Navy continued its maneuvers close to Soviet waters in the North Pacific. Seymour Hersh:

> One night in early April, the *Midway,* after cutting off all electronic equipment whose emissions could be monitored by the Soviets, slipped away from the flotilla and steamed south toward the Kuriles. The Soviets did not track it. "When he [the *Midway*] popped up southeast of Kamchatka [by turning its electronics back on]," one Navy intelligence officer recalled, "they were clearly surprised." The *Midway*'s next act surprised not only the Soviets but also the senior commanders of the U.S. Pacific Fleet. On April 4, a group of at least six Navy planes from the *Midway* and the *Enterprise* violated Soviet borders by overflying the island of Zeleny in the Kurile archipelago. . . .
>
> The incident inevitably was viewed by the Kremlin as highly provocative and an explicit challenge to Soviet sovereignty over the heavily fortified Kurile Islands. . . . Within twenty-four hours, Soviet aircraft responded with a direct overflight of American territory in the Aleutian Islands; there was no doubt in the U.S. government that the Soviet overflights were, as one State Department official put it, "clear retaliation." . . .

> Within hours of the overflight, the Soviet Air Defense Forces in the Far East were put on alert. They would stay that way through much of the spring and summer. The stakes, already high, had become higher.

Andropov responded to the April 4 Zeleny overflight by ordering more than simply a Soviet retaliatory overflight of the Aleutians. According to the investigative journalist Murray Sayle, he also ordered a new law added to the Soviet Air Code, Article 53, to complement Article 36 of the Law on the State Border of the U.S.S.R. that had been promulgated the previous November. "Read together," Sayle writes, "these two laws closed the whole of Soviet airspace to 'intruder' aircraft, and 'in instances in which the violation cannot be stopped or the violator detained by any other means,' Article 36 *instructed* the 'frontier guard troops and air-defense forces . . . to use weapons and combat equipment' . . . to shoot the intruder down."

Andropov warned the Central Committee in late June, Andrew and Gordievsky report, of an "unprecedented sharpening of the struggle" between the United States and the Soviet Union; he said "the threat of nuclear war [was] hanging over mankind." Another telegram went out to Soviet NATO residencies urging close attention to RYAN. Ironically, now that SDI was in release Reagan was contemplating not nuclear war but nuclear abolition, much to the dismay of his advisers. In a letter responding to one from Andropov that Reagan drafted by hand in mid-July, he wrote, "If we can agree on mutual, verifiable reductions in the number of nuclear weapons we both hold, could this not be a first step toward the elimination of all such weapons? What a blessing this would be for the people we both represent. You and I have the ability to bring this about through our negotiators in the arms reduction talks. . . . ~~that could lead to the total elimination of all such weap~~ [ons]" [*sic*]. Impatiently, on the advice of his second national security adviser, William Clark, the president agreed to delete the paragraph, including the line he had struck through himself, from the rewritten copy he sent to Andropov.

AN HOUR BEFORE DAWN ON THE MORNING of 1 September 1983, beyond the Kuriles above Sakhalin Island in the Sea of Okhotsk, a Soviet Sukhoi-15 fighter jet prepared to shoot down a Boeing 747 civilian airliner, Korean Airlines flight KE007, off course en route to Seoul from a refueling stop in Anchorage. KE007, which originated in New York, carried 269 passengers, sixty-one of whom were U.S. citizens, including Rep. Larry P. McDonald of Georgia, the national chairman of the far-right-wing John Birch Society. The airliner was 360 miles off course because its overworked captain, Chun Byung-in, had set the automatic pilot to fly on its magnetic compass rather than its more accurate inertial guidance system. It had already overflown the southern tip of the Kamchatka Peninsula; it would have been intercepted there had the Soviet fighters scrambling to intercept it not run short of fuel. Their tanks were deliberately kept only lightly filled to prevent their pilots from defecting, as one had done in 1976.

KE007 had crossed flight paths with a U.S. Air Force RC-135 reconnaissance aircraft, a Boeing 707, east of Kamchatka. The RC-135 had been sent out, legally, to monitor a Soviet missile test. The test had been scrubbed and the military aircraft was returning home. The appearance of the airliner, far off course, had sufficiently confused Soviet radar monitors on Kamchatka when the two planes crossed paths that they had assigned it the RC-135's track number, 6065. They told Sakhalin command center when they handed it off that it had been "provisionally identified as an RC-135."

Sakhalin sent up the Sukhoi-15, radio identifier 805, and a trailing MiG-23. Eight zero five located KE007, tracked it, observed its lights. (Eight zero five to ground station *Deputat*: "The air navigation lights are burning. The light is flashing.") Orders to close on it came from *Deputat*. The 805 pilot began to do so, and swore when he discovered his missiles were prematurely live and locked on. Turning off lock-on, he approached the target.

After KE007 crashed into the Sea of Okhotsk, the Soviets secretly recovered the downed plane and played back its flight recorders. The recordings revealed that the sleepy Korean Airlines pilots had been unaware that they had drifted over forbidden Soviet territory. The Soviets had taped their own communications as well. Andropov received transcriptions of the several recordings on 18 November 1983; thereafter they were hidden away in the GRU archives in Moscow. A decade later, Boris Yeltsin handed them over to the U.N.'s International Civil Aviation Organization. Murray Sayle quoted them in his comprehensive 1993 account of the incident:

> The Soviet tapes confirm that a hurried, half-hearted attempt was indeed made to intercept the straying airliner, and, at the same time, the tapes show that the Soviet air defense never made up its collective mind what the "target" was. The fighter pilot broke his electronic lock on KE007, approached the airliner from the right side . . . and fired a warning burst of cannon shells, which were invisible to the airliner. By now, KE007 is a few seconds from safety [it was nearing neutral waters], and [ground control] General Kornukov has made a decision:
> "Has he fired the warning burst?"

"Affirmative, he has."

"Destroy the target."

"Task received. Destroy Target Six-oh-six-five with missile fire."

As the fighter positions itself to fire, Kornukov worries that KE007 may escape. "Oh, fuck. He is already getting out into neutral waters. Engage afterburner immediately. Bring in the MIG-23 as well. While you are wasting time, it will fly right out."

"He has launched. He fired both missiles."

In three quick transmissions just seconds apart, 805 radioed to *Deputat*, "I have executed the launch. . . . The target is destroyed. . . . I am breaking off attack." When KE007, its tail damaged and one wing destroyed, slammed into the Sea of Okhotsk twelve minutes later at 600 miles per hour, all 269 people aboard were killed instantly. Sayle argues that the deaths "were mandated by Andropov's pitiless laws sealing the Soviet air borders, which must share much of the blame. . . . The laws had no requirement for intruders to be identified, or for them to be guilty of anything at all, beyond mere intrusion." Since the laws, however cruel, had responded to John Lehman's belligerent policies of naval threat display, of showing the Soviets who was boss, some share of blame for the loss of innocent life surely belongs as well to the Reagan administration.

Reagan called the destruction of KE007 "an act of barbarism" and a "crime against nature." He was still speaking months later of "the murder of 269 innocent people in a defenseless airliner." Secretary of State George Shultz, scheduled to hold private talks with Andrey Gromyko during a meeting of the Conference on Security and Cooperation in Europe in Madrid on 8 September 1983, kept his appointment but used the occasion to deride the Soviet government coldly for shooting down the plane and blaming the incursion on the United States. Gromyko's responding statement "was astonishingly brutal," Schultz wrote in his memoirs, adding, "The meeting became so outrageous and pointless that we just ended it."

The national security lesson Andropov learned from the airliner incursion was the vulnerability of his borders, now evident to the world, which may explain the belligerence of his response. "The 747 had been in Soviet airspace for over two hours before Soviet air defense forces were able to approach the aircraft," writes the University of Toronto scholar Beth Fischer. "Even more disturbing, eight of the eleven Soviet tracking stations on the Kamchatka Peninsula and Sakhalin Island had failed to detect the plane." Beleaguered, with advanced diabetes, his kidneys failing, his life sustained by dialysis, Andropov issued a statement from his hospital bed on 28 September

1983 that George Kennan described as the kind of invective that would once have been a prelude to war.

The mortally ill general secretary said that the United States was on "a militarist course which poses a grave threat to peace." He spoke of "the unprecedented build-up of U.S. military potential, the large-scale programs of manufacturing weapons of all types—nuclear, chemical and conventional," adding, "Now it is planned to project the unrestricted arms race into outer space as well." For the sake of its "imperial ambitions," he cautioned severely, "[the American] Administration goes to such lengths that one begins to doubt whether Washington has any brakes at all to prevent it from crossing the line before which any sober-minded person must stop." Not yet knowing what the flight recorders would reveal, he accused the United States of an "insidious provocation involving a South Korean plane engineered by U.S. special services," a conspiracy that was "also an example of extreme adventurism in politics." He said the United States was "a country where an outrageous militarist psychosis is being implanted" and warned Europe away.

October 1983 brought more conflict and suffering. On 23 October, a suicide bomber driving a yellow Mercedes delivery truck loaded with six tons of explosives barreled into a U.S. Marine barracks at Beirut International Airport in Lebanon and detonated his load. The building shattered and collapsed and 241 American service personnel were killed. A parallel attack seconds later at a French barracks in West Beirut killed fifty-eight French paratroopers. The Iranian-funded Lebanese terrorist group Hezbollah was eventually charged with the attacks. Two days later, coincidentally, Reagan ordered the invasion of Grenada, the small, formerly British island in the eastern Caribbean where Cuban forces and workers had been building a large airport and advising a new Revolutionary Military Council that had installed itself after a coup. In the back of Reagan's mind and of George Shultz's was concern that a thousand American students attending medical school on the island might be taken hostage as Americans had been taken in Tehran during the revolution there in 1979—an event that had sunk Jimmy Carter's chances for reelection. The marines who liberated Grenada— diverted from their transport by sea to Beirut to replace those killed there in the terror bombing at the airport—captured Soviet advisers as well as Cuban.

The culminating and most dangerous misunderstanding in that year of misunderstandings involved a nine-day NATO military exercise designated ABLE ARCHER 83, scheduled for 2 through 11 November 1983. NATO annually conducted multinational exercises called AUTUMN FORGE from its northern to its southern flank, mobilizing aircraft and moving tanks, troops, and artillery across rivers and through mud in realistic battle simulations. In some years AUTUMN FORGE ended with a command-post exercise, ABLE ARCHER, that practiced the coordinated consultations among NATO national leaderships necessary to authorize the use of nuclear weapons, just the procedure that the KGB's Project RYAN directives of the previous February had instructed its residencies to be particularly alert for—"to ascertain in good time the moment when nuclear consultations begin inside NATO." ABLE ARCHER 83 differed from previous command-post exercises in involving the actual participation of senior U.S. and NATO leaders who would have had to approve such nuclear releases. Reagan himself had been expected to participate as well as Vice President George H. W. Bush, Caspar Weinberger, and the chairman of the Joint Chiefs. "I had serious misgivings about approving the drill as originally planned," Reagan's third national security adviser, Robert McFarlane, told the scholar Beth Fischer. "There were concerns that superpower relations were too tense. There was a concern with how Moscow would perceive such a realistic drill." McFarlane scrubbed participation by the highest-level U.S. leaders, but British prime minister Margaret Thatcher and German chancellor Helmut Kohl both took part. Even McFarlane's caution was subject to misinterpretation in the fog of cold war. "The sudden disappearance of such figures," the British correspondent Martin Walker noted, "the disruption of usual schedules and the swift movement of the military high command around Washington were precisely the signs the Soviet intelligence had been told to look for under RYAN."

James Buchan had reported seeing Moscow officials the previous summer running around like chickens without heads. "They were extremely frightened of some kind of large military exercise by NATO in the autumn of '83," he recalled, "after the Bundestag [the parliament of the Federal Republic of Germany] had approved the [Pershing] missile deployments." By late 1983, the CIA's Ben Fischer writes, "the entire [Soviet Union] was in a frenzy, stimulated by peace rallies, civil defense drills and classified briefings for the party *aktiv* on the war danger. (Photographs from this period show students practicing air-raid and gas-mask drills.) A foreign ministry official returning to Moscow in November 1983 described the atmosphere as 'pre-war.' " Melvin Goodman, a senior analyst at the CIA at the time, recalls seeing "some clandestine reports that suggested great alarm in Moscow. But frankly they weren't taken very seriously by anyone but the analysts." Angelo Codevilla, a conservative analyst for the Senate Select Committee on Intelligence in 1983, told Beth Fischer, "When the report surfaced that the KGB was worried about an American first strike, there was a great deal of incredulity: How could anyone be this ignorant of America?" The KGB was mirror-imaging, as Richard Pipes might have put it: The Soviet war plan proposed disguising a move toward nuclear war within a seemingly routine military exercise. The Soviet leadership had every reason, including knowledge gained from spying, to believe that a NATO attack would begin the same way. And indeed, starting a war from within an exercise was NATO's strategy as well.

Robert Gates came to be convinced that the Soviet scare over ABLE ARCHER 83 was far more serious than the CIA judged it to be at the time. According to the KGB defector Oleg Gordievsky, Gates writes, "the exercise especially alarmed Moscow because (1) the procedures and message formats used in the transition from conventional to nuclear war were different from those used before, and (2) in this exercise the NATO forces went through all of the alert phases from normal readiness to general alert. Further, he says that alarmist KGB reporting persuaded 'the Center' that there was a real alert involving real troops. Also, surveillance around U.S. bases in Europe reported changed patterns of officer movement. Thus 'the KGB concluded that American forces had been placed on alert—and might even have begun the countdown to nuclear war.' " The former CIA director describes a pattern of Warsaw Pact alerting:

> Between November 2 and 11, there had been considerable activity by Soviet and other Warsaw Pact forces in the Baltic Military District as well as by East German, Polish and Czechoslovak forces in response to preparations for the exercise and the exercise itself. Elements of the air forces of the Group of Soviet Forces Germany had gone on heightened alert because, according to the commander, of the increase in the threat of possible aggression against the USSR and its Warsaw Pact allies during the exercise. Soviet military meteorological broadcasts were taken off the air during the exercise. Units of the Soviet Fourth Air Army had gone to increased readiness and all combat flight operations were suspended from November 4 to 10.

The director of the Australian Defense Intelligence Organization at that time, Paul Dibb, adds a further detail to Gates's account. "The Group of Soviet Air Forces in East Germany was forward-loading tactical nuclear weapons onto Sukhoi-17 long-range strike aircraft to strike West Germany," he reports. "They were tactical nuclear weapons to bomb military and other targets just across the border from East Germany in West Germany."

All this evidence points to the same conclusion: that the United States and the Soviet Union, apes on a treadmill, inadvertently blundered close to nuclear war in November 1983. That, and not the decline and fall of the Soviet Union, was the return on the neoconservatives' long, cynical, and radically partisan investment in threat inflation and arms-race escalation.

During the Cuban confrontation, when American nuclear weapons were ready to launch or already aloft and moving toward their Soviet targets on hundreds of SAC bombers, both sides were at least aware of the danger and working intensely to resolve the dispute. During ABLE ARCHER 83, in contrast, an American renewal of high Cold War rhetoric, aggressive and perilous threat displays, and naïve incredulity were combined with Soviet arms-race and surprise-attack insecurities and heavy-handed war-scare propaganda in a nearly lethal mix. Gates reviews the episode from a post–Cold War perspective, to the same conclusion:

> Information about the peculiar and remarkably skewed frame of mind of the Soviet leaders during those times that has emerged since the collapse of the Soviet Union makes me think there is a good chance—with all of the other events in 1983—that they really felt a NATO attack was at least possible and that they took a number of measures to enhance their military readiness short of mobilization. After going through the experience at the time, then through the postmortems, and now through the documents, I don't think the Soviets were crying wolf. They may not have believed a NATO attack was imminent in November 1983, but they did seem to believe that the situation was very dangerous. And U.S. intelligence had failed to grasp the true extent of their anxiety. A reexamination of the whole episode by the President's Foreign Intelligence Advisory Board in 1990 concluded that the intelligence community's confidence that this all had been Soviet posturing for political effect was misplaced.

As if ABLE ARCHER 83 were not enough, the first sixteen Tomahawks arrived at England's Greenham Common Air Force Base, west of London near Newbury, on 14 November. Eight days later the United States began deploying the first Pershing 2 missiles in West Germany and the Soviet delegation walked out of the Intermediate Nuclear Forces talks in Geneva. Ustinov, the Soviet defense minister, announced at a meeting of Warsaw Pact defense ministers on 6 December that the Soviet Union was "lifting its voluntary moratorium on the deployment of intermediate-range Soviet nuclear weapons in the European part of the country. These weapons will now also be deployed at locations from which they could reach the territories of the relevant West European countries." On 8 December the Soviets suspended the Strategic Arms Reduction Talks (START) as well—the Reagan administration's answer to Jimmy Carter's SALT II negotiations—which in any case had been deliberately held to a glacial pace for months by the administration's self-important negotiator Edward Rowny, a retired Army general. "Never, perhaps, in the postwar decades," Gorbachev would summarize later, "has the situation in the world been as explosive . . . as in the first half of the eighties."

Reagan was surprised and shocked that the Soviets had taken his years of militant rhetoric and his massive arms buildup seriously. He belittled their concerns in his diary on 14 November: "I feel the Soviets are so defense minded, so paranoid about being attacked that without being in any way soft on them, we ought to tell them no one here has any intention of doing anything like that. What have they got that anyone would want?" A few weeks later William Casey returned from meeting with British intelligence in London and briefed Reagan further on RYAN and ABLE ARCHER 83. "Do you suppose they really believe that?" the president of the United States asked McFarlane less defensively afterward, the truth finally dawning. "I don't see how they could believe that—but it's something to think about."

THE PIVOTAL YEAR 1983 WAS CROWDED with experiences that gave Ronald Reagan, as he said, "something to think about." Besides the hostile Soviet reaction to Reagan's announcement of his Strategic Defense Initiative, the suicide bombing of the U.S. Marine barracks in Beirut, the destruction of Korean Airlines flight KE007, and the Soviet war scare around ABLE ARCHER 83, several more personal experiences also influenced the president to rethink his approach to superpower relations.

"Columbus Day," Reagan began a diary entry on Monday, 10 October 1983. "In the morning at Camp David I ran the tape of the movie ABC is running on Nov. 20. It's called 'The Day After' in which Lawrence, Kansas, is wiped out in a nuclear war with Russia. It is powerfully done, all $7 million worth. It is very effective and left me greatly depressed. So far they haven't sold any of the 25 ads scheduled and I can see why. . . . My own reaction: we have to do all we can . . . to see that there is never a nuclear war." *The Day After,* a television film that Nicholas Meyer directed for the ABC network, graphically depicted the effects of a nuclear war between the United States and the Soviet Union on the people and buildings of Lawrence, Kansas, a quiet university town in the hilly eastern part of the state, and on Kansas City, Missouri, and its rural surroundings. Jason Robards played a country doctor overwhelmed with wounded and dying victims, JoBeth Williams a compassionate nurse, John Lithgow a college professor, and Steve Guttenberg and Amy Madigan two young people caught up in the disaster.

In 1983 I was in the midst of writing *The Making of the Atomic Bomb;* I lived in Kansas City at the time and remember well the shock of seeing simulated mushroom clouds rising over the city where I grew up and Minutemen launched in reprisal from the missile silos that punctuated the abundant farmlands to the east. I had lived in Lawrence as well and used the University of Kansas library there for research. Having visited Hiroshima and Nagasaki by then, having interviewed survivors, walked the ground, and studied photographs and film of the aftermath of the atomic bombings, I understood that the ABC production underplayed the destruction it depicted, a point the popular astrophysicist Carl Sagan made in an interview after the broadcast when he discussed the possibility of nuclear winter—a possibility that he and other scientists had only just proposed in a controversial paper in *Science* that year. But if it pulled its punches, *The Day After* was nevertheless sufficiently realistic to stir national angst and extensive debate, some of it partisan, even before the production's late-November airing. Liberals worried that such a universal disaster might be a real possibility given Reagan's hostile anti-Soviet rhetoric and trillion-dollar rearmament program. Conservatives suspected that the production was part of a liberal plot to scare the country into arms negotiations. Educators feared that it would give children nightmares, and no doubt it did.

As a former movie actor, Reagan was famously responsive to stories told on film. "I knew from Sacramento days that he liked celluloid," the national security adviser and former California Supreme Court Justice William Clark told Reagan's biographer Lou Cannon. Film became a way to educate a president who had come to the White House notoriously ill-informed about foreign affairs, Cannon writes:

> When Bill Clark became Reagan's second national security adviser at the beginning of 1982, he found that the president knew next to nothing about what was going on in many corners of the globe. . . . Clark . . . realized from his first day at the White House that the gaps in the president's knowledge were potentially dangerous ones that needed to be filled. His technique for doing this demonstrated an understanding of Reagan's mental processes and work habits that was unmatched in the White House. Clark knew that the president responded to visual aids and reasoned that he would be most receptive of all to films. So he took Reagan to the movies. Clark obtained Defense Department movies on "the Soviet threat," the problems of the Middle East and other issues and showed them to Reagan in the White House theater. [He] asked the CIA to provide a "profile movie documentary" on world leaders Reagan was scheduled to meet. "And the agency started producing some great stuff that was enjoyable for all of us," Clark said. "[It was] far more interesting to see a movie on Mrs. [Indira] Gandhi covering her life than sitting down with the usual tome the agency would produce."

To the point, Edmund Morris, another Reagan biographer, commented that Reagan's diary entry about *The Day After* was "the first and only admission I have been able to find in his papers that he was 'greatly depressed.' "

For a president who shied from personal conflict and stopped his ears against bad news, viewing *The Day After* was an unsettling experience.

The experience in turn affected Reagan's reaction to an extensive briefing on the SIOP (the Single Integrated Operational Plan) that he received in preparation for ABLE ARCHER 83. By 1983, the SIOP had been distended to an attack on five thousand decapitation targets among a preposterous total of fifty thousand targets of military, industrial, or economic significance. Beth Fischer interviewed several officials who attended the late October briefing. They reported, she writes, that the president "was 'chastened' by what he witnessed and became withdrawn. Weinberger has attested that the president found the briefing to be a terribly disturbing experience. 'He had a very deep revulsion to the whole idea of nuclear weapons,' the defense secretary explained. 'These war games brought home to anybody the fantastically horrible events that would surround such a scenario.' " Afterward, Reagan wrote in his diary: "A most sobering experience with Cap W [i.e., Weinberger] and Gen. Vessy [*sic:* JCS chairman Gen. John W. Vessey, Jr.] in the Situation room, a briefing on our complete plan in the event of a nuclear attack. . . . In several ways, the sequence of events described in the briefings paralleled those in the ABC movie. Yet there were still some people at the Pentagon who claimed a nuclear war was 'winnable.' I thought they were crazy."

How Reagan's mind worked was a subject of considerable discussion during the years of his presidency and among his biographers afterward. Most discussants came to similar conclusions, although their estimates of the quality of Reagan's thinking depended on whether they were promoters or detractors of his goals. In a word, Reagan thought "anecdotally, not analytically," as the journalist and former assistant secretary of state Leslie Gelb put it. The president organized events and ideas on a Procrustean bed of personal experiences and rigid beliefs. Taxes stifled enterprise because in the 1950s a top federal income tax rate of 91 percent on earned income had led him and other movie stars to limit their acting work to four films a year. Communists were cynical, brutal, cold-blooded, and completely lacking in morality because the Communists he believed he had fought for control of the Screen Actors Guild when he was its president had seemed to him to be such people. "Firsthand discoveries are the ones that matter to Reagan," Cannon confirms. "When he expressed his view of Communist morality at his first presidential news conference, he believed he was talking from experience."

Cannon found that "most of his aides thought of him as intelligent, but many also considered him intellectually lazy." In fact, they laughed at him behind his back. He was Joe Six-pack, they told each other, his opinions and judgments exactly those guileless truisms you would expect to find among patrons of a neighborhood bar. "The sad, shared secret of the Reagan White House," Cannon writes, "was that no one in the presidential entourage had confidence in the judgment or capacities of the president. Often, they took advantage of Reagan's niceness and naïveté to indulge competing concepts of the presidency and advance their own ambitions. Pragmatists and conservatives alike treated Reagan as if he were a child monarch in need of constant protection. They paid homage to him, but gave him no respect." A book in his hand was more likely to be a Tom Clancy novel than a Henry Kissinger memoir—though the same could be said for many Americans. "Not one of the friends and aides" Leslie Gelb interviewed "suggested that the President was, in any conventional sense, analytical, intellectually curious or well-informed—even though it would have been easy and natural for them to say so. They clearly did not think it necessary. Time and again, they painted a picture of a man who had serious intellectual shortcomings but was a political heavyweight, a leader whose instincts and intuition were right more often than their own analyses. His mind, they said, is shaped almost entirely by his own personal history, not by pondering on history books." For George Shultz, in Cannon's paraphrase, "Reagan's seemingly irrelevant anecdotes were tools that the president used to comprehend the world. 'He often reduced his thinking to a joke,' Shultz said. 'That doesn't mean it didn't have a heavy element to it.'" Cannon counters that Reagan "sometimes used humor to avoid facing issues he ought to have faced, particularly the reality that it was impossible to increase military spending, reduce taxes and balance the budget simultaneously." Reagan's difficulty with governing went deeper, Cannon insists:

> His biggest problem was that he didn't know enough about public policy to participate fully in his presidency—and often didn't realize how much he didn't know. Reagan's legal advisers learned that he knew little about the law, his national security advisers found that he was devoid of knowledge on the capabilities of most U.S. and Soviet weapons systems and his economists discovered that he was poorly informed on economics, even though he sometimes reminded them that he had majored in economics and sociology at Eureka College.

("Playing it safe," the cultural historian Garry Wills writes, explaining Reagan's economic lacunae, "he majored in economics—[economics professor] Archibald Gray was the most notoriously easy grader on the campus.")

Less politely, the political scientist Richard M. Pious, reviewing Cannon's biography and other studies of the president, reduced their findings to three parallel axioms: "Reagan could only understand things if they were presented as a story; he could only explain something if he narrated it; he could only think about principles if they involved metaphor and analogy." For Sidney Blumenthal, who contrasts Reagan's triumphant promotion of political conservatism with Barry Goldwater's failure, the president's storytelling was the secret of his success:

> With him, facts don't determine the case; they don't make his beliefs true. Rather, his beliefs give life to the facts, which are tailored to have a moral. Reagan doesn't use stories the way experts use statistics. They seek mathematical certainty, whereas he has moral certainty. He asks listeners to trust the tale, not necessarily the detail. If the facts belie his premises, then the facts are at fault, and he can shift ground without making any fundamental change in his beliefs. His policies might be contradictory and counterproductive, but his mythology remains appealing. . . . His life experience vindicates his nostalgic approach to the future; he feels what he says, and that gives it authenticity and force.

Such a mode of thought, far from being baffling or unique, is characteristic of religious, and particularly of fundamentalist, thinking, an archaic mode in which facts are allegorized into parables or reinterpreted to match doctrine. If the Bible says the world was created in seven days and humankind is a separate creation, then evolution must be an unsupportable theory and fossils simply traps God has set to confound unbelievers. If homosexuality is proscribed in Genesis and Leviticus, then it must be a lifestyle choice, not a biologically determined orientation. If religious belief is necessary to morality, then Communists—atheists by definition—must be amoral.

Reagan's fundamentalist mentation encouraged him to find the supernatural as credible as the natural. He had been convinced since at least his days as governor of California that the end of the world was approaching. He believed that the Bible predicted the future. "Everything is in place for the battle of Armageddon and the second coming of Christ," he told a surprised California state senator one day in 1971, citing as a sign his understanding that Libya had gone Communist. The founding of Israel in 1948, the Jews thus reclaiming their homeland, was another sign Reagan credited as meaning that a great final battle between good and evil would soon be fought on the plain of Armageddon. The atomic bombings of Hiroshima and Nagasaki, he believed, fulfilled the prediction in Revelation of an army out of Asia of "twice ten thousand times ten thousand" routed by plagues of "fire and smoke and sulfur." He added Chernobyl to his list when he learned that the name of the old town was the Byelorussian word for wormwood, fulfilling the prophecy of "a great star [that] fell from heaven, blazing like a torch, and it fell on a third of the rivers and on the fountains of water. The name of the star is Wormwood."

Cannon describes an occasion in 1970 when the singer Pat Boone and two radio evangelists visited Ronald and Nancy Reagan at their residence in Sacramento; while the five were holding hands and praying together, the evangelist George Otis "was seized by what he took to be a visitation of the Holy Spirit [when] he prophesied that Reagan would become president." Otis's hands were shaking, Cannon reports, and so were Reagan's. The visit "stirred Reagan's interest in Armageddon," a story that "appealed to Reagan's adventurous imagination and met his requirement of a happy ending. As Reagan understood the story, Russia would be defeated by an acclaimed leader of the West who would [then] be revealed as the Antichrist. He, too, would fall, and Jesus Christ would triumph."

Robert McFarlane concluded that Reagan's commitment to strategic defense derived primarily from his belief that Armageddon was approaching. "From the time he adopted the Armageddon thesis," the national security adviser told Cannon, "he saw it as a nuclear catastrophe. Well, what do you do about that? Reagan's answer was that you build a tent or a bubble and protect your country. This was one of the intellectual contradictions in Reagan's thinking. He sees himself as a romantic, heroic figure who believes in the power of a hero to overcome even Armageddon. I think it may come from Hollywood. Wherever it came from, he believes that the power of a person and an idea could change the outcome of something even as terrible as Armageddon. This was the greatest challenge of all. . . . He didn't see himself as God, but he saw himself as a heroic figure on earth." Frank Carlucci, deputy secretary of defense under Caspar Weinberger and subsequently one of Reagan's five national security advisers, confirmed that Reagan connected Armageddon with nuclear war. "He would say to me that nuclear weapons are inherently evil," Carlucci told Cannon. When Carlucci argued the case for nuclear deterrence, Cannon paraphrases, "he did not convince Reagan, who responded to the argument by telling Carlucci about Armageddon."

If Reagan actually believed he might be the "acclaimed leader of the West" who might beat Russia, the evil empire, then he must also have considered the possibility that he himself might be the Antichrist, Christ's opposite, the disguised embodiment of evil. Better to rewrite the script to give it a happy ending, to prevent the "hail and fire, mixed with blood," falling on the earth, the burning up of "a third of the earth . . . a third of the trees . . . and all green grass." Better to prevent a nuclear war. Evidently the president didn't dwell on the unintended consequences of his rewrite, that saving the world from Armageddon would also delay the second coming of Christ.

Beliefs are often not logical, though they are anchored in the inner logic of profound personal experience. The inner logic of Reagan's life, as he himself testified, posited that "God has a plan for everyone," an idea that came to him originally from his devout Disciple of Christ mother, Nelle. He practiced the plan that God had for him, he wrote in his autobiography, in "seven summers [as] a lifeguard at Lowell Park" on the Rock River, which ran through Dixon, Illinois, a hundred miles from Chicago. Dixon was where he moved with his father, mother, and older brother, Neil, when he was nine and where he lived, he wrote, "the life that . . . shaped my body and mind for all the years to come after":

> Lifeguarding provides one of the best vantage points in the world to learn about people. During my career at this park, I saved seventy-seven people. I guarantee you they needed saving—no lifeguard gets wet without good reason. In my case it really took an emergency because my job was seven days a week, and from morning until they got tired of swimming at night. A wet suit was a real hardship and I was too money-conscious to have a spare. Not many thanked me, much less gave me a reward, and being a little money-hungry I'd done a little daydreaming about this. They felt insulted. . . .
>
> I got to recognize that people hate to be saved: almost every one of them later sought me out and angrily denounced me for dragging them to shore. "I would have been fine if you'd let me alone," was their theme. "You made a fool out of me trying to make a hero out of yourself."

The ingratitude of the rescued may have been the basis for a platitude Reagan adopted as his own and often quoted to his advisers; as William Clark rather stiffly recalled it: "We can accomplish almost anything together, if we do not concern ourselves with the question of who might receive the credit." Curiously, and noted as such by those who worked with him, Reagan insisted that the Strategic Defense Initiative was his idea and his alone. "The SDI program was very much driven by Ronald Reagan," Shultz would recall. "It was personal." At a press conference two days after his announcement, Reagan told reporters, "I've been having this idea, and it's been kicking around in my mind for some time here. I brought this up one day in a meeting [at] which the Chiefs of Staff were present and others, and we talked about it and discussed it and then discussed it some more." Several years later he told a reporter, more impatiently, "It kind of amuses me that everybody is so sure I must have heard about it, that I never thought of it myself. The truth is, I did." Reagan didn't mean that he originated the idea of ballistic missile defenses, of course; research and even deployment of various versions of such defenses, none of them effective, had been under way since the 1950s in both the United States and the Soviet Union. He meant he originated his own grandiose version of strategic defense (which he described, in his original announcement of the initiative on 23 March 1983, as having the "ultimate goal of eliminating the threat posed by strategic nuclear missiles") as providing "the means of rendering these nuclear weapons impotent and obsolete." In later speeches he would describe his goal even more specifically as a system "that might one day enable us to put in space a shield that missiles could not penetrate, a shield that could protect us from nuclear missiles just as a roof protects a family from rain."

"Lifeguards are solitary objects of adoration," Cannon writes, "who intervene in moments of crisis and perform heroic acts without becoming involved in the lives of those they rescue." Cannon's description might apply as well to the kind of movie star Reagan became, one who played the role of genial hero in movies that invariably ended happily. Next he scaled the role up to politics, becoming a two-term governor of California and then running for president once unsuccessfully before finally winning—twice—that most powerful of all roles.

He wanted to be president to accomplish a great rescue, he told his campaign manager, Stuart Spencer. "The sum total of him is simply this," Spencer recalled in an oral history interview: "Here's a man who had a basic belief, who thought America was a wonderful, great country. . . . This guy came from an alcoholic family, no money, no nothing. He was a kid who was a dreamer. He dreamed dreams and dreamed big dreams and went out to fulfill those dreams with his life and he did it. . . . [And] he had real concerns about all this leaving us because of communism. . . . It was the only thing that he really thought about in depth, intellectualized, thought about what you can do, what you can't do, how you can do it." Spencer told the future secretary of the Air Force Thomas Reed of a conversation he had with Reagan on the flight from Los Angeles to Detroit to join the 1980 Republican National Convention, where Reagan would be nominated as the party's presidential candidate:

> In the afternoon the conversation turned philosophical. Spencer asked the question all political pros learn to ask their candidates early on. "Why are you doing this, Ron? Why do you want to be President?"

Without a moment's hesitation Reagan answered, "To end the Cold War."

Spencer: "How do you plan to do that?"

Reagan: "I'm not sure, but there has got to be a way."

Reagan went on at length about the weakness of the Soviet system, about his horror at the thought of nuclear war, and about his annoyance with the accommodating, détente-oriented posture of the incumbent and preceding Presidents. Reagan was not a hawk. He did not want to "beat" the Soviets. He simply felt that it would be in the best interests of both countries, or at least of their general citizenry, to "end this thing." If the United States was strong enough, it could capitalize on the Soviet weaknesses that Reagan knew were there.

"There has to be a way, and it's time."

Michael Deaver, who became Reagan's deputy chief of staff, understood him similarly. "Reagan thought that he had to run for president," Deaver told the historian Paul Lettow. "He was the guy that could get the Soviets to the table and end nuclear war. . . . This was a guy who believed in predestination, who believed that there was a purpose for everybody's life and we had to fulfill it. And that was his purpose. . . . He was running for president because he believed he was destined to do away with nuclear weapons."

A sense of destiny muscled Reagan's dream of doing away with nuclear weapons, but its driving force was visceral dread, much as Curtis LeMay's had been when he came home to green Ohio after masterminding the devastating firebombing of Japan. LeMay's answer was preventive war before the Soviets acquired enough bombs to retaliate, or, failing that, early crisis preemption. Reagan, for all his totalistic anti-communism, sought a less dangerous solution. "One of the first statistics I saw as president," he recalled in his 1990 memoir, *An American Life,* "was one of the most sober and startling I've ever heard. I'll never forget it: The Pentagon said at least 150 million American lives would be lost in a nuclear war with the Soviet Union—even if we 'won.' For Americans who survived such a war, I couldn't imagine what life would be like. The planet would be so poisoned the 'survivors' would have no place to live. Even if nuclear war did not mean the extinction of mankind, it would certainly mean the end of civilization as we knew it. No one could 'win' a nuclear war." As Spencer saw him, "He was willing to roll those dice, because he absolutely had an utter fear of the consequences of nuclear warfare." Richard Pipes told Lettow smugly, "Reagan, for all his toughness, was terribly afraid of nuclear war."

In the spring of 1981, after Reagan was shot by John Hinckley, Jr., in an assassination attempt, and nearly died of blood loss, he wrote in his diary, "Whatever happens now, I owe my life to God and will try to serve him every way I can." Having come so close to death, he recalled in his memoir, "made me feel I should do whatever I could in the years God had given me to reduce the threat of nuclear war." The career diplomat Jack Matlock, Jr., who served as Reagan's principal adviser on Soviet affairs from 1983 to 1987 and then as ambassador to the Soviet Union, confirmed Reagan's horror of nuclear war in an interview with Lettow:

> Matlock . . . suspected Reagan would not retaliate in the event of a nuclear attack: "I think deep down he doubted that, even if the United States was struck, that he could bring himself to strike another country with [nuclear weapons]. He could never hint, but I sort of sensed [that]." Matlock believed that Reagan's unwillingness to retaliate against a nuclear attack contributed further to his desire for a missile defense. Matlock paraphrased Reagan's thoughts as: "How can you tell me, the president of the United States, that the only way I can defend my people is by threatening other people and maybe civilization itself? That is unacceptable."

Pipes's phrase "for all his toughness" in his comment on Reagan's fear of nuclear war implies that such fear was a weakness, a common attitude among nuclear strategists inside and outside the government. Shultz caught a glimpse of the strategists' protective alienation from the destruction they were contemplating during a briefing he received from Paul Nitze: "I listened as Nitze described these horrible, cataclysmic weapons of mass destruction in his genteel, bland manner, as if he were talking about baby farm animals." And easy enough for Pipes to say; the self-important academic never had to be responsible for the terrible decision that would face a president (or a general secretary) if deterrence failed and his country absorbed the devastation of a successful first strike: whether or not to respond with what was left of his nuclear arsenal, potentially killing millions more human beings for no other purpose than revenge. Far from being signs of weakness, Reagan's fear of nuclear war and his determination to reduce its risks measured his maturity as a human being—but also the extent to which he was and remained an outsider to the government over which he presided. At least twice during the first two years of his presidency, the diplomatic correspondent John New-house reports, "Reagan asked the bureaucracy to give him a plan to eliminate nuclear weapons. The bureaucracy did not respond." Nor did the problem go away.

Negotiation had been a traditional approach to limiting nuclear arms. The United States had negotiated nuclear issues with the Soviet Union and with other countries since shortly after the Second World War, when it offered the Baruch Plan for international control of atomic energy to the United Nations in 1946 (a negotiation that failed, a fact that Reagan sometimes lamented). The Limited Test Ban Treaty, the Outer Space Treaty, several Nuclear-Weapon-Free-Zone Treaties, the Nuclear Non-Proliferation Treaty, the Seabed Arms Control Treaty, the Anti-ballistic Missile Treaty, and the Threshold Test Ban Treaty, as well as the several SALT agreements, had all been designed to limit the development, deployment, and use of nuclear weapons. A president determined to "do away with nuclear weapons" might well be able to negotiate dramatic nuclear reductions or even nuclear abolition, especially one as popular and otherwise conservative as Reagan, who was elected to a second term by an overwhelming majority, carrying every state in the Union except Minnesota, his opponent's home state, and winning nearly 60 percent of the popular vote. He could hardly endorse such changes without intrusive programs of verification, of course, but those would be matters of negotiation as well.

Unfortunately for the world, one dimension of Reagan's Procrustean bed of fixed opinions prevented him from trusting negotiation as a path to ending the nuclear arms race. He discussed it at a West Point commencement on 27 May 1981. "Already," he told the graduating class, "the Congress has . . . mightily increased the spending for the military. The argument, if there is any, will be over which weapons, not whether we should forsake weaponry for treaties and agreements." Then he mentioned a book by a former Screen Actors Guild attorney that had settled his opinion about treaties and agreements, a book he called "the best book written on defense": "My good friend Laurence Beilenson authored a book a few years ago called *The Treaty Trap*. It was the result of years of research, and it makes plain that no nation that placed its faith in parchment or paper, while at the same time it gave up its protective hardware, ever lasted long enough to write many pages in history. Now this is not to say that we shouldn't seek treaties and understandings and even mutual reduction of strategic weapons. The search for peace must go on, but we have a better chance of finding it if we maintain our strength while we're searching." (Later in the address, the president referred obliquely to the Soviet Union, if not indeed to the Antichrist. "Today," he told the graduates, "you are that chain holding back an evil force that would extinguish the light we've been tending for 6,000 years.")

But if deterrence doesn't work, and treaties fail, and your opponent is prepared to lie, cheat, and steal to have his way, what's left? That would seem to be the question Reagan pondered once he decided that his personal destiny was to prevent Armageddon; he "thought about what you can do," as

Stuart Spencer understood Reagan's engagement with the challenge, "what you can't do, how you can do it." Edward Teller pointed him down the garden path of strategic defense when he visited Teller's Lawrence Livermore National Laboratory in 1967 as governor of California, introducing him to what Teller presented as defensive systems but what in later congressional testimony the Hungarian-born physicist would characterize as a "third generation of nuclear weapons." (The first generation of nuclear weapons were fission weapons, the second thermonuclear. The third generation that Teller had in mind would focus and transform the enormous energy of a nuclear explosion to drive directed-energy devices such as lasers, particle accelerators, or microwave beams—rifles, as it were, rather than firecrackers.) Lettow found "no documentary evidence that Reagan wrote or spoke of missile defense before 1967," which points to the governor's visit to Livermore as his earliest exposure to the idea.

"He took fifteen years to make up his mind" about strategic defense, Teller would say. Along the way he was encouraged by a self-appointed group of millionaire friends banded together into an organization they called High Frontier, founded by a founding member of the Committee on the Present Danger, Karl R. Bendetsen, who had the distinction of having directed the confinement of more than 100,000 Japanese-Americans in internment camps during the Second World War. Others who joined High Frontier included Joseph Coors, the right-wing Colorado brewer; an oilman, William Wilson; Jacquelin Hume, a friend of White House counselor Edwin Meese through the Bohemian Club, a men's club in San Francisco, and thus a direct link to Reagan; and Teller, the only scientist among them but one with a reputation for exaggeration and partisanship. Bendetsen recruited retired lieutenant general Daniel Graham, of the CPD and Team B, to run the organization. Unlike most military technologies, in other words, strategic defense as its proponents conceived it did not emerge from new developments in science and technology; it was instead a political concept, technologically barefoot, something that the United States could buy that would obviate any need to negotiate with the Soviets and that might restore the lost U.S. capability to destroy the Communist world in an overwhelming first strike.

SDI in Reagan's mind was never about any specific technology, however, not Teller's oversold and unproven X-ray laser nor Graham's off-the-shelf battle stations in space. Strategic defense was a dream, a fantasy, an uninformed, winner-take-all bet that American technology could make miracles happen if only a sufficiently committed leader stepped forward to offer support and run interference. It was a fond wish, as Reagan said in the speech when he announced it, "that the human spirit must be capable of rising above dealing with other nations and human beings by threatening their existence." Unlike Teller and the Bohemian Club Edisons of High Frontier, the president linked it quite specifically, then and later, to nuclear abolition. "I would hope that if such a weapon proves practical," he said in 1985, "that we can realistically eliminate these horrible offensive weapons, nuclear weapons, entirely."

But the warheads will always get through, political scientist Kerry L. Hunter reminds us:

> The truth is, SDI could have never provided a way out of the world of mutual assured destruction. Though MAD may feel morally bankrupt, there is no escaping the vulnerability caused by nuclear weapons. . . .
>
> The power of Reagan's Star Wars vision . . . lay in its utopian characteristics. It did not matter that Star Wars ignored reality. In fact, it was for this reason that the ideal was so appealing. The Star Wars dream allowed Americans to avoid a very stark truth that was practically intolerable to face: there was nothing they could do to protect themselves from nuclear annihilation outside of cooperating with the Soviets. Reagan seemed to sense this. Accordingly, he never did participate in discussion over the difficult questions the actual SDI program created. Even when the goals of the program were limited to seeking measures for protecting missiles, Reagan continued to believe in and espouse the vision of population defense—a total security from nuclear weapons, not security by having them. . . . The world his Star Wars dream promised was symbolic of how things ought to be, of what American presidents ought to be dreaming of.

And if wishes were horses, beggars would ride.

WHETHER REAGAN BELIEVED SDI WAS POSSIBLE, or only hoped it would be, he knew when he learned of the Soviet war scare in the midst of ABLE ARCHER 83 that weapons were armed and ready and no defenses had yet come to hand. Surprised, angered, chagrined that his hot rhetoric could be so coldly misunderstood, he moved quickly to send a message to the Soviet leadership that he was not preparing to attack. "President Reagan was not able to discount the Soviets' alarm as readily as his advisers did," writes Beth Fischer. "According to McFarlane, the president responded with 'genuine anxiety' to the news of the Soviet panic. Reagan was visibly shaken by the Soviets' misinterpretation of the NATO drill. The president had never believed that his war of words would lead to an armed conflict with the Soviet Union. More ominously, he had always felt that, in the face of an impending nuclear exchange, reason would not prevail. As he saw it, both sides 'had many contingency plans for responding to a nuclear attack. But everything would happen so fast that I wondered how much planning or reason could be applied in such a crisis.' "

On the last day of ABLE ARCHER 83, 11 November, Reagan spoke to the Soviet alarm—appropriately, in a speech before the Japanese Diet in Tokyo, in the only nation where atomic bombs had ever been used in war. He (or his speechwriters) could not resist continuing his attacks on the Soviet system, aligning the United States with Japan as nations that "do not build walls to keep our people in. We do not have armies of secret police to keep them quiet. We do not throw dissidents into so-called mental hospitals. And we would never cold-bloodedly shoot a defenseless airliner out of the sky." With the boilerplate delivered, he then reemphasized a conviction he had expressed before, at the United Nations and during one of his radio addresses. "I believe there can be only one policy for preserving our precious civilization in this modern age," he told the Japanese legislators. "*A nuclear war can never be won and must never be fought.* The only value in possessing nuclear weapons is to make sure they can't be used, ever. I know I speak for people everywhere when I say our dream is to see the day when nuclear weapons will be banished from the face of the Earth."

Several weeks later Reagan followed up his Diet signal with a further initiative, Shultz recalls: "When I met with the president on Saturday, December 17, he said he wanted to make a major Soviet speech and include in it his readiness to get rid of nuclear weapons. He told me he had noticed that Soviet Defense Minister Ustinov, in a speech two days previously, had proposed a ban on all nuclear weapons. By Monday, December 19, we had a good draft speech in the president's hands." That speech, which Reagan delivered from the White House on 16 January 1984, the morning before the first meeting of the Conference on Security and Cooperation in Europe (CSCE) in Stockholm—a "European disarmament conference" in Reagan's formulation—repeated the usual boilerplate, but in muted voice.

In the last ten years, Reagan said, the Soviets had "produced six times as many ICBM's, four times as many tanks, twice as many combat aircraft" as well as its SS-20s. He chose not to mention that the United States during the same period had deployed fifty-five hundred new warheads, five hundred more than the Soviets. He did say that his arms buildup had "halted America's decline." That made deterrence more credible, he added, but it might also be "the reason that we've been hearing such strident rhetoric from the Kremlin recently." He made clear that he was alluding to the war scare of the previous months: "These harsh words have led some to speak of heightened uncertainty and an increased danger of conflict. This is understandable but profoundly mistaken." Restored deterrence had made the world safer, but nuclear arsenals were still "far too high, and our working relationship with the Soviet Union is not what it must be." What he wanted it to be—the speech's central message to the Kremlin—was buried deep in the text:

> In our approach to negotiations, reducing the risk of war, and especially nuclear war, is priority number one. A nuclear conflict could well be mankind's last. And that is why I proposed over 2 years ago the zero option for intermediate-range missiles. Our aim was and continues to be to eliminate an entire class of nuclear arms. Indeed, I support a zero option for all nuclear arms. As I've said before, my dream is to see the day when nuclear weapons will be banished from the face of the earth.
>
> Last month the Soviet Defense Minister stated that his country would do everything to avert the threat of war. Well, these are encouraging words, but now is the time to move from words to deed. The opportunity for progress in arms control exists. The Soviet leaders should take advantage of it.

He might as well have been talking to a wall. Andropov, now mortally ill, had already dismissed the Reagan administration as beyond the pale. A "hackneyed ploy," Andrey Gromyko said, condemning the speech. When Andropov died, in early February 1984, Reagan pointedly chose not to attend his funeral, sending George H. W. Bush and Senate Majority Leader Howard Baker to Moscow instead. Reagan and Andropov's successor, the emphysemic seventy-three-year-old Konstantin Chernenko, exchanged letters—five were sent and answered between February and May—but made little progress. The Soviets were prepared to talk only if the United States first renounced SDI; as Chernenko put it, "What is needed is not the negotiations on what such systems might be, but a resolute and unequivocal renunciation of the very idea of creating such systems." In May, Tass compared Reagan to Hitler and called one of his speeches "a shameless lie from beginning to end." In July 1984, the Soviet Union boycotted the Los Angeles Olympics in retaliation for Jimmy Carter's boycott four years before.

By now Nancy Reagan, worried about her husband's place in history, had weighed in on the side of negotiations. According to Shultz, "hints came in" during August "that Gromyko might be looking for a chance to meet the president." Though he was nearly at the end of his first term, Reagan had not yet actually talked to a member of the Politburo. He did so, finally, in late September. "The president later told me," Shultz writes, "that in their private conversation he had been struck by Gromyko's description of the two super-powers sitting on top of ever-rising stockpiles of nuclear weapons and by Gromyko's statement that the Soviet Union wished to reduce the size of those piles. 'My dream,' Reagan had told him, 'is for a world where there are no nuclear weapons.' "

Once Reagan was reelected, in November 1984, the Politburo had little choice but to deal with him. Preparations went forward on both sides for a meeting between Gromyko and Shultz in Geneva in January 1985 to plan three independent, concurrent negotiations on strategic weapons, intermediate-range weapons, and defensive systems. With Chernenko still officially in charge, Gorbachev made his debut in London in December and Margaret Thatcher hallmarked him. In a speech before Parliament he took a cue from Willy Brandt and spoke of a common European heritage: "What-ever is dividing us, we live on the same planet and Europe is our common home—a home, not a theater of military operations." Reagan, dreaming his dream, noticed in a news report a pledge Gorbachev had made during a luncheon speech: "The Soviet Union is prepared . . . to advance towards the complete prohibition and eventual elimination of nuclear weapons." Thatcher joined Reagan at Camp David three days before Christmas to report on her conversations with Gorbachev and dropped the other shoe; as the official memorandum of conversation has it, "Gorbachev had told her 'tell your friend President Reagan not to go ahead with space weapons.' He suggested if you develop SDI the Russians would either develop their own, or more probably, develop new offensive systems superior to SDI."

Shultz fought off the assaults of the Weinberger-Perle faction to organize his meetings with Gromyko, noting as others have noted that "the toughest negotiations take place within your own team, on your own side of the table." His toughest negotiation may have been with Reagan himself:

> Ronald Reagan's views were definite: all nuclear weapons should be eliminated, and strategic defense should take over the role of deterrence. He was annoyed with me for expressing reservations. I pointed out that offensive weapons were needed and that even the most far-reaching version of his dream of strategic defense was incomplete. What about defense against bombers, stealth aircraft, sea-launched cruise missiles? SDI wouldn't cover them. The Soviets didn't need to be convinced about the importance of strategic defense; they had always val-ued it. It was the United States that had deprived itself intellectually and actu-ally of such defenses. SDI was essential, I agreed, but it was not everything. The president listened, but he didn't give any ground.

In Geneva, Gromyko played bait-and-switch games with the agreed text that the two sides put together on Monday and Tuesday, 7 and 8 January 1985. Monday night, at the inevitable reception, Shultz was amused "to see hard-line cavemen with their muscle-bound approach to the Kremlin sporting big but uncertain smiles on their faces, elbowing each other to get close enough to be photographed with Gromyko." The agreement that the foreign minister and the secretary of state finally forged, at eleven p.m. on Tuesday evening, included an allusion to abolition: "The sides believe that ultimately the forthcoming negotiations, just as efforts in general to limit and reduce arms, should lead to the complete elimination of nuclear arms everywhere."

There was more infighting in Washington afterward to pick the chief negotiator who would oversee the three deliberations. Shultz had been studying nuclear strategy with Paul Nitze and would have chosen him but for the illness of Nitze's wife, which precluded his moving to Geneva. Weinberger suggested Edward Teller, of all people, on the grounds, says Shultz, that "no one else could be trusted to be totally committed to SDI." All sides finally agreed on Max Kampelman, a soft-spoken lawyer and ambassadorial diplomat. Negotiations were set to begin on 12 March 1985. They did, but in the immediate days before and after that beginning, Reagan was diagnosed with colon cancer and underwent surgery, Chernenko died, and Gorbachev assumed the leadership of the Soviet Union. Shultz and Bush met Gorbachev for the first time in the Kremlin late on the evening of 13 March 1985, the day of Chernenko's funeral. "The USSR has never intended to fight the United States," Gorbachev told the two U.S. leaders candidly, "and does not have such intentions now. There have never been such madmen within the Soviet leadership, and there are none now." Shultz registered the impression Gorbachev made on the many leaders he spoke with that day; "the result was a certain Gorbachev euphoria in the air." The fifty-three-year-old former minister of agriculture was totally different from any Soviet leader he'd ever met, the secretary of state concluded. By late March, Gorbachev had written Reagan proposing that they hold "a personal meeting . . . to search for mutual understanding."

Shultz, normally so deliberately impassive that one observer compared him to a Toby jug, seems to have smiled at the shift in policy he had managed to organize for his strange but agreeable president: "We were smack in the middle of what was ever more clearly shaping up to be the endgame of the cold war."

PART THREE

COMMON SECURITY

Security can now only be achieved in common. No longer against each other but only with each other shall we be secure.

EGON BAHR

Government secrecy, risky design, and human error all contributed to the explosion and burnout of Reactor Number Four at Chernobyl, in northern Ukraine, on 26 April 1986. Millions of Soviet citizens learned that the state had lied to them and was powerless to protect them. Mikhail Gorbachev took away a deep sense of the unlimited destructiveness of nuclear war.

Intensely radioactive blocks of burning graphite blew out of the destroyed
Chernobyl reactor; to save the other reactors, firemen cleared their roofs
with wheelbarrows, shovels, and bare hands.

Left: Byelorussian physicist
Stanislav Shushkevich (here
with the author in 2005), later
the first Belarusian head of state,
deplored Moscow's failure to
allow protective measures after
Chernobyl. *Above:* International
Atomic Energy Agency director-
general Hans Blix was the first
outsider allowed to visit the
burning reactor.

Mikhail Gorbachev, a farmer's son, was born in 1931, the time of terror famine in the U.S.S.R. when Stalin used mass starvation to force Soviet farmers onto collective farms. Gorbachev's own family suffered.

Left: Gorbachev as a small boy with his grandparents. In the mistreatment of his own family, Gorbachev learned early of the corruption of the Soviet state.

Above: Wedding portrait, 1953. Gorbachev met Raisa at Moscow University. Her childhood had also been scarred.

Above: Moscow University prepared Gorbachev for a government career. *Below:* In his native North Caucasus, Gorbachev struggled to improve Soviet agriculture.

Opposite, top to bottom: The brutal suppression of Czech liberalization during the 1968 Prague Spring intensified Gorbachev's doubts about the Soviet political system. Under Leonid Brezhnev (here with Jimmy Carter) the Soviet economy stagnated. In 1969 Gorbachev found a Politburo patron in Yuri Andropov, who called him "a brilliant man working in Stavropol." He would not move to Moscow for ten more years.

On 29 August 1949, Joe 1, the first Soviet atomic bomb test, ended the American atomic monopoly and set the stage for the nuclear arms race that followed.

Right: Already in September 1945, the U.S. Air Force had plotted the ranges of its strategic bombers against a map of the U.S.S.R. to determine how many atomic bombs it would need. Even if 50% were duds, planners estimated, 466 20-kiloton bombs would destroy 66 Russian cities and obliterate its military and industry.

Below: Air Force chief of staff Curtis LeMay with John F. Kennedy. By 1960, the U.S. strategic nuclear arsenal exceeded 3,000 weapons and would ultimately number 16,000.

The B-52 bomber, first flown in 1954,
became the Strategic Air Command's workhorse.

In 1950 the State Department's Paul Nitze (*left*) and Secretary of State Dean Acheson (*center*)
deliberately exaggerated the Soviet threat in the founding document of the Cold War, NSC-68,
to boost defense spending. Dwight Eisenhower (*right*) pushed for moderation when
he became president in 1953. The Navy offered a less grandiose deterrent than bombers
and ICBMs, the ballistic missile nuclear submarine (*below*).

Top: Humiliated during the Cuban Missile Crisis, the Soviet Union in 1963 began an all-out effort to match the U.S. nuclear arsenal.

Center: Kennedy *(back to camera)* and Secretary of Defense Robert McNamara *(right)* tried to limit nuclear proliferation. Flanking Kennedy to his left and right, McGeorge Bundy, Paul Nitze, and Gen. Maxwell Taylor.

Bottom: Dick Cheney and Donald Rumsfeld, a durable team, first emerged into prominence in the administration of Gerald Ford.

Left: Sen. Henry "Scoop" Jackson and staffer Dorothy Fosdick with Richard Perle, who used Jackson's authority to attack U.S.-Soviet détente. Richard Pipes *(center left)*, Paul Wolfowitz *(center)*, Edward Teller and John S. Foster, Jr., *(bottom)* inflated CIA estimates of Soviet intentions as advisers to "Team B"; Wolfowitz coauthored the Team B report.
Center right: Nuclear strategist Albert Wohlstetter was a Perle and Wolfowitz mentor.

Opposite page, top: The Soviet invasion of Afghanistan in late 1979 soured U.S.-Soviet relations; Carter sharply increased defense spending.

Center: Ronald Reagan used his overwhelming 1980 electoral mandate to justify a trillion-dollar armaments program, including new missiles and bombers, and a more belligerently anti-Soviet policy.

Bottom: CIA director William Casey invented provocations, including a Saudi oil price cut that cost the U.S.S.R. billions of dollars.

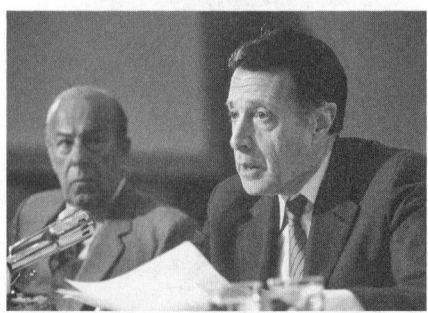

Above: Bellicose Navy secretary John Lehman invented more provocations, including overflights of the Soviet Far East and aggressive naval exercises that set the stage for the Soviet shootdown of Korean Airlines flight KE007 in September 1983.

Left: Secretary of State George P. Shultz, who favored diplomacy, and Secretary of Defense Caspar Weinberger, who took his cues from Richard Perle, battled for Reagan's soul.

A massive new U.S. "Peacekeeper" missile with ten warheads fueled Soviet suspicions of U.S. war preparations. Reagan, as a young lifeguard who saved 77 lives, secretly dreamed of eliminating nuclear weapons and ending the Cold War.

Above: Reagan nearly bled to death after his attempted assassination; he concluded God had spared him for the great purpose of negotiating peace between the superpowers. *Below:* Reagan thought strategic defense—space-based antimissile systems—would protect the U.S. from hold-outs and "madmen." Though Edward Teller promoted it, SDI was a political concept with no technological base.

Above: When the Soviets upgraded an old medium-range missile deployed in Eastern Europe with a solid-fueled mobile SS-20, the U.S. responded in late 1983 by threatening to deploy Pershing 2s (*below*) which could reach Moscow in 10 minutes or less. *Opposite, top:* Deployment went ahead despite Reagan's increasing uneasiness, fueled by grisly war-plan briefings and a television movie, *The Day After,* about nuclear war. *Bottom:* NATO exercises in November 1983 nearly led to a Soviet first strike.

Right: Bobbies arrested anti-U.S. demonstrators at Greenham Common, west of London, in November 1983.

Old warhorse Andrei Gromyko, the Soviet foreign minister,
nominated Gorbachev to lead the U.S.S.R. on 11 March 1985.

Gorbachev, here with Defense Minister Sergei Sokolov and Nikolai Tikhonov
on the Lenin Mausoleum, was a new kind of Soviet leader,
eager for reform and chary of using violence.

Gorbachev soon replaced Gromyko with Eduard Shevardnadze *(left)*
as foreign minister; shrewd Anatoly Chernyaev became a close adviser.
Both counseled ending the Cold War.

Gorbachev and Reagan met for the first time at the Geneva summit in November 1985. The Soviet premier broached the idea of "common security" rather than unending competition and attacked Reagan's Strategic Defense Initiative. The president defended his dream of a shield against nuclear weapons and surprised his advisers by offering to share the system. *Below:* Two months later the space shuttle *Challenger* exploded on ascent when hot gas leaked from a failed seal—a lesson, ignored by Reagan, in the unpredictability of complex technological systems.

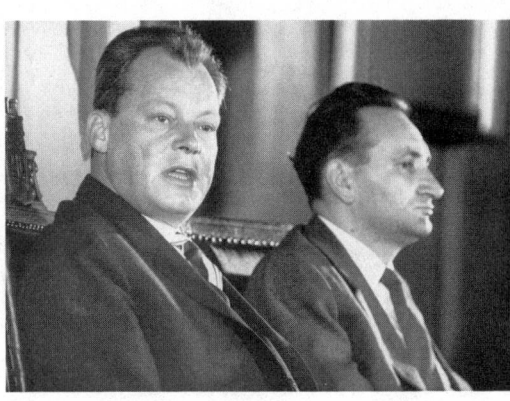

Gorbachev borrowed the idea of common security from a U.N. commission led by Sweden's Olof Palme *(left)*; Gorbachev adviser Georgi Arbatov *(left in group photo at bottom)*, a member of the commission, carried the message home. The new approach originated in the *Ostpolitik* of German chancellor Willy Brandt and his adviser Egon Bahr *(above)*. "No longer against each other," Bahr wrote, "but only with each other shall we be secure." A back channel of Soviet and American scientists also encouraged arms reduction: Gorbachev advisers Yevgeny Velikov *(left)*, Roald Sagdeev and Nikolai Shishlin *(bottom, with Susan Eisenhower)*. Eisenhower, the president's granddaughter, and Sagdeev would marry, another opening between the two nations.

The scientists' back channel: Richard Garwin, Ann Druyan, Evgeny Chasov, Bernard Lown, Carl Sagan. *Center left:* Stanford physicist Sidney Drell. *Center right:* Gorbachev released Andrei Sakharov from exile to demonstrate his commitment to glasnost.

Gorbachev maneuvered the Soviet military to support nuclear abolition. *Below right:* Marshall Sergei Akhromeyev. Paul Nitze *(below)* advised pocketing Gorbachev's offers at the October 1986 Reykjavik summit without offering concessions.

Gorbachev arrived at Reykjavik with major arms concessions, including eliminating medium-range missiles in Europe and all strategic nuclear weapons. At one point he and Reagan nearly agreed to abolish all nuclear weapons if Reagan would limit SDI to laboratory research for ten years. On Richard Perle's advice, Reagan refused. An angry Reagan left the meeting feeling cheated, but Gorbachev saw that they had broken through.

German student pilot Matthias Rust's penetration of Soviet air defenses allowed Gorbachev to purge his military of resistance to perestroika.

Below: Lithuania led the way in breaking free of Soviet rule. KGB violence there tarnished Gorbachev's record.

At the UN on 7 December 1988 Gorbachev proposed reducing strategic arms and withdrew half a million troops from Europe.

Below: A year later, in November 1989, the Berlin Wall fell.

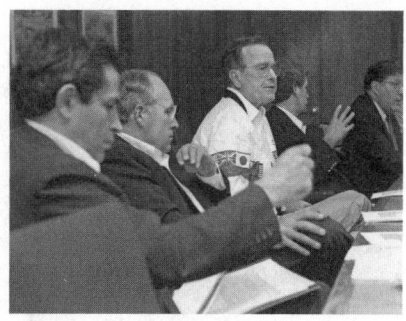

Right: A new administration doubted Gorbachev's sincerity and sat on its hands. Cheney thought that encouraging regime change could make the U.S.S.R. a democracy. *Left to right:* Wolfowitz, Cheney, George H. W. Bush, vice president Dan Quayle, chief of staff John Sununu.

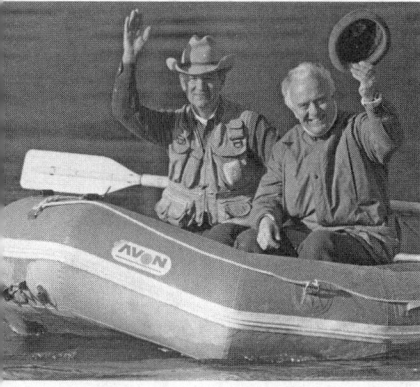

Left: Cooperation between the U.S.S.R. and the U.S. during the first Gulf War improved relations; Secretary of State James A. Baker III and Foreign Minister Eduard Shevardnadze (seen here fishing at Baker's ranch in Jackson Hole) became good friends.

The signing of the Conventional Forces in Europe Treaty in November 1990 marked the real end of the Cold War. Under its terms, Warsaw Pact and NATO forces had to be equal and balanced, making aggressive war impossible. The Soviets destroyed 28,000 battle tanks.

Above: In August 1991, when a right-wing junta arrested Gorbachev and tried to stage a coup, Boris Yeltsin rallied Muscovites to resist. Gorbachev returned to find his presidency obsolete.

Below: Nationalism and ethnic identity proved to be the centrifugal forces that pulled the U.S.S.R. apart. Ukraine's Leonid Kravchuk, Shushkevich of Belarus, and Yeltsin met in December to draft the document that dissolved the Soviet Union. Gorbachev resigned on Christmas Day, 1991.

ELEVEN **GOING AROUND IN CIRCLES**

MIKHAIL GORBACHEV AND RONALD REAGAN MET for the first time on 19 November 1985, a cold, gray Tuesday, near Geneva, the substantial Swiss guildhall of international diplomacy mortared around the lower end of Western Europe's largest lake. The United States had rented the Château Fleur d'Eau on the western shore of Lake Leman for the summit meeting; Reagan, the host of the first morning's tête-à-tête, thrilled his staff by emerging hatless and coatless from the château's glassed-in atrium as the Soviet limousines arrived and bounding down the steps to greet a Gorbachev carefully bundled against the cold. The trivial upstaging had been the last-minute inspiration of a White House advance man, but such was the freight of public attention to the first U.S.-Soviet summit in more than six years—some thirty-five hundred journalists had been granted credentials to read the tea leaves—that Gorbachev needled Reagan thereafter at the end of each session, "The next time we meet, will it be coats on or coats off?"

Leaders who make history are often provincials: Provincials attempt what sophisticates consider naïve. The two current candidates for world leadership were both country boys, a state park lifeguard and a champion harvester, each an outsider to the inner elites of the government he headed, each in his own way an idealist determined to push beyond the status quo. Reagan had been tailored in Hollywood, but the sophistries of Washington's nuclear mandarins had failed to complicate his apocalyptic Dixon, Illinois, worldview. Gorbachev's southern Russian accent and hillbilly grammar offended the ears of the suave Moscow bureaucracy he outmanipulated a dozen times on any ordinary day.

Their handlers had scheduled only fifteen minutes for their first morning meeting, the two of them alone with their translators. They took an hour. The official photographers left, the doors closed, the general secretary said they could really talk now, and the president held forth. Both he and Gorbachev had come from similarly modest beginnings, he said, and now the two of them held the fate of the world in their hands. Their countries were superpowers, the only countries that could start World War III but also the only countries that could bring peace to the world. They would talk about many things in the plenary sessions to come; perhaps now, at the beginning, they should try to eliminate their suspicions of each other. And then a Reagan truism, repeated in speeches and private conversations for decades: Countries don't mistrust each other because of armaments; they build up their armaments because they mistrust each other. (While his aides believed the maxim was a Reagan coinage, he had in fact borrowed it without attribution from the writings of the Spanish historian and diplomat Salvador de Madariaga, who had headed the League of Nations disarmament section for six years in the 1930s and written a bittersweet memoir about the experience—although a likelier source of the Madariaga maxim was Reagan's friend Lawrence Beilenson's disquisition on treaties.)

Gorbachev thanked the president for receiving him. He had prepared for their meeting for months, he said, studying all the president's statements. His main conclusion was that he and the president could not ignore each other. He was convinced that they could begin to change their relations for the better. He'd reviewed his conclusion a thousand times, wondering if it was too simplistic with two countries so tremendously different. Certainly they were different, but they had a long history of cooperation.

They had disagreed, Gorbachev went on. There had been squalls, some of them extreme. But the Soviet people and the Soviet leadership recognized the role of the United States in the world and wished it no harm. They realized that international relations could not be built on a desire to harm American interests.

A rich history lay behind Gorbachev's opening argument, his first statement at Geneva of a theme central to what he and the reformers who advised him called their "new thinking": the idea of common security. Framed as a negative ("international relations could not be built . . . to harm"), it may have sounded to Reagan like boilerplate. The record does not indicate that he acknowledged it, and later in this first conversation he told Gorbachev that the Soviet belief "that the Marxist system should prevail" was one reason the United States distrusted the Soviet Union. Yet by assigning common security a higher value than class conflict, Gorbachev was repudiating both Marxist theory and long-standing Soviet practice.

The idea of common security had come to Gorbachev from the social democrats of Europe, in particular Olof Palme of Sweden and Willy Brandt of the Federal Republic of Germany. Brandt's adviser and Bundestag member Egon Bahr had formulated the concept succinctly in May 1981: "Security can now only be achieved in common. No longer against each other but only with each other shall we be secure." The venue of Bahr's formulation was a high-level international commission, the Independent Commission on Disarmament and Security Issues, convened in 1980 to prepare a report for the Second United Nations Special Session on Disarmament, scheduled for June 1982. A previous commission that Brandt had chaired considered conventional military forces; the new commission focused on nuclear forces. Palme, the prime minister of Sweden, was its chairman. Its membership included Bahr, the former British foreign secretary David Owen, the French parliamentarian Jean-Marie Daillet, the Norwegian parliamentarian Gro Harlem Brundtland, the former secretary of state Cyrus Vance, representatives of India, Japan, Indonesia, Mexico, Canada, Tanzania, and several other countries, and, most significantly, Georgi Arbatov, the director of the Soviet Institute for the U.S.A. and Canada, who later served as Gorbachev's principal adviser on foreign affairs prior to Eduard Shevardnadze's appointment as foreign minister in July 1985. ("We met many times," Arbatov said later of his work with the general secretary, "usually at his invitation, and I sent him scores of memos.") Gorbachev had read the Palme Commission report, *Common Security: A Blueprint for Survival,* had reviewed its ideas with Arbatov as well as with Brandt, Bahr, and Palme himself, and had seized on common security as a more realistic national-security policy than those of his predecessors for dealing with the hard realities of the nuclear age.

Before Gorbachev, even during the years of détente, the Soviet military had operated on the assumption (however unrealistic) that it should plan to win a nuclear war should one be fought—a strategy built on the Soviet experience of fighting Germany during the Second World War. Partly because a massive surprise attack had initiated that nearly fatal conflict, the Soviet military had been and still was deeply skeptical of relying on deterrence to prevent an enemy attack. For different reasons, so were the proponents of common security. Brandt, who followed the Palme Commission's deliberations closely, wrote that he "shared the conclusions [the commission] came to: collective security as an essential political task in the nuclear age, and partnership in security as a military concept to take over gradually from the strategy of nuclear deterrence; [because] deterrence threatens to destroy what it is supposed to be defending, and thereby increasingly loses credibility."

One explanation bruited today for Gorbachev's decision to change official Soviet policy from war-fighting, with its essentially limitless demand for resources, to common security is that he needed to reduce his defense budgets to save the Soviet Union from imminent economic collapse. According to this triumphalist argument, the United States drove the Soviet Union to rein in its imperial ambitions by outspending it. But the evidence does not support this self-congratulatory claim. The Soviet arms buildup of the 1970s was largely complete by the time Reagan became president in 1981, and in any case Soviet defense budgets gradually increased, not decreased, through 1988.

Neither George Shultz nor even Caspar Weinberger credited the triumphalist theory of Cold War victory. "I never really bought that," Shultz told an interviewer. "The idea of building up our military capability was not to outspend them but to provide ourselves with adequate defenses." Weinberger commented similarly in 2002, "There were some people who said that the whole thing was just an attempt to run the Soviet Union into bankruptcy," not acknowledging that he had once been one of them. He went on: "Actually it was not, in my view. What [the president] needed, what we needed—and we were in full agreement on it—was to restore our military deterrent capability—to get a capability that would make it quite clear to the Soviets that they couldn't win a war against us—in such black and white terms as that."

Jack Matlock, Jr., Reagan's adviser on Soviet affairs on the National Security Council, and former Soviet ambassador Anatoly Dobrynin both concur. "None of the key players were operating from the assumption that we were going to do the Soviet Union in," Matlock said in 1998, "or that the purpose of the pressure was to bring them down. . . . Our goal was always to give the Soviets incentives to bring the Cold War to an end." And as Dobrynin points out in his memoirs, "Reagan's second term coincided with the appearance of a new Soviet leader, Mikhail Gorbachev. Without Gorbachev, there is no way that the Cold War would have ended. But if Reagan had also been farsighted enough to divine the Soviet Union's true motives and agree to the disarmament treaties that were already on the table, that would have ended the Cold War without the crushing military expenditures he laid on the backs of the American people." Dobrynin adds:

> Throughout the Reagan presidency, the rising Soviet defense effort contributed to [the Soviet Union's] economic decline, but only marginally as it had in previous years. The troubles in our economy were the result of our own internal contradictions of autarky [i.e., economic self-sufficiency], low investment and lack of innovation, as even Western economic specialists at the World Bank and elsewhere now believe. . . .

If the president had not abandoned his hostile stance toward the Soviet Union for a more constructive one during his second term, Gorbachev would not have been able to launch his reforms and his "new thinking." Quite the contrary, Gorbachev would have been forced to continue the conservative foreign and domestic policies of his predecessors in defense of the nation against America. And who knows how the world would have developed?

Certainly Gorbachev saw the Soviet defense budget as a sump from which he might siphon funds for modernizing and upgrading Soviet industry. "Although the Defense Ministry was well aware of the price the arms race extracted from the country," he writes sardonically, "in all the years of my work in Moscow they never made any suggestions for cuts in defense spending." His suggestions were blunt: "What are you doing?" he would ask anyone who presumed to lay claim to state funds for new weapons systems. "Still preparing to fight a nuclear war? Well, I'm not." Anatoly Chernyaev adds: "Since there was no real threat of an attack from the United States against the Soviet Union, and Gorbachev felt so, he assumed the need for an arms reduction process, and this was what underlay his thinking from the start."

Common security for Gorbachev was first of all a response to the dangers implicit in the vast nuclear arsenals of the two superpowers, dangers he had come to understand in searching conversations with Soviet scientists as well as European political leaders. He paid special attention to the conclusions of the assembly of presidents of scientific academies and other prominent scientists convened by Pope John Paul II in the summer of 1982. The declaration the assembly presented to the pope that September predicted the immediate deaths of "many hundreds of millions of people" in the aftermath of a major nuclear war, denied the prospect of "making defenses sufficiently effective to protect cities, since even a single penetrating nuclear weapon can cause massive destruction," and appealed to national leaders "to take the initiative in seeking steps to reduce the risk of nuclear war . . . and to eschew military conflict as a means of resolving disputes." The declaration evoked a "common responsibility" to avoid war and defined an "ultimate goal of complete nuclear disarmament."

The physicist Yevgeni Velikhov, the sturdy, ruddy vice president of the Soviet Academy of Sciences, had represented the Soviet Union among the sixty-four scientists at the assembly. Velikhov worked for reform within the Soviet system during the Brezhnev era and would become Gorbachev's chief scientific adviser. In Rome he had met the Austrian-born American theoretical physicist Victor Weisskopf, one of the most principled alumni of the United States's atomic bomb program during the Second World War.

Weisskopf, Velikhov said later, "made a great impression on me by his commitment to abolishing nuclear weapons. It's one thing when preachers say this must be done, but Weisskopf had worked on the Manhattan Project and lived through all of atomic history. He and I worked together on [the] declaration. . . . If you read it you'll see some of the ideas we now call the new thinking—the need for a nuclear-free world, the impossibility of nuclear superiority or of a defense against nuclear weapons. I won't say that the declaration influenced Gorbachev, but I know that he read it and reached his own conclusions." Velikhov, along with the astrophysicist Roald Sagdeev, a Tatar who was the director of the Soviet space program, and the historian and engineer Andrei Kokoshin of Arbatov's institute also participated in semiofficial back-channel talks with American scientists interested in arms control during the early 1980s. These included Jerome Wiesner, a former president of MIT; the IBM physicist Richard Garwin, a protégé of Italian physicist Enrico Fermi who had worked on the design of the first U.S. hydrogen bomb; the Stanford physicist Sidney Drell; and Carl Sagan.

"The task of insuring security," Gorbachev would tell the 27th Party Congress a few months after the Geneva summit, "is more and more taking the form of a political task and can be resolved only by political means." In that statement he echoed, perhaps unknowingly, Niels Bohr's formulation of the central paradox of the introduction of nuclear weapons into the world: "We are in an entirely new situation that cannot be resolved by war." Nor could the situation be resolved by deterrence, which, as Brandt said, risked destroying, if it failed, what it was meant to protect. "In our time," Gorbachev continued, "genuine equal security is guaranteed not by the highest possible, but by the lowest possible level of strategic balance, from which it is essential to exclude entirely nuclear and other types of weapons of mass destruction."

Ironically, one important source of the idea of common security was the program Willy Brandt had championed with Egon Bahr in West Germany in the 1960s and 1970s, a program they called *Ostpolitik*—"East policy." As early as 1963, Brandt writes, "I criticized the official attitude in Bonn that we were engaged in a race, and that we must 'always be swift and firm in rejecting any suggestion from the East just because it comes from the East. . . . Progress with the problems of Germany, I said, was unthinkable without détente. . . . There was no mistaking the fact that '*no solution to the German question can be found in opposition to the Soviet Union, only with it.* We cannot give up our rights, but . . . to realize them we need a new relation between East and West, and with it a new relation between Germany and the Soviet Union.' " Central to *Ostpolitik,* Bahr adds, was making "renunciation of force the guiding principle in relations between ourselves and Eastern Europe."

This bilateral version of common security led West Germany to sign a treaty with Moscow acknowledging the sovereignty of its Communist East German counterpart, the German Democratic Republic. From there the West Germans moved to "raise our principle of renunciation of force to a European level." They succeeded, Bahr goes on, "insofar as the wording of the Moscow Treaty was also used in the Helsinki Final Act" of 1975. The Helsinki Final Act, signed by thirty-five countries including the United States, the Soviet Union, and all the states of Europe, acknowledged the existing borders of the nations of Europe, both Eastern and Western, and renounced the use of force in changing them—seemingly a triumph for the Soviet Union and its control of its Eastern European satellites, but in fact the beginning of the end of that control. This larger success underlay the work of the Palme Commission and its formulation: "The principle of common security asserts that countries can only find security in cooperation with their competitors, not against them." In meetings in Moscow between Gorbachev and Brandt in which Bahr personally participated, Bahr heard Gorbachev "make reference to the reports of the Brandt and Palme Commissions" in discussing "global problems." In rethinking the superpower arms race and the sources of superpower conflict, Gorbachev took his most valuable lessons not from the Reagan administration's hostile rhetoric and reassertion of trillion-dollar military power but from the ideas and experiences of the European community, with which he identified his country strongly as part of a "common European home."

HOWEVER WELL BRIEFED REAGAN might have been at Geneva, he could hardly have known that all this background lay behind Gorbachev's opening remarks in that first morning tête-à-tête. In fact, Gorbachev had led off with his central argument for changing the direction of U.S.-Soviet relations. Having done so, he suggested that the president speak, reserving time later to talk about the current international situation.

Reagan responded with one of the nuggets he always carried in his possibles pouch: There was no question, he said, that the Soviet and American peoples, if they learned more about each other, would find that they had many things in common and that friendship between them would grow. It wasn't people who created armaments, he said, but governments. A wave of good wishes for this meeting had come from the people of the United States, primarily hopes for peace. He knew the Soviet Union had suffered greatly during the Second World War and knew it was concerned about war. People don't like war. Americans hate war.

Reagan had been reading from a pocket set of cue cards he carried. He produced another nugget: People don't get into trouble when they talk *to* each other, he said, but rather when they talk *about* each other. There had been too much of that kind of talk from both sides. When he and the general secretary met in plenary session with their advisers—they should go in to that meeting soon—they could discuss such mistrust and make a start at moving beyond it.

Gorbachev spoke up again, impatient with the president's clichés and determined to put his points on the table before the two leaders joined the plenary. (He was appalled at Reagan's cue cards and his initial unwillingness to engage Gorbachev directly, recalling "the blank, uncomprehending eyes of the president, who mumbled banalities from a piece of paper.") A new policy was needed, Gorbachev said, one that would be adequate to the present international situation. It ought to be aimed at resolving the central issue of the age, which was the question of war and peace. If they could reach a substantive agreement in Geneva it would be a great accomplishment. (Eight months earlier, on the day Gorbachev took office, he had asked his principal adviser, Alexander Yakovlev, to assess Reagan's motives for proposing a meeting, as Reagan had done in a letter delivered that day. "He would like to solve a number of problems," Yakovlev had responded, "in the context of his dream about [being] a 'great peacemaker President.' " So Gorbachev was baiting his hook with Reagan's presumed ambition when he talked about "a great accomplishment.") Young people were worried about whether they would live or die. So was the older generation, which had already endured so much suffering. They needed to get things moving or there would be great disappointment. People would say that they were irresponsible. They shouldn't subject themselves to such a fate.

There were many problems in the world, Gorbachev continued—problems between capitalist and socialist countries, problems in the Third World as well. There was hunger, illiteracy, and disease. These problems demanded their attention. They required solutions based on cooperation rather than confrontation. He was speaking sincerely, he insisted. The Soviet Union wasn't playing a game with the United States. It wasn't being duplicitous. If it were, if it harbored secret intentions, then the relationship couldn't be improved.

(Outside the room, White House Chief of Staff Donald Regan and National Security Adviser Robert McFarlane worried about the schedule—or, more likely, about what their maverick president might be giving away. They pushed the president's assistant, Jim Kuhn, the coat-switch specialist, to break into the meeting before it ran any longer. Knowing better than to interrupt the president of the United States at his deliberations, Kuhn proposed asking George Shultz, who was meeting in another room with Shevardnadze. "Bud and Don are concerned about the Reagan-Gorbachev meeting," Kuhn remembers whispering to Shultz. Shultz responded full-voice: "Are you out of your mind? This is what it's about. The longer they talk, the better it is." Kuhn retreated to the anteroom and told Regan and McFarlane that Shultz had just "ripped my neck off in front of Shevard-nadze." They left the president and the general secretary alone, facing each other in their fireside chairs.)

Reagan said he wanted to make a brief reply, after which he thought it would be best for them to join the rest of the group. The two countries could mutually help the developing countries, he agreed, but the U.S.S.R. created mistrust with its Marxist idea of helping socialist "revolutions" throughout the world and—Reagan repeated—its belief that the Marxist system should prevail. The United States felt to the contrary that what was most important to a country was its right to self-determination. The Soviet Union tried to use force to shape the developing countries to the Soviets' own pattern, and too often such force was used only by a minority.

Reagan tried again to herd his guest into the plenary session. When they moved on to the plenary, he told the general secretary, they would each greet the members of the opposite delegation, then they would have a photo opportunity beside the fireplace before they joined the others at the table.

Gorbachev had no intention of leaving the tête-à-tête with Reagan's last accusation hanging in the air. People had believed that the American Revolution should be crushed, he challenged the president—and the French and Soviet Revolutions as well. Millions of people had engaged in similar struggles in India, in Indonesia, in Algeria, where 1.5 million people had died in their struggle for freedom. The Soviet Union didn't believe a way of life could be imposed on a society if the society wasn't ready for it. These revolutions had their national roots. Moscow wasn't omnipotent. Gorbachev didn't wake up every morning thinking which country should have a revolution today.

THAT MUCH HAVING BEEN SAID, the two leaders moved over to the first plenary session—"wreathed in smiles," according to Jim Kuhn. Gorbachev joined Shevardnadze, Dobrynin, Yakovlev, Deputy Foreign Minister Georgi Kornienko, and other Soviet advisers on one side of the table; Reagan joined

Shultz, McFarlane, Nitze, Matlock, Donald Regan, and other American advisers on the other side. The president offered Gorbachev the floor and the general secretary reiterated what he had told the president in their private session. If they couldn't deal with the critical, pivotal issue of peace and war, he repeated, they would devalue the whole process. The situation was so acute that if they returned to their home countries without saying anything about arms control, people would say the meeting had given birth to a mouse.

Gorbachev said he knew what American think tanks such as the Heritage Foundation were advising. They advised that the United States should use the arms race to frustrate his plans, to weaken the Soviet Union. But history taught that such a program of intimidation hadn't been possible even earlier, when the Soviet Union wasn't as strong as now. Such a program was a delusion.

He saw a basis for movement on the issues between them, Gorbachev concluded. The president had said recently that there should be no nuclear war. (So Gorbachev had noted Reagan's deliberate repetition of the phrase "a nuclear war can never be won and must never be fought.") Gorbachev agreed. The president had said that they should proceed as equals. Gorbachev agreed. The president had said that he was in favor of exchanges among our peoples. The Soviet side agreed with that as well, Gorbachev said, provided such exchanges took place within a framework of respect for sovereignty and each society's values. (This proviso was Gorbachev's response to U.S. demands for Jewish and other emigration, demands responding to Soviet persecution of dissidents and refuseniks that Gorbachev deeply resented.) But the central question, Gorbachev concluded forcefully, was how to halt the arms race and disarm. The two countries could only live in the world together, so both had to think how to put their relations on a new track.

Reagan took up his version of the history of the arms race, which quickly resolved itself into his standard anti-Communist stump speech. Why did the United States distrust the Soviet Union? he asked rhetorically. After all, the two countries had fought together in two wars. Americans who had delivered supplies to help the Soviet Union during the Second World War were buried near the Soviet port of Murmansk. When that war ended, the United States was the only country whose industry had not been bombed and which had not sustained great losses. It was the only country as well to have built atomic bombs. It could have used them on the Soviet Union if it had chosen to. It didn't. Instead it reduced its armed forces from 12.5 to 1.5 million men, its navy from a thousand ships to fewer than half that number. It began proposing to do away with nuclear weapons and share nuclear technology with the world. Eighteen times before this meeting, said Reagan, the United States had proposed such meetings to deal with the divisions between the two countries, and on twelve of those occasions the United States had nuclear superiority. His country had been willing to give up that superiority, but most of the time Gorbachev's predecessors had refused to cooperate.

The eighteen meetings before this one had only addressed regulating the increase in nuclear weapons, Reagan contradicted himself. Now for the first time the United States was seeking with the Soviet Union actually to reduce the mountain of weapons. But the Soviet government talked about a one-world Communist state. It had inspired revolutions around the world. The United States was fully aware of the Soviet military buildup, including in nuclear weapons, which continued even after dozens of American arms-control proposals had been put on the table. The United States had fewer nuclear weapons now than in 1969 (which was true, but with MIRVing, more of them were targeted on the Soviet homeland). The Soviet Union had the largest military in history, with 5.4 million men in arms compared to the United States's 2.4 million. The United States had a Soviet satellite state, Cuba, just ninety miles off its shores. There had been problems in Cuba with nuclear missiles, but those had been settled. Now the Soviets were involved in Afghanistan, Ethiopia, Angola, and Yemen, with thirty-five thousand Cubans in Angola, for example. Reagan explained that he mentioned all these things because they were reasons for America's concern and distrust.

Warming to his subject, Reagan proceeded to relieve Gorbachev of any illusions about the burden of military spending on the U.S. economy. The United States spends more for its elderly, its handicapped, and for other social needs than it does for the military, he informed the general secretary. Two-thirds of U.S. military spending paid for manpower; only a very small percentage of the American gross national product (GNP) was spent on weapons. (Two weeks earlier, when Gorbachev had first heard these figures from Shultz and Robert McFarlane—McFarlane had specified defense spending at 6 percent of U.S. GNP—he had been "astonished," McFarlane says.) But spending none at all would be even better, the president said; the United States had no interest in carrying on an arms race.

Maybe the Soviets didn't want war, Reagan challenged, but they seemed to want to have their way. There had been violations of arms-control agreements already signed. (This assertion was a neocon theme and a Richard Perle favorite, by which, writes the arms-control analyst Michael Krepon,

Perle had "succeeded in transforming modest compliance flaps into serious violations, while blocking any diplomatic resolution of these problems.") The United States was ready to try to meet Soviet concerns if they were ready to reciprocate. It would take more than words. The two sides needed to get on to deeds.

After summarizing the general argument he had offered Gorbachev in their tête-à-tête—theirs were the only nations that could cause a world war, the United States had no hostile designs and hadn't taken advantage when it had been in a position to do so—Reagan said he wanted to bring up one specific question. It concerned SDI. He said Gorbachev had claimed the United States was pursuing strategic defense, a shield against missiles, because it wanted to achieve a first-strike capability. Well, he didn't know if a shield would be possible; the United States had a research program and the Soviet Union had a similar program. But if both sides continued their research and if one or both came up with a system, then they should sit down and make it available to everyone so that no one would have a fear of a nuclear strike. A madman might turn up with a nuclear weapon. If the United States and the U.S.S.R. could develop a shield and share it, then nobody would worry about a madman. Reagan said he didn't even want to call SDI a weapon; it was a defensive system.

Gorbachev, eager to challenge Reagan's arguments, asked if there was any time left. Should they stick to their schedule? Reagan joked that they should stick to their schedule because the next item on the schedule was lunch. Gorbachev reserved the right to open the next session with his response to the president's remarks. He said he hoped they would get to more specific discussion in the afternoon. Reagan agreed, and the two delegations left the large table (hauled all the way from New York on an Air Force cargo plane) and went their separate ways.

Both men had been anxious about their first encounter. They were relieved to have taken each other's measure but frustrated to be—as they saw it—misunderstood. The Gorbachevs were staying at the Soviet Embassy on the Avenue de la Paix in Geneva, and Gorbachev and his party now drove there for lunch. "I returned at the break to meet my colleagues," Gorbachev recalled. "They asked, 'What's your impression?' I said 'I have met a caveman—a dinosaur!' "

Reagan's party returned to the Maison de Saussure, an eighteenth-century residence where the Reagans were guests of the Aga Khan. Kenneth Adelman, the brash associate director of the U.S. Arms Control and Disarmament Agency, remembered the president arriving to be scolded by his son

Ronald Reagan, Jr., who had been granted credentials for the summit as a journalist writing for *Playboy:*

> The first words I heard were Ronnie's, saying, "Dad, you know you're late, we've been waiting for you to have lunch." Reagan says, "It's those interpreters." The translations that morning reminded the ex-actor of foreign films wherein someone on screen talks endlessly while a one-sentence subtitle—like "That's fine"—flashes on the bottom of the screen.
>
> Reagan said, "Excuse me," and headed for the men's room. . . . So we all stood at the [dining] table waiting for Reagan. . . .
>
> When he came out, Reagan stood at his place and had a grin like a cat who had just swallowed a canary. He was just so beaming. Then one by one all of us realized that one of his arms was in his suit coat [but] the other [sleeve] was just hanging down [empty]. . . . Then the whole room started laughing. I was one of the last to catch on. Finally someone next to me [asked], "Where's your arm?" And Reagan burst out [laughing] and said, "Well, it was here before I met Gorbachev. I don't where it is now." He just got the biggest kick out of it, all of us laughed. It . . . really put all of us at ease.

AT THE BEGINNING OF THE AFTERNOON plenary session, Gorbachev tried to avoid what he called "a big debate" over Reagan's accusations at the plenary that morning. He felt the need to defend himself nevertheless. He reminded Reagan that the Soviet leadership wasn't "primitive," meaning unsophisticated. Soviet policy, he said, wasn't based on some global plan for supremacy, on empire-building. He agreed that there were hotbeds of conflict that caused problems with the relationship between the superpowers, but he couldn't agree that Soviet "expansionism" was responsible—that idea was either a misunderstanding or a deliberate distortion, and if the United States based its policy on such a view it would be hard to find a way to move forward.

Reagan overemphasized the power of the Soviet Union, Gorbachev scolded him; it had no secret plans for world domination. It was unreal anyway to think that a small group of people could dominate the world with all its millions. Turning to Afghanistan, where the Soviet Union had been at war since 1979, Gorbachev offered a significant concession: He would support a political settlement in Afghanistan, he said, a political settlement under the United Nations. The United States could help. But while it claimed it wanted his country to withdraw its troops, it actually wanted them engaged there, and the longer the better. (Implicit in Gorbachev's accusation was his understanding that the war, as he would say frequently in the years to come, was a "bleeding wound," and that the United States was happy to see the flow of Soviet blood, treasure, and credibility left unstanched.) His country had no plan to use the war to gain access to a warm-water port or to the Persian Gulf, or to infringe on U.S. interests in any way; no such plan existed.

Having thus briefly responded to Reagan's conviction that the Soviet Union ran an evil empire and schemed to dominate the world, Gorbachev returned to the subject of armaments, his primary focus at the Geneva summit. Reagan had said that the Soviet Union built and the United States lagged behind. The president had claimed they were committed to an arms race. He'd charged that while the United States was showing restraint, the Soviet Union was building up its military potential. But twenty years ago there was no strategic balance. The United States had deployed four times as many strategic delivery systems as the U.S.S.R. and forward-based systems as well. The Soviet leadership had needed to offset the American advantage, just as the United States would have done, to avoid being manipulated. But since 1960, the United States had tripled the number of its warheads, and even now it had more nuclear weapons than the Soviet Union. The U.S.S.R. didn't want to lag behind, but neither was it trying to get ahead. Superiority didn't lead to normal relations, so it wasn't productive, even if the imbalance had been in the Soviet Union's favor. All the institutes that studied the problem, including the IISS* in London and Reagan's own Joint Chiefs of Staff, had concluded that their two countries had strategic parity. The forces were different, but they supported different strategies.

Now, Gorbachev continued, they needed to reduce parity to lower levels. He was all in favor of equal security at lower levels of force. That's why he came to Geneva. If they were to reduce strategic weapons, they needed to meet each other halfway. Of course America could meet any challenge from the Soviet Union—and the Soviet Union could meet any challenge from America. It was time for them to muster the realism and the political will to stop trying to outsmart or overrun each other.

The key disagreement on Gorbachev's mind was SDI, against which he now marshaled every argument he had. The Soviet Union, he said, believed that SDI could lead to an arms race in space, not simply a defensive arms race but an offensive arms race with space weapons. Space weapons would be harder to verify and would feed suspicions and mistrust. Why not take the obvious next step?

* The International Institute for Strategic Studies.

His scientists told him that any shield could be pierced, Gorbachev said. If SDI couldn't save America, why create it? It only made sense if its purpose was to cope with a weakened Soviet retaliatory strike after a U.S. first strike. Reagan's own defense secretary, Caspar Weinberger, had said that it would be bad for the world if the U.S.S.R. achieved such a defensive system first. What would the West think, Gorbachev asked sharply, if the Soviet Union were developing these weapons? It would react with horror. (Someone on Gorbachev's staff read *The Wall Street Journal,* which on 7 December 1983 had quoted Weinberger seemingly giving away the game: "I can't imagine a more destabilizing factor for the world than if the Soviets should acquire a thoroughly reliable defense against these missiles before we did." Weinberger, however, like Reagan and others in the Reagan administration, claimed to believe that an antimissile system in U.S. hands ought to threaten no one, since the United States had pledged to use it only for defense and in the context of reductions in offensive missiles.)

Gorbachev said he knew that the president was attached to the program, and because of his endorsement, Soviet scientists had studied it seriously. The conclusion they came to was that it would lead to an arms race on earth and in space. The Soviet Union would not cooperate in a plan intended to achieve superiority. It seemed that the United States had military aims in space that would violate the ABM Treaty—a treaty of fundamental importance. Testing, he said, was also inconsistent with the treaty, which could only exacerbate mistrust.

If the United States embarked on its Strategic Defense Initiative, Gorbachev predicted, two things would happen: One, there would be no reduction in offensive weapons; and, two, the Soviet Union would respond. "We will build up in order to smash your shield," Jack Matlock, who was there, says Gorbachev "thundered." Their response would not be a mirror of the American program, Gorbachev added, but a simpler, more effective system. What would happen if the United States put up "seven layers" of defenses in space? It would just destabilize the situation, generate mistrust, and waste resources. All of the American SDI schemes were based on using computers to monitor thousands of targets. They would all be holed up in bunkers, Gorbachev predicted, with the computers making the decisions. The world could end because a meteor passed by. Reagan hadn't thought it through, he scolded the president. It would be a waste of money and it would cause more distrust and more weapons. America didn't need SDI to avoid a madman with a bomb. Both countries had mounted sufficient retaliatory capability to deal with that problem for many years. And if they both began to disarm, other states would join them and aid in verification. The Soviet Union was prepared for full verification.

Concluding his argument, Gorbachev offered a carrot and a stick. If America agreed to ban space weapons, he told the president and the secretary of state, then the two nations could negotiate on their respective proposals for offensive weapons reduction. He was ready to compromise, he added earnestly. If space weapons were banned, it would create a new attitude on the Soviet side. The result would be very different if Reagan and Gorbachev left Geneva without any agreements. Then, Gorbachev threatened, the Soviet Union would have to rethink its offers.

Matlock, a seasoned negotiator, was not impressed with Gorbachev's negotiating skills at Geneva. "I observed him from across the table with growing disbelief," he writes. "Here was a man reputed to be a formidable debater. . . . But now he was leading with his chin" by denying the obvious and painting himself into a corner by reacting so strongly against SDI.

THE SOVIET SCIENTISTS WHO HAD studied SDI included Yevgeni Velikhov and Roald Sagdeev as well as engineer and historian Andrei Kokoshin and young Alexi Arbatov, Georgi's son, a political scientist. "Velikhov and I were in Washington just prior to Reagan's Star Wars speech," Sagdeev told me. "We learned of it from the newspapers on the plane out of Washington. Nothing could have predicted such an unexpected speech. We had been talking to our back-channel contacts at the National Academy of Sciences, scientific people such as Richard Garwin, and we learned later that they were just as surprised as we were. We saw that investigating Reagan's proposal was the first thing we had to do coming back to Russia. You know what the major argument was for investigating? What we were most afraid of? We were afraid that the industrialists in our military-industrial complex would say, 'Great, we should do the same thing.' "

Sagdeev laughs when he tells that story, but it almost came true. At a meeting sometime after Geneva in Gorbachev's office in the Kremlin, Sagdeev wrote in a memoir, the head of commercial services for the Soviet space program, noticing "Gorbachev's genuine involvement in strategic thinking," wheedled, " 'Dear Mikhail Sergeyevich, I completely understand your concerns. Trust me. We are losing time while doing nothing to build our own counterpart to the American SDI program.' " Sagdeev writes that he "almost died from suppressing my laughter," but adds soberly, "this brief episode gives at least a clue as to why we Russians were, as many in the West thought, overescalating the anti-SDI rhetoric. In my own frame of reference, I always had in mind the potential danger that could arise if . . . influential members of the military and industrial sectors in our own country were to involve us in a nonstop escalation of an SDI budget at that time, at the expense of the deteriorating strategic stability and our economy."

The scientists' investigation, which took the form of an extended meeting in April 1983 at the Soviet Academy of Sciences and culminated in a book, benefited from what Velikhov calls the Soviet government's previous "vaccinations" against strategic defense systems. The Soviet military had begun discussing strategic defenses in the late 1960s, Velikhov writes, when "the idea emerged of using lasers or charged-particle beams to hit warheads as they approached their targets." The scientists, led by Lev Artsimovich, quickly pointed out the futility of the scheme, however: "Compact reentry vehicles, specially designed to withstand the high temperatures of reentry from space, are hard to locate and lock on to for enough time to administer fatal doses of energy." Nor would such beams easily pass through the atmosphere. Yuli Khariton, the director of the Soviet Union's primary weapons-design laboratory, Arzamas-16, since the beginning of the Soviet nuclear-weapons program in 1946, insisted that "an honest and principled critique" be written and given to the government, "which decided to stop the program around the time the antiballistic-missile treaty was concluded in 1972."

The second vaccination came in 1980, when a Soviet engineer who designed booster rockets managed to slip a proposal to Leonid Brezhnev to create "a space-based defense using interceptor missiles"—a proposal similar to Daniel Graham's High Frontier program for battle stations in space. "Owing to the principled stand of a number of scientists and military experts," Velikhov writes with relief, "the heated debate resulted in a correct decision: The proposal was turned down."

Armed with these experiences, Velikhov and his group prepared an extended report on strategic defense in 1983 that Velikhov, Sagdeev, and Kokoshin edited and published in 1986 as a book, *Weaponry in Space: The Dilemma of Security.* The report reviewed the history and science of strategic defenses, but its essence was a careful analysis of the destabilizing consequences of an ABM-system buildup for strategic balance and of relatively inexpensive countermeasures that could foil any anticipated strategic defense. "The 'balance of terror,' " the report argued, "is a precarious balance. A really secure and peaceful world is only possible when both sides (and any other nations) have no nuclear arms. The world would be much safer if it were free of nuclear weapons and respective delivery vehicles, if all conflicts were tackled by negotiations, if economic, scientific and cultural international cooperation were improved and expanded." Nuclear abolition was a brave and radical argument to make in the Soviet Union of Yuri Andropov in 1983, the year of the Soviet war scare and ABLE ARCHER 83.

The "simpler, more effective system" that Gorbachev threatened to build to penetrate Reagan's defensive shield incorporated several of the countermeasures described in *Weaponry in Space*. "Our response to SDI will be effective," Gorbachev told Chernyaev. "The United States expects us to create analogous systems, they hope to outrun us technologically. . . . But . . . for only 10 percent of its cost we can produce a countersystem capable of nullifying SDI." Among the countersystems Gorbachev had in mind was an advanced version of a three-stage, solid-fueled mobile ICBM, the Topol-M (SS-27), with a 550-kiloton warhead with a maximum error of nine hundred meters across a range of eleven thousand kilometers (6,900 miles). The Topol-M's short engine burn time, flat ballistic trajectory that minimizes its time in space, maneuverable reentry vehicle, and advanced penetration aids, all discussed in the scientists' report, were intended to avoid or defeat antimissile attacks. Design of the advanced Topol system began in 1985, and development survived the dissolution of the Soviet Union. The Topol (silo-based) and Topol-M (mobile) missile is Russia's designated primary ICBM today; by 2006, 312 had been deployed.

But if Gorbachev had a system already under design that could nullify SDI (if indeed a comprehensive system of strategic defense could ever be made to work in the first place, which is highly unlikely), why was he so determined to convince Reagan to abandon it? Or as the American physics Nobel laureate Steven Weinberg would ask later, "How could Gorbachev have been worried about something so silly?"

The answer seems to lie primarily with the Soviet military, and behind the military with the large and powerful bureaucracy of the Soviet military-industrial complex—the nine ministries overseen by the Military Industrial Commission (known by its Russian initials as the VPK) and the eight additional ministries that supported them. "Experts at the Soviet Academy of Sciences," writes the foreign correspondent Don Oberdorfer, "argued that the Star Wars program was impractical and that any partial success it might achieve could be nullified by modest countermeasures. But despite such advice and doubts about its practicality, the Soviet leaders 'could not ignore such a position' as that outlined by Reagan on March 23, [1983,] especially since it was soon to be backed up by many billions of dollars, according to Andropov's foreign policy assistant, Andrei Aleksandrov-Agentov. 'So whether it was a practical idea or not, they had to account for the reality—the real factor in the policy of the United States.' " And if the Soviet military worried about the danger that a multibillion-dollar U.S. research program into strategic defense could turn up new offensive weapons along the way, the VPK might well, as Sagdeev feared, take the opportunity to press Gorbachev for a larger share of the Soviet budget to carry on parallel research and development to forestall an American breakout. William Odom, the lieutenant general who directed the National Security Agency during Reagan's second term, judges Gorbachev's primary opposition on the question of reform within the Soviet government to have been the VPK:

> A surprisingly broad consensus existed among most of the Soviet elite that the Soviet economy was in serious trouble and that the burden of military expenditures was much to blame. To reduce it, Gorbachev turned to disarmament through arms control. That was impossible, he realized, without a fundamental change in the Soviet Union's relationship with the world, both the capitalist world and foreign communist parties.
>
> To set a new course in military policy, therefore, Gorbachev quite logically began by changing Soviet foreign policy. His breakthrough in personal relations with Western political leaders convinced most of them that he was serious. Soviet negotiators returned to Geneva and Vienna, and under Shevardnadze's determined guidance, they surprised Western leaders with major changes in traditional Soviet positions.

"Disarmament through arms control"—seemingly the key to relieving the Soviet economy and improving the quality of life for the Soviet people—meant major reductions in the Soviet military. "Cutting military forces," Odom continues, "could free manpower for the civilian economy's workforce, but it would not save significant military expenditures because military pay was abysmally low—five or six rubles per month for conscripts. A very large part of the military budget went to the VPK for constant modernization of weaponry." (Which was how, for example, the Soviet Union came to replace its old first-generation liquid-fueled missiles in Europe with more modern solid-fueled SS-20s, and why it had produced so many more ICBM models than the United States.) "The key point," Odom writes, "is that Gorbachev confronted more than the uniformed military in this cat-and-mouse game. Somewhere between 20 and 40 percent of the state economy was tied up in military production. The issue of military reform, therefore, set Gorbachev and his allies against this large and privileged sector of the economy as well as against the conservative elements of the uniformed military leadership." He might win their grudging agreement to some degree of arms reduction, but they expected him in return to smother SDI in its crib.

REAGAN'S RESPONSE TO GORBACHEV'S CHALLENGES surprised some of his own advisers. He said the general secretary's presentation illustrated the lack of trust between their two governments. He proceeded to read through a list of twelve U.S. nuclear initiatives, beginning all the way back in 1946. He counted up the warheads the Soviets had added since SALT II and denied that the two nations' arsenals were presently equal. "With righteous indignation," Gorbachev writes sarcastically, "President Reagan tore apart the American policy of deterrence, which had triggered the arms race and led mankind to the brink of destruction." Reagan claimed proudly that SDI was his idea. There had never been a weapon without a defense, he said. He was talking about a shield. No one knew yet if it was possible. But if such a weapon could be produced, it shouldn't be added to present offensive forces. The two sides should sit down and get rid of nuclear weapons, and with them the threat of war. And defenses should be shared—they should be made available to all.

Sharing a high-tech weapons system that would have cost the United States many billions of dollars to invent was the proposal that surprised some of Reagan's advisers. "We had no idea where the idea had come from," Kenneth Adelman recalled, "none of us. We thought it was wacko." Evidently Adelman had been asleep at the switch. Reagan had discussed sharing strategic defenses during his second debate with the Democratic presidential candidate Walter Mondale in Kansas City in 1984. Since Adelman, like many others in the Reagan administration, found themselves unable to take their president seriously on questions of arms control, his lapse of memory probably reflects his contempt for the idea. Mondale took Reagan seriously. He rejoined that he "sharply disagree[d] with the President on sharing the most advanced, the most dangerous, the most important technology in America with the Soviet Union."

Reagan in Geneva talked for a while about Third-World conflicts, but soon returned to SDI. Gorbachev, trying a different tack, interrupted to ask what directions they should give to their negotiators. Reagan proposed that Shevardnadze, Shultz, and their advisers work on the structures of forces that would allow the two superpowers to reduce their nuclear arsenals by 50 percent. Gorbachev reminded the president that their foreign ministers (Shultz and Gromyko) had agreed in January 1985 that there should be no